D1014318

MUSTARD SEED VERSUS McWORLD

'Tom Sine's *Mustard Seed Conspiracy* was a prophetic challenge to the international church and deeply affected the course of world mission. This new book had me totally riveted. Here, at last, is a user-friendly analysis of the forces which are shaping our culture, and some clue as to how we can best respond. A book no church leader in the new millennium can ignore.'

– Rev. Dr Rob Frost
National Methodist evangelist

'Tom has produced *the* primer for millennium III. Whether you view the future through the lens of a church leader, a mission director, a business executive or a concerned Christian, Tom defines the issues and provides the tools to place you at the sharp end of shaping the future. This book is compulsory reading for all leaders… read it as a priority!'

– Mike Morris
Director of Peaceworks and member of Pioneer

'Tom is not only concerned about future trends, he is also concerned with God's purposes for the future of the church. Somehow he manages to help us see the broad picture more clearly without losing sight of people. This is essential reading for Christians who want to position themselves for the 21st century.'

– Rev. Joel Edwards, General Director
Evangelical Alliance, UK

'In the meltdown to the new millennium this is a *"must read"* for all who care about the future of the church and the world. A profoundly challenging book.'

– Roger and Faith Forster
Ichthus Christian Fellowship

'An important book about our globalised society and the consumer values which drive it. This is essential reading for all western Christians committed to shaping their lifestyle according to the teaching of Christ.'

– Rev. Graham Cray, Principal
Ridley College, Cambridge

'A powerful prophetic vision that screams hope in the face of modern day fatalism. We are educated about our world, challenged to change it and given the tools and inspiration to do so.'

– Phil Wall
Salvation Army

'Wide-ranging and stimulating. Most important, it inspires us with many stories of practical prophetic models of faithful Christian witness amidst the shifting sands of contemporary culture.'

– Luke Bretherton

'Arresting, inspiring, challenging, disturbing, faith-filled and hope-soaked… If you've ever stood in a car park full of Volvos wondering why the church has lost its edge, this book is for you.'

– Gerard Kelly, chairman
youth & r:age programmes, Spring Harvest

'This book should be read by every Christian leader. Tom Sine's ability to define the issues, envisage the future, question the present and bring biblical clarity and hope for the church of tomorrow is a gift to the wider church. We must take heed to what he is saying.'

– Rev. Brian Hathaway, facilitator
VISION, New Zealand

'Tom Sine has been invaluable in helping Tearfund assess and anticipate future international challenges. Tom's gift is the way he applies impersonal global trends to everyday lifestyle choices that you and I make. A must for anyone who cares about bringing the Kingdom into the next generation.'

– Doug Balfour, General Director
Tearfund

Mustard Seed versus McWorld

*Reinventing Christian Life
and Mission For a New Millennium*

TOM SINE

MONARCH
BOOKS

Copyright © Tom Sine 1999
The right of Tom Sine to be identified
as author of this work has been asserted by him in
accordance with the Copyright, Designs
and Patents Act 1988

First published by Monarch Books 1999
Reprinted 1999

ISBN 1 85424 435 3

All rights reserved.
No part of this publication may be reproduced or
transmitted in any form or by any means, electronic
or mechanical, including photocopy, recording, or any
information storage and retrieval system, without
permission in writing from Monarch Books
in association with Angus Hudson Ltd,
Concorde House, Grenville Place,
Mill Hill, London, NW7 3SA.

Unless otherwise stated, Scripture quotations are taken
from *The New Revised Standard Version* copyright © 1989
by the Division of Christian Education of the National
Council of the Churches of Christ in the USA.

British Library Cataloguing Data
A catalogue record for this book is available
from the British Library.

Designed and produced for the publishers by
Bookprint Creative Services
P.O. Box 827, BN21 3YJ, England
Printed in Great Britain.

CONTENTS

DEDICATION

Over the years I have tried to pay attention to the lively edge of what God is doing in our world. As a result Jesus people in the sixties taught me about whole hearted devotion to Jesus Christ. In the seventies my friends in Haiti taught me a great deal about what it means to trust God in good times and tough times. In the eighties I was repeatedly challenged by the staying power of the black church in America in our cities.

In the nineties I believe God is raising up a new generation of young people all over the world to lead the church into a new millennium. I discovered these young leaders first in Great Britain. In the early days of this decade I discovered a remarkable number of young Christians planting churches, starting urban ministries and reaching out to their contemporaries through very creative alternative worship services. In succeeding years I have found them starting performance night clubs in New Zealand and rehabilitating delinquents in Australia.

It got a little later start in North America. But in the last few years hundreds of young people have planted new churches in the States to reach out to a postmodern generation and develop drama and arts groups in Canada to share the story through new images. I am challenged not only by the commitment of this generation to Jesus Christ, but by the risks they are taking in living their lives and sharing their faith to advance God's kingdom.

Therefore I want to dedicate this book to a new generation of Christian leaders that is being raised up by God to lead the church into a new millennium.

ACKNOWLEDGEMENTS

I am deeply grateful for the family, friends and associates who have been so supportive in this project. My wife Christine has spent countless hours reading and critiquing this manuscript. I sincerely appreciate the support of my sons and their partners, Clint and Jenn and Wes and Emily. Dorsey and Betsy McConnell have encouraged our church to pray for us. I am particularly indebted to those who were kind enough to take the time to read and give me candid feed back on rough copy including: Norm Ewert, Tom Balke, Richard Kew, Craig Gay, Rodney Clapp, Graham Fawcett, Mike Morris, Mike Crook, Graham Cray, Paul McKaughan, Bill O'Brien, Mark Driscoll, Linda Fuller and Doug Paggitt. I appreciate the patient guidance of my two editors Tony Collins with Monarch UK and Paul Engle with Baker US. And I am very much aware of the prayers of those who have gone before including my parents Tom and Katherine and that huge family that will welcome us at the Great Homecoming.

FOREWORD

Sometimes Christian leadership feels like tight-rope walking without a safety net. On other days it feels like tight-rope walking without a tight-rope! So many questions, so few answers.

All the significant forms of leadership are future-focused. What will the world look like in the third millennium? How will the work-place be different? What forms of family life will be most common? And perhaps, most crucially of all, how must the Church change to make an impact on this new environment?

Any leader, indeed any thinking Christian, will find this book full of rich stimuli for the brain, passion enough for the biggest heart and prophetic vision in significant doses, to stir the will and feed the soul. But, not without cost to our comfort zones!

There is plenty to argue with, lots to pray about, much to discuss—if this book is to fulfil its potential. I'm sure Tom will feel that much has been accomplished if only we will take the future seriously. His goal, and mine, is that the Church places its full trust in an unchanging God, who will give us the courage to change everything that hinders our task of mission.

Stephen Gaukroger
Senior Minister, Gold Hill Baptist Church

PREFACE

I like the man and I like the book. I don't have a lot of time for the standard, manipulative futurologist. They tell me what is obvious to any informed citizen and simply press all the panic buttons of an insecure society, while laughing all the way to the bank with a best seller success based on market research of current buzz words. Tom is different. He dares to approach truth and evidence whether it is popular or not.

Here is a futurologist who is interested in meanings, not just markets. Here is a brother who is cyber serious. Here is someone who recognises that *business as usual won't touch it.* Here is someone who recognises that tomorrow can only be seen at the margins of today.

In a world where globalisation is the buzz word, this brother dares to contest a future McWorld with images of a *mustard seed faith conspiracy.* This is a day when people who are interested in their own pocket books write books about feeling good but this courageous brother dares to challenge us about being radical subversives who dare to believe that the Kingdom of God is more relevant and more accessible than the World Bank and McDonald's Corporation. In this book, you will find practical designs for a subversive hope. Beyond the overrated Millennium Bug lies the reality that Jesus, not the computer, is the stable point of a rapidly spinning world. However, Tom will show you that Jesus takes both the computer and your world seriously.

In a time of crisis, as W. S. Sloan has observed, we can become 'sanctuaries of frightened Christians, recruiting grounds for authoritarian figures or movements or centres of creative and courageous thinking. Will be we scared to death or be brought to life?'

Hey cyber freaks, this book may not make you feel good, but it will certainly help you be informed for the inevitable future.

John Smith
Care & Communication Concern
Australia

Introduction

A ride on the wild side—hurtling into a global future

We hurtled down the mountain highway in Haiti at ninety-five miles an hour—on the wrong side of the road! As the highway took a sharp turn to the right I could actually feel the tyres begin to lift up on the right side. The old Daihatsu truck had a very high centre of gravity that was aggravated by twenty-five Haitians standing in the back holding on for dear life. Clint, my fifteen-year-old son, and I urged our Haitian driver to slow down. But he continued driving with absolute abandon as though involved in a race to the death with every other vehicle on the road.

Suddenly a huge bus loaded with people careered round the corner at an outrageous speed—also on the wrong side of the road. The two vehicles rushed towards each other like enraged bulls. Both drivers furiously fought the G-forces to avoid an almost certain head-on collision.

Miraculously both vehicles veered back into their respective lanes barely avoiding what appeared to be certain disaster. Incredibly, in that three-hour ride to Port au Prince my son and I experienced at least half a dozen near-death experiences. It did wonders for our prayer life but our focus became very immediate and completely excluded the larger world around us. It was a ride on the wild side that focused us totally on the immediacy of survival.

How many of you are experiencing a ride on the wild side? What kind of pressures are you under in your families and congregations? Are those of you in leadership finding the resources you need not only to make sense of our rapidly changing future but also to creatively engage change? You are not alone. As my wife, Christine, and I have the opportunity to work with families, pastors and those in leadership of Christian organisations in Britain, Australia, New Zealand, Canada and the United States, we hear an urgent cry for help.

Racing into the third millennium—a cry for help

As we race into a new millennium the rate of change seems to be accelerating. We will all have to deal with more change than we are experiencing today. El niño, floods and tornadoes seem to be increasingly shaking our planet. Global economic meltdown is imperiling many economies. Threats of biological terrorism, nuclear proliferation and global plagues menace our future. Web-trekking, cyber-freaks and virtual communities are dramatically changing how we relate to one another.

We are rapidly entering a new global society in which ninety per cent of the computers world-wide rely on software from Microsoft, Saddam Hussein watches CNN daily and they are selling Hard Rock Café T-shirts in Sarajevo with bullet holes printed on them. Global change is what's happening. It feels like the 'pedal to the metal'. Rapid change can be very unsettling and disorienting. And there are virtually no resources available to help parents, pastors or Christian leaders get ready for the new challenges of a new millennium.

Quite honestly I struggle with change when I travel. Apparently I am one of those born with the 'gift' of disorientation—which makes change even a little more confusing. When I travel without my wife, I frequently get off the track and have adventures I never intended. In my wanderings I have become acquainted with some charming cows in the south of France and some very friendly monkeys on a seldom travelled road in Nepal.

I have learned to be philosophical and to maintain a sense of humour about my disorientation and the unexpected changes it brings into my life. But growing numbers of individuals, families and churches are being hammered by change they did not create—and it isn't funny. As we race into a new century we are going to get ripped off by change if we don't get ready.

A cry for help from families

As Christine and I work with parents, pastors and mission executives from Western countries, we hear the same urgent cry for help. Many of these good people tell us they are experiencing a ride on the wild side and feel like they are losing control. Families from Pasadena to Liverpool tell us they are working harder and longer just to stay even. They are so busy driving their kids to activities that they have precious little time left over for family life. Many of them feel guilty because they are not as involved in the life of their churches as they would like to be and they report they have little time left over for prayer or ministry to others. Numbers of parents tell us that they are routinely skipping worship service on Sunday morning to take their kids to soccer matches.

But we haven't seen much in the way of practical materials designed to prepare Christians for a future in which there is likely to be mounting pressure on their lives and families. And people have no idea of how to take whatever is preached on Sunday morning and make good decisions from Monday to Saturday. There are virtually no resources to help Christians put first things first in a rapidly changing world.

A cry for help from the Christian young

Recently, university graduates in both Seattle and London told us a very similar story. A surprising number of them are working as temps or at entry-level jobs. Many of them have moved back in with their parents. In the book *The Thirteenth Gen* there is a cartoon about the young moving back home to the 'Boomerang Motel'. Signs on the front include: 'Mum's Diner', 'Dad's Rent-A-Car', 'Laundromat: we fold and iron at no extra cost!', 'Instant Cash', and 'Nintendo Video Arcade'.[1]

The reason so many of the young are moving back home is the cost of housing. A large number of the under-thirty-five generation in the US and UK tell us they are spending over half their income for rent or mortgage. They report that they are frustrated because they have very little time or money left over to invest in the work of God's kingdom.

I have found virtually no Christian ministries to university-age adults that are preparing them for a future in which many of them are likely to have less, economically speaking, than their parents' generation. Nor have I seen many stewardship education efforts to enable a new generation to find creative ways to reduce their housing costs so they have more time and money left over to advance God's purposes.

A cry for help from churches

Pastors tell us they are feeling overwhelmed by change too. They tell us that programmes which worked well for decades don't work at all any more. Groups like the Alban Institute, which works primarily with mainline churches, and Saddle Back Church, which relates primarily to evangelical churches, are keen advocates of equipping the laity to do the work of the

Church. This is a position I strongly endorse.

But pastors tell us that even their most active members are getting busier and busier and have less time left over for the work of the Church. In this book we will show why our people are likely to become significantly busier in the future, seriously compromising the ability to find laity who have time to be equipped. Therefore, for those of us who are advocates of equipping the laity to do the work of the Church, I believe we will have to fundamentally reinvent how we equip Christians. – That includes serious timestyle and lifestyle change.

A cry for help from Christian mission organisations

Christine and I also work with a broad spectrum of mission organisations, helping them to create new strategies to address the new challenges of the twenty-first century. From Open Doors Holland, Tearfund England, World Vision Australia, the Baptist Board of Foreign Missions in New Zealand and World Concern in the US, we hear the same cry for help. These leaders are struggling to understand how both the fields in which they do mission, and their donor support base, are likely to change in the coming decade as we rocket into a very uncertain future.

For example, Open Doors Holland is concerned that persecution of Christians in Muslim countries seems to be mounting. Many new converts in Islamic countries not only lose their families but are also fired from their jobs. Open Doors is seriously considering how they might use microenterprise projects to help the persecuted Church.

God hasn't lost control!

What all these people have in common is that they all want more for their lives, families, churches and Christian organisations than to simply survive a ride on the wild side. They are looking for resources, not only so they can make sense of their future, but also so they can creatively engage these challenges for God's kingdom.

If you are among those who are experiencing a ride on the wild side, if you are feeling out of control, let me whisper an important word in your ear. All appearances to the contrary, the creator God is quietly transforming our 'future-shocked' world. While we may feel out of control, our God isn't. At the very core of our being we are people of a wild outrageous hope. We believe that the God who began this entire venture will write the final chapter and make all things new. And Scripture tells us that God invites us to be a part of this venture.

In the early chapters of this book we will examine some waves of change we are likely to face in the future that can be a little overwhelming. Please remember that for the people of God all tomorrow's challenges are really opportunities to manifest something of God's compassionate love. Henri Nouwen used to remind us that Jesus Christ is present in every aspect of our world in both crucifixion and resurrection. Jesus is present in crucifixion in death squad activity in Honduras and in the persecution of his followers in China.

Jesus is also present in resurrection in the community in Pasadena that John and Vera May Perkins took back from the drug dealers, and in a run-down tenement called Easterhouse, Glasgow where Christians have helped the poor help themselves by starting a credit union. We all have the opportunity to be a part of God's resurrection response as we discover how God wants to use our mustard seeds to make a difference.

Business as usual won't touch it!

 As we listen to these cries for help, one thing is transparently clear. Business as usual won't begin to equip us to deal with the new challenges of a new millennium. A number of our tried and true methods of being the Church simply won't carry us very far into the future. And I am convinced that a little tinkering and fine tuning won't be of much help in our lives, churches or Christian organisations. We will need to find ways to fundamentally reinvent how we live out our lives and act out our faith if we hope to effectively address the new challenges of a new millennium.

The place to begin this journey towards creating the new is by paying attention to what God is stirring up. We need to pay attention to how God is at work in our world today through the mustard seed. And then we need prayerfully to ask God how we can join that part of the lively edge of what the creator God is doing to make a world new.

Paying attention to the lively edge of the global Church

Mustard Seed Versus McWorld will take you on a global tour of ways the Holy Spirit is stirring up Christians all over the world to make a difference for God's kingdom. Christine and I have the opportunity to work with churches in Britain, continental Europe, Australia, New Zealand as well as Canada and the United States. We have also both had the opportunity to work in countries in the Two-Thirds world. Frankly, we often find more creativity per square mile in Britain, Australia and New Zealand than we do in the States.

I sense God is giving birth to something altogether new in

the Church, particularly through a post-modern generation. As we work with twenty and thirty-year-olds, we are not only impressed by their uncommon commitment to Christ and his mission in the world but by the imaginative ways they are finding to give expression to their faith. They are not simply creating younger versions of older models. God is inspiring them to create some innovative new approaches that I believe we can all learn from.

We see the post-modern young relocating to an inner-city community in London to start a food co-operative with the poor, starting performance cafés to reach their peers in New Zealand, designing WEB pages in Vancouver BC to promote missions, and planting post-modern churches all over the US with the support of the Leadership Network. For example, Mars Hill Fellowship planted a church a little over a year ago in Seattle that has grown from zero to over 400.

Unlike many of the successful boomer churches of the nineties, post-modern churches are not interested in highly programmatic 'user friendly' models that can be replicated. They are creating models that are much more relational and that are unique to each situation. Most importantly they are both reaching the young and discipling them to make a difference.

We need to pay attention not only to what the Spirit of God is stirring up in the Church today, but also to the new challenges and opportunities that are likely to be a part of the third millennium and to which we need to respond.

One world, ready or not!

It is no accident that families, our young people, pastors and those leading our missions organisations are feeling so overwhelmed by change. Not only does the rate of change seem to be accelerating, but new driving forces have emerged in the past decade which are decisively altering the direction and character of change. Futurists not only attempt to make sense of change but to identify the driving forces that are directing its course. It is the contention of this book that one of the primary forces directing change, as we race into a new century, is *globalisation*.

We are hardwiring our planet electronically into a single global system of satellites, fax machines and internet communications. Borders are melting away. Distance is disappearing. $1.5 trillion dollars flash around the planet every day as we witness the rapid creation of a *one world economic order*. However, we are belatedly discovering that this new global economic order was not carefully constructed. As I write we have no idea how long it will take to overcome the global economic meltdown or create a more reliable structure for the twenty-first century.

With the sudden end of the cold war, for the first time in history virtually all the nations in the world have joined in the capitalist race to the top. Not only has capitalism triumphed but so has McDonald's. It has just passed Coca Cola as the most widely recognised logo in the world. As a consequence we will join others in using McWorld as a way to characterise the process of globalisation.

Jerry Mander, a senior at the Public Media Center, states: 'Economic globalisation involves arguably the most fundamental redesign of the planet's political and economic arrangements since at least the industrial revolution. Yet the profound implications of these fundamental changes have barely been exposed to serious public scrutiny or debate. Despite the scale of reordering, neither our elected officials nor our educational institutions nor the mass media have made credible effort to describe what is being formulated or to explain its root philosophies.'[2]

One of the reasons we are experiencing a ride on the wild side is that this new global economy is turning out to be fiercely competitive. Sudden decisions half a world away are increasingly impacting our lives regardless of whether we live in London, Sao Paulo, Chicago or Sydney. None of us were ever given an opportunity to vote as to whether we or our respective countries wanted to be a part of a one world economic order. National leaders seem to have reached some kind of a worldwide consensus, without our input, that it is the only game in town. And now we are all on board this global race to the top, like it or not. It's like going to sleep in your bed in your own home and waking up jammed into a gigantic global rocket ship with 6 billion others all hurtling through space at fantastic speeds with absolutely no notion of the destination.

Many of us are already benefiting in a myriad ways from globalisation. We are able to purchase an expanding array of products from all over the world and travel to virtually any place on the planet. We can suddenly be on-line with people half a world away. New technologies that will make our lives more efficient are coming at us at blinding speed. But there are a growing number of voices from all over the world that argue that globalism not only brings many benefits but also raises a number of new concerns.

Mustard seed versus McWorld—a global contest

In every era the Church of Jesus Christ has found itself in a deadly contest with the principalities and powers of this world. Throughout this book we will argue that we will increasingly find ourselves contending with not only escalating global change but also a system of values that is often fundamentally at counter-point to the values of the gospel of Christ.

Defining the contest

Let me be very clear. As I describe this contest between economic globalisation and God's agenda for our global future, my battle is not with free market economics. Centrally planned economies have been abandoned for a good reason: they don't work very well. The free market is more effective at producing goods and services than any system we know. Throughout the book I will be arguing that we need to promote growth in our respective economies and at the same time make a massive effort to assist those who are marginalised to start small businesses and credit unions to help them move out of poverty and achieve a decent way of life for their families.

The efforts to create a new one world economic order is raising some new challenges that deserve a much more thoughtful response by people of faith. I am very concerned about some of the consequences of economic globalisation and particularly about the values that are driving it. As I will point out in this book, early evidence suggests that globalisation doesn't seem to work as well for the global poor as for those who have resources to take advantage of the lift-off. More concerning is the centralisation of economic power that seems to be one of the consequences of the rapid creation of a one world economic order.

There are those on both the right and the left who talk about globalism in conspiratorial terms. As I will show I don't believe that there is any conspiracy but there is a consensus among those who are strong advocates of economic globalisation about what the ideal future looks like and how to get there. Therefore, when I use the phrase 'McWorld' I am simply describing this shared consensus as well as the process of globalisation itself.

When I talk about the contest between the mustard seed and McWorld I am primarily talking about the contest between two very different visions for our global future and two very different systems of values. As I will show, the aspirations and values that are driving globalisation are a product of the

Enlightenment and modernity and are, in many ways, directly counter-point to the aspirations and values of God's new global order. Therefore, those of us of Christian faith have the challenging task of finding a way to be a part of this world, in all of its dimensions, while doing serious battle with any values that we believe are contrary to the inbreaking of God's new global order.

We will show both some of the promised benefits of globalisation as well as some of the potential drawbacks. But we will also argue that McWorld is about much more than creating a global economic system. The architects of McWorld are not simply trying to increase global free trade and free enterprise. They are, I believe, working to redefine what is important and what is of value in people's lives all over the planet in order to sell their wares.

Pope John Paul, making what is likely to be his last trip to the Americas in 1999, focused on the challenges facing humankind in a new millennium. The centrepiece of his concern is this new reality of economic globalisation. He also outlined some of the upsides and downsides of globalisation. He also shares our concerns regarding 'the absolutising of the economy', the growing distance between rich and poor, and global media imposing materialistic values 'in the face of which it is difficult to maintain a lively commitment to the values of the gospel'. (*'Excerpts from John Paul's Message About the Poor and the Rich', New York Times,* 24 January 1999, p.6)

For example, I was attending a conference sponsored by World Evangelical Fellowship in Abbottsford, Canada, when two Pentecostal pastors from the Dominican Republic came up to me after I had shared how globalisation is already changing the future of their communities and their congregations. They told me, 'Five years ago we lost the young people from a number of our Pentecostal churches. It was right after

MTV and an invasion of American pop culture came into the Dominican Republic. And to be honest we haven't been able to find a way yet to win them back.'

More than any of us in the Western Church seem to recognise, the merchants of McWorld are also influencing people of serious faith to buy into the aspirations and values of modern culture. In a fascinating book called *Material World: A Global Family Portrait*, the photojournalists persuaded families all over the world to move all their worldly possessions into their front yards and then they took a picture of the family with their belongings.

What I found particularly telling was the portrait of the one American family from Texas. Compared to all the other family portraits their yard was flooded with a huge range of consumer possessions including: three radios, three stereos, five phones, two TV sets, one VCR, one computer, one car, one truck, one dune buggy and loads of furniture. And this Texas family, who are believers, stood in front of all their things holding their big family Bible open, apparently oblivious to the image it communicated.[3]

This American family is not unusual. I think most of us Western Christians would be embarrassed to have a picture taken in front of our accumulation of things—particularly if it was in a volume with pictures of many of our poorest neighbours. Everywhere we travel, Christine and I see the Church losing out big time to the seductions of modernity and the allures of the Western dream. As the values of modernity go global, Christians everywhere, our young in particular, will increasingly find ourselves in a contest in which we will have to choose between the aspirations and values of the mustard seed and those of McWorld.

An invitation to join the subversive mustard seed movement

In *Jihad vs McWorld*, Benjamin Barber argues that the two

major forces shaping the human future are the forces of globalisation (McWorld) and the forces of fragmentation (Jihad).
The reader is left with the clear impression that one must
choose between the two.[4] I am arguing that we don't have to
choose sides between the forces of globalisation and fragmentation. The Scripture teaches that there is a third force at work
in human society that isn't apparent to those outside the community of faith. The creator God who passionately loves a
people and a world is working through the subversion of the
mustard seed to make all things new.

The power of this new global economic order is awesome
and it has brilliantly demonstrated its ability to market not
only its products but its values all over our small world. But I
believe that God's mustard seed agenda, with a very different
approach to globalisation, will win the day.

> Jesus let us in on an astonishing secret. God has chosen to
> change the world through the lowly, the unassuming and the
> imperceptible. Jesus said, 'With whom can we compare the king-
> dom of God, or what parable shall we use for it? It is like a grain
> of mustard seed, which when sown upon the ground is the small-
> est of all seeds on earth; yet when it is sown it grows up and
> becomes the greatest of all shrubs and puts forth large branches,
> so that the birds of the air can make nests in its shade.'[5]

Economic globalisation is being advanced by powerful
financiers, influential CEOs of transnational corporations and
international political brokers. The mustard seed agenda for
globalisation on the other hand is led by one who comes on a
donkey's back. The mustard seed movement defines the
ultimate in terms of God's kingdom breaking into the world
to redeem a new global community from every tongue, tribe
and nation. And Jesus tells us that we will find our ultimate
satisfaction not in seeking life but in losing it in service to
others.

God's plan has always been to work through the small and insignificant to bring his new global order into being. This book is an invitation to set aside our lesser agendas and join with sisters and brothers all over the world who are finding the enormous satisfaction of God using their mustard seeds to make a little difference in the world in anticipation of Christ's return when God will make all things new.

Recently I was at an urban ministries conference, sponsored by the Christian Community Development Association. Half a dozen people came up and told me that the reason they are in urban ministry today is because they read a book nearly two decades ago, called *The Mustard Seed Conspiracy*. For instance, Al Tizon and his wife Janet were so challenged by the stories of how God used ordinary people to make a difference that he quit his government job in Oregon and Janet quit hers in nursing. They left their comfortable way of life in Oregon and moved to the slums of Manila. Al said he was both surprised and gratified to discover that God was able to use their lives to make a difference in the lives of their new friends.

This book is offered to others who are interested in discovering what God can do with their lives if they put first things first. While we will benefit in many different ways from globalisation, I will show that God's vision for the better future has much more to do with making a difference than with making a dollar. It has more to do with creating a new reconciled global community of justice and celebration than with the production of a new global community of consumption. It has more to do with coming home to Jerusalem than Babylon. It is through the death and resurrection of Jesus Christ that we are all invited to devote our lives to the subversive cause of the mustard seed that is destined to redeem a people and transform a world.

In search of a user's guide to the third millennium

Frankly, there aren't many books available to enable Christians and those in leadership to make sense of the rapidly changing landscape of tomorrow's world or to help them find innovative ways to deal with that change. As we cross the threshold into a new millennium there are, predictably, a growing number of books on various end time theories like *Left Behind* by Tim LaHay and Jerry B. Jenkins and *End of the Age* by Pat Robertson.

But these books not only offer little help in making sense of change, they consistently try to force various global events into a particular end times theory. They unintentionally tend to reinforce the fatalistic assumption that we can't make a difference because everything is destined to get worse and nothing can improve.

Let me be clear. I look forward to the return of Christ with great anticipation. But the Bible tells us that the timetable of the last days is God's business not ours. What is our business? As followers of Jesus Christ our business is to do what Jesus did and make God's purposes our purposes. In other words in this book we will work from scripture to outline something of God's purposes for the human future. And then we will show how putting God's purposes first not only helps us to face the future with hope but with a growing realisation that God can use our mustard seeds to make a real difference in our rapidly changing world.

There are a growing number of books attempting to help the Church change but most of them don't take the future seriously. They attempt to enable the Church to plan as though the future is simply going to be an extension of what is happening now. Even the spate of books on the future and the Church, written over the past decade, tend to focus on the future of the Church instead of the future of the larger society.

There are a few welcome exceptions to this pattern. George Barna, in a recent work, *Generation Next*, does an excellent job of profiling some of the ways our youth culture in the United States is changing. Leonard Sweet provides some very vivid impressions of post-modern culture and the Church in his new book *11 Genetics Gateways to Spiritual Awakening*. Peter Brierley (in Britain) has published a very helpful book on the changing demographics of the Church entitled *Future Church*.

But I haven't located any books that try to help the reader learn to anticipate change or that attempt to look more broadly at global and national challenges likely to shape our common future. Nor is there much conversation about how we can create new biblical responses to tomorrow's emerging opportunities.

While there is increasing interest by Church leaders in post-modernity, very little has been written about the extent to which the Church has caved into modernity. In fact, many books that are attempting to help the Church get its act together are unconsciously promoting values of modern culture that have much more in common with McWorld than with the mustard seed. Rodney Clapp's book, *A Peculiar People*, and Craig Gay's *The Way of the [Modern] World* are two of the few recent publications attempting to challenge the Church to become liberated from the seductions of modern culture.

A user's guide to the third millennium—defining the direction

Mustard Seed Versus McWorld: Reinventing Christian Life and Mission for a New Millennium is written to respond to this cry for help. It is intended to enable Christians, particularly those in leadership, to more fully anticipate and more creatively respond to the challenges of our global future in a way that advances the purposes of God's new order. It is a book designed to help you find creative ways to put God's purposes first so you can live, thrive and serve God in a rapidly changing future.

This book is written to address three serious crises (that receive virtually no attention in the literature) that threaten the ability of the Church to carry out its mission in the twenty-first century: 1) a crisis of foresight—a failure to take the future seriously; 2) a crisis of vision—a failure to take the future of God seriously; 3) a crisis of creativity—a failure to take our God-given imagination seriously.

Essentially the book will be broken into three sections:
1. *A crisis of foresight.* In chapter 1 I will explain why it is essential that all Christians, particularly those in leadership, learn to take the future seriously. Then I will outline specific practical ways in which those in leadership can anticipate how their churches and the communities in which they minister are likely to change. In chapters 2—6 we will explore how globalisation is likely to impact our lives, families, churches and larger world. We will explain how all of tomorrow's challenges, for people of faith, are really opportunities for creative biblical response.
2. *A crisis of vision.* In chapter 7 we will argue that many of us Western Christians have unwittingly allowed modern culture to define much of the direction of our lives and those of Christian organisations instead of Scripture because we haven't given enough thought to *why we do what we do*. As you will see, one of the reasons many of us are out of control in our personal lives is that the aspirations and values of modernity have really set the primary agendas of our lives and shaped much of the character of our churches and Christian organisations. In chapter 8 we go back to the Bible and discover an alternative vision to the Western dream—one that can help us find a new reason for being and a new sense of

purpose for our churches. We will show that God can help us live our lives and steward our churches with a much greater sense of advancing God's new order.

3. *A crisis of creativity.* In chapter 9 we will outline how Christians can put God's purposes at the centre of their lives and then find innovative ways to reinvent their lives and reorder their priorities to put first things first. We help you think 'out of the box'. We will describe how we can as 'whole life' disciples create a way of life that is more festive and less stressed than the rat race—a way of life in which God can use our mustard seeds to make a difference in our rapidly changing world. In chapter 10 we explore how to reinvent our churches and Christian organisations to more creatively and effectively advance God's mission purposes in response to the challenges of tomorrow's world. Finally, in the epilogue we will invite you to join with Christians all over the world on our WEB page at www.bakerbooks.com. (go to <u>Mustard Seed vs McWorld</u> and click on.) in creating new possibilities for life and mission for a new millennium.

Essentially we will define the future in three different ways:

1. The future as anticipation is the likely future—the new challenges that are coming at us whether we like it or not.

2. The future as vision is the ideal or preferred future—God's new order, the future we want to see come into being.

3. The future as creativity is God's Spirit working through our imagination to enable us to create ways to advance God's vision that addresses the anticipated challenges.

A reader's road map

Since people are very busy, particularly those in leadership, we want to make this book as reader friendly as possible. We have attempted to open it up a bit with graphics and provide icons to help you find your way through the book as easily as possible. If you find a section a little hard going feel free to skip ahead. The most important thing is to prayerfully pay attention to what God is saying to you and act on it. Throughout the book you will find the following icons to make your journey as easy as possible:

- *Finding the focus of the chapter icon* will tell you the aim of every chapter.
- *Key points icon* will highlight the key points of every chapter.
- *Seeds of hope icon* will describe creative ways people are finding to make a difference.
- *Leadership opportunity icon* will outline specific ways those in leadership can both respond to new challenges and create new possibilities.
- *Questions for discussion and action icon* will provide questions at the end of each chapter.

This book is designed to be used as a text book in seminaries, colleges and church study groups. We hope this graphic format enables you to find your way and to use the book for group discussion. I don't expect readers to agree with all my analysis or my proposals but I do hope the book stimulates a serious discussion about how to live our lives, lead our churches and carry out God's mission in a rapidly changing world.

One last word. I am not an economist but a historian and a futurist trying to make sense of very complex economic change. As a lay person I have made my best effort at trying to share with other non-economists what I have been learning about globalisation with help from a friend and economist from Wheaton College, Norm Ewert. I recognise that on our best day we all 'see through a glass darkly'. The aim of this book is not to offer definitive answers but to raise important questions about the future and the Church as we charge into a globalised new millennium. I pray that this book is of help in preparing you to serve God effectively in a rapidly changing future.

Notes

1   Neil Howe and Bill Strauss, *The Thirteenth Gen: Abort, Retry, Ignore, Fail?* (Vintage Books: New York, 1993) p.105.

2   Jerry Mander, Edward Goldsmith, editors, *The Case Against the Global Economy: and for a turn toward the local* (Sierra Club Book: San Francisco, 1996) p.3.

3   Peter Menzal, *Material World: A Global Family Portrait* (Sierra Club Book: San Francisco, 1994) p.132-138.

4   Benjamin R. Barber, *Jihad vs McWorld* (Times Books: New York, 1995).

5   Tom Sine, *The Mustard Seed Conspiracy* (Word Books: Waco, Texas, 1981; MARC Europe, London, 1985).

SECTION ONE

A Crisis of Foresight—Learning to Take the Future Seriously

While working with a group of aboriginal Christian leaders in Sydney, Australia, where my wife Christine is from, we were introduced to a more relaxed form of holding conferences. When these Christians get together they don't hold conferences day and night. They have their formal meetings in the daytime then party and tell stories at night. An aboriginal pastor came up to me on the first night of enjoying each other and caught me a bit off guard.

The pastor said, 'We wouldn't have this mess we have in the world today if we aboriginals had been the ones in the Garden of Eden instead of you guys.' I said, 'What are you talking about?' He replied, 'If we had been the ones in the Garden of Eden instead of you guys we would have thrown away the fruit and eaten the snake and we wouldn't have any of these problems we are dealing with today!'

To get ready for the third millennium we are all going to need a new perspective.

Speaking to sixty Christian businessmen in Christchurch, New Zealand, I asked, 'How many of you forecast before you plan in your business?' Every hand in the room went up. 'Now,' I asked, 'how many of you as leaders in your churches forecast before you plan?' Not a single hand went up. While corporations routinely make an effort to make sense of how the future is likely to change before they plan, churches and Christian organisations rarely do. We plan as though we are frozen in a time warp.

Why it is essential that leaders take the future seriously

I have been consulting with denominations, Christian colleges and mission organisations for twenty years and have discovered that it is extremely rare to find any Christian organisations or churches that make an effort to systematically research how the context in which they carry out missions or how their donor support base is likely to change in the future before they plan. We do so-called long range or strategic planning as though the future is simply going to be an extension of the past. Anyone who has lived through the last three decades knows that this assumption is false.

We are living in a world changing at blinding speed and yet in our homes, churches and Christian colleges we unconsciously prepare our young to live and serve God in the world their parents grew up in instead of the Third Millennium. Don't we have a responsibility to prepare our young to live in tomorrow's world?

As a consequence of leaders failing to lead with foresight, churches and Christian organisations have, in recent years, been repeatedly hammered by change and missed a lot of opportunities to bring the gospel of Christ to a changing world. Instead of driving into the future with our eyes firmly fixed on our rear-view mirrors we need a new generation of leaders who learn to lead with foresight.

Leading with foresight

We can no longer do planning in the church, raise our young or order our lives as though the future is simply going to be static. Those of us in leadership need to learn to lead with foresight. We need to anticipate the change that is rushing towards us and grasp how globalisation is likely to drastically alter our common future. Globalisation will offer us a huge range of benefits in the future, some of which may come with a high price tag.

To the extent that those in leadership can anticipate possible areas of change in our lives, churches and communities we have lead time to create new biblical responses; we have lead time to be proactive instead of reactive.

In the first chapter in this section we will ask, 'What are the tools that are available for those of us in leadership to anticipate areas of change that are likely to confront our lives, churches and the larger world?' Then in chapters 2–5 we will ask, 'What are likely to be the new needs, challenges and opportunities likely to face us in our lives, churches and mission organisations as we race into an increasingly global future?' Finally in chapter 6 we will ask, 'How effectively is the Church going to be able to respond to these challenges given changes that are also taking place in the Church?'

Enjoy your trips back to the future!

I

A ride on the wet side –
learning to surf with
Shakespeare

I dug hard into the choppy waves with both arms. My huge surfboard breached the final wave and I joined the small cluster of surfers waiting for my first ride back to the shore. It had taken me fifteen minutes to paddle out from the shore near Lahaina, Maui and I was winded. It was a hot April day on this Hawaiian island and I decided to lie on my board and watch the other surfers while I caught my breath. One after another they positioned themselves to an inbound wave. Then they paddled like fury and suddenly were lifted to the crest of the wave like a feather on the wind. The surfers catapulted towards the beach with tremendous speed. I watched one Filipino lad turn into the curl and ride down the pipeline with all the grace of an Olympic figure skater.

How hard could it be? Ten years before I had mastered skiing the first time I hit the slopes. By the end of the day I was thoroughly enjoying myself. My friends were amazed that I got up the first time I went water-skiing on Strawberry Lake in California. I did a complete circuit of the lake. No problem.

I took a deep breath and did exactly what I saw the others do, I turned my board towards the shore and paddled with all my strength. A huge wave hit me and the board and sent us both to the bottom with tremendous force. As I swam back up to the surface, I looked above me and there was my nine-foot board hurtling right down towards my head. I dived, and I barely escaped decapitation. When I finally swam back to shore, there was my board lying innocently on the beach. Instead of catching the wave I had a ride on the wet side.

Over the next three hours, amazingly I repeated this exercise over a dozen times with the same result—getting dumped into the deep. Sometimes the waves passed me by entirely and I just found myself sitting in the doldrums. I simply didn't have a clue as to how to anticipate which waves would give me a ride or how to catch them. Exhausted, after one final ride on the wet side I called it a day and dragged my board ashore watched by the amused surfers. Do you know what it's like either to get hammered by waves or have them pass you by?

Believe it or not, William Shakespeare had some important insights on surfing. In his play *Julius Caesar*, he has Brutus address Cassius after the slaying of Caesar, attempting to refocus the political life of that community: 'There is a tide in the affairs of men which taken at the flood leads on to fortune; amid it all the voyage of their life is bound in the shallows and in miseries. On such a full sea are we now afloat, and we must take the current when it serves us or lose our ventures.'[1]

I am persuaded that Shakespeare's counsel is spot on. In a world changing as rapidly as ours we must either learn to surf with Shakespeare or experience repeated rides on the wet side. Wayne Burkan, a corporate futurist, puts it in slightly different terms: 'To survive in an ever changing world, it is vital to anticipate the future.'[2]

Looking back on rides on the wet side

One has only to look back on the waves of change that have

battered the Church in the last four decades and see the waves we have missed to realise there must be a better way. For example, we failed to anticipate the impact of MTV and video games on the young in the eighties and nineties. And the Church has been decades late in waking up to the growing need for racial reconciliation in America. Belatedly, Promise Keepers, 'a group which encourages men to live truly Christian lives', discovered that this is a serious issue that Evangelical Christians need to address.

Too often in the past the Church has either been jolted by waves of change or allowed them to pass us by altogether—because we have made virtually no effort to anticipate them. Too many of us in leadership have been operating as if we are frozen in a time warp. As a consequence we have missed repeated opportunities to make a difference. In the third millennium the Church needs leaders who can lead with foresight.

Looking forward to surfing with Shakespeare

As I complete this book, millennial fever is growing. The most exotic destinations in the world from the Sphinx in Egypt to the Space Needle in Seattle have been booked years ahead as sites for lavish celebrations to welcome a new millennium. Prime Minister Tony Blair is building a huge Millennium Dome as a centre to focus people in Britain on the new opportunities for the UK in a new millennium. For others the journey into a new millennium is whipping up an apocalyptic frenzy. New Agers are flocking to Brasilia in their thousands to await the dawn of a new era. Some survivalists are certain that the millennium bug is going to usher in the end of the world and are building survivalist camps in the mountains. Reportedly, militia groups in the US are arming to the teeth because they believe that crossing the threshold into the year 2000 will ignite Armageddon.

Regardless of whether you view crossing the threshold into a new millennium with apprehension or anticipation, entering a new millennium is causing us all to give much more thought to the future. The aim of this book is to persuade those in leadership to wake up to the changes that are likely to confront us in a new millennium—and to take seriously the responsibility to prepare the Church to find creative ways to address those changes with full confidence that we can trust God to guide us.

Eventually I learned the secret of catching a wave instead of getting hammered by it. All it required was simply to anticipate the wave's arrival. The first time I finally caught a wave it was like getting shot out of a cannon. Riding the power of the crest is much more exhilarating than getting dunked in the deep. I strongly recommend it!

Finding a focus

 Therefore, the purpose of this chapter is to provide specific practical ways for you to learn to lead with foresight. It is designed to provide you with a tool kit to enable Christian leaders not only to anticipate but creatively to respond to the waves of change rushing towards us. I am sure that you too will find riding the crest is a lot more satisfying than dredging the bottom.

First, it is essential to remind the reader that we have an unprecedented tsunami racing towards us. It is called globalisation. You can be certain that this McWorld tsunami will repeatedly swamp all our boats if we don't make an effort to take the future seriously. As we rush into a new millennium we need to anticipate both the opportunities and challenges that globalisation will present to us, our families, our churches and the world God has called us to care for.

Back to the future—identifying the fingerprints of God

The first way that people of faith seek to make sense of change is beyond the scope of secular futurists. We believe that our God is not only alive and well but active in history. Therefore, the first way we need to make sense of change is to pay attention to how the creator God seems to be at work within history, based upon what the Bible teaches us about God and the growth of God's subversive mustard seed.

In *Wild Hope* I wrote that some of the important changes of the past decade seemed to reflect something of the work of God. I wrote that I believed the dance on the Berlin Wall was the dance of God. The joyous songs sung by children at the release of Nelson Mandela, and now the re-unification of South Africa for all its people, are the songs of God. And the prayers increasingly raised all over the world for the peace of Jerusalem are certainly the prayers of God.[3]

In other words, the first way to lead with foresight is to discern how God seems to be at work through the inbreaking of God's mustard seed in human history—so we can consciously seek to collaborate with a God intent on subverting human arrogance and invading human history through the small and the insignificant.

Back to the future—is forecasting possible?

People often ask me: how do futurists try to predict the future? I usually respond, 'I prefer using sheep entrails, I don't find tea leaves terribly reliable.' Seriously, Christians often ask if it is even possible to make sense of the future. Only the Lord Almighty knows fully what the future holds. We need to remember that we live in a very complex world with an incredible number of variables, a world in which both natural and supernatural forces are at work over which we have very little understanding or control.

In spite of that I am convinced that we can use the intelligence the good Lord gave us and a little discernment to read some of 'the signs of the times'. I believe we can anticipate some of the change coming at us and find ways to creatively respond before the waves actually reach us. While the planning and forecasting methods we are discussing in this chapter are certainly a product of modernity and to some extent post-modernity, I believe these tools can enable people of faith to become more creative stewards of our lives and churches.

Forecasting is a very messy art

Let me say right up front that trying to make sense of the future is not a science. It is a very messy art. And futurists often get it wrong. Herman Kahn was one of the leading corporate futurists who in the seventies predicted a future of ever-increasing prosperity for everyone on the planet with no mention of any possible dislocations. Both Richard Naisbitt's optimistic projections for the future and Faith Popcorn's consumer snapshots have sometimes proven to be dead wrong.[4]

While I accurately predicted a widening gap between rich and poor in America in the eighties and nineties and a period of growing political conservatism in the US in *Mustard Seed Conspiracy* (circa 1981), I missed a major change when I wrote *Wild Hope*, published in 1991. I correctly projected the creation of three major economic coalitions in America, Europe and Asia. But I didn't anticipate the decline in the Japanese economy even though I had a colleague, a businessman who accurately predicted what has happened.

 In spite of the fact that we sometimes get it wrong in this business of attempting to make sense of the future, we really have only two options. Either we can ignore change entirely and live our lives, raise our young and run our organisations as though the future is simply going to be more of what's happening now—and enjoy repeated rides on the wet side. Or we can make our best effort to anticipate some of the change racing towards us so that we have lead time to respond to it. I for one think Shakespeare is right. It makes more sense to 'take the current when it serves'.

Futuring—the possible and the impossible

'Merely to survive, churches must learn not simply to ride each wave of change . . . we should be finding out how to anticipate, as far as possible, what the future holds in store for us,' urges Richard Kew and Roger White in their helpful book *Towards 2015.*[5] Of course there is no way we can accurately predict even a relative representation of what the landscape of tomorrow's world will look like in its entirety. There are, however, some areas of change that we can predict with a fairly high level of confidence. Other forms of futuring are highly speculative. And it is essential that those in leadership learn to distinguish.

To illustrate the point, demographic projections ten to fifteen years into the future are usually very reliable. For example, one can predict with a fairly high degree of certainty how many Americans will reach retirement age in 2010 when the boomers start to retire. We can, with a fairly high degree of certainty, predict some of the new technologies that are likely to invade our homes, lives and churches in the next ten years. Virtual reality will certainly be one of those new technologies. Armed with the forecast that various forms of virtual reality will be available in our stores within ten years, a Christian organisation could test a process called 'consequence forecasting'. I am confident that if we did solid research on this new technology we could successfully predict some of the possible positive and negative applications of virtual reality in our homes, schools and churches.

Other forms of forecasting are much less reliable. Personally, I have little confidence in those who claim to predict how the stock market will be performing in two years. And I don't believe anyone can predict with any degree of confidence what the youth culture will look like five years from now. These kinds of forecasting border on pure speculation. Christian leaders can learn reliable ways to make sense of some of the changing landscape of tomorrow's world by learning from those who have the most experience.

Back to the future—learning from the horizon watchers

Those who have the best track record in attempting to make sense of the future are those in the corporate world. I have yet to find a major corporation that doesn't do some form of forecasting before they do planning. And there are over three dozen major consulting firms in the USA from the Centre For Alternative Futures and Coates and Jarratt to Brain Trust that offer sophisticated forecasts at expensive prices for their corporate clients. It is obvious that corporations wouldn't spend money for these kinds of forecasting services if they didn't have real value.

We at Mustard Seeds Associates work with Christian organisations and churches to help them anticipate new challenges and opportunities. But there are very few other groups who work with Christian organisations to help them make sense of change.

Of course, the reason why corporate leaders are so keen to anticipate change is because they have learned from bitter experience that repeated rides on the wet side can be very expensive. Christian leaders need to anticipate change not to make a profit but so that we have lead time to create new ministry responses.

Even the book *Fortune Sellers*, which is very critical of all types of forecasting from weather forecasting to speculating on the stock market, still recognises the value of taking the future seriously. Author William Sherden states that we dare not ignore the future. 'We must continue to plan for the future by considering scenarios of what might happen and adapting our plans accordingly. To do otherwise would be foolhardy. We cannot blind ourselves to all predictions, because some contain vital information about our environment—not necessarily what *will* happen but what *could* happen.'⁶

User's guide for surfing with Shakespeare

A futures tool kit for leaders
Over the last four decades the corporate world has pioneered most of the methods and developed most of the tools designed to make sense of how the future is likely to change. We will briefly overview these tools then recommend specific tools those in Christian leadership might use.

1. *Trend extrapolation.* Economists and demographers use trend extrapolation as one of their basic tools. They simply extrapolate how many people are likely to be available to join the work force in the next five years in Canada or the US based on recent birth rates.

2. *Issues analysis.* This is one of the newest tools in the kit.

Essentially, business or government leaders identify ten to fifteen key issues on the horizon to monitor what could either send them to the bottom or enable them to catch the crest of change.

3. *Delphi polling.* Delphi polling is simply a method of gathering expert opinions about how the future is likely to change. For example, one might survey 100 of the top leaders in cancer research to predict the likelihood of a cure for the various forms of cancer by 2010.

4. *Intuitive insight.* Intuitive insight simply relies on subjective hunches about how the future is likely to change. Faith Popcorn's predictions about the future are based on substantial research. But she takes intuitive leaps to interpret this data to her clients. She creates terms to reflect these subjective leaps such as: 'cocooning', 'mum-food' and 'down-aging'.

Bill O'Brien, Director of the Global Center at Beeson Divinity School has worked with John Andersen from NASA to develop a non-linear forecasting method they call Horizon Mission Methodology. Essentially in this more intuitive method they project on the screen of tomorrow's world a possible future. For example, at a recent workshop they projected the emergence of Africa as a global power by 2050. Then participants were invited to identify the conditions, enterprises and relationships that would have to be formed to bring this possible future into being.[7]

5. *Prophetic insight.* One has only to read the prophets of the Old Testament to realise that at times God gifted some with prophetic insight about the future. I believe this gift is still operational in the Church today and I think I have seen some examples. But quite honestly the majority of cases I have heard of have often missed the mark. Having said that, I believe prophetic insights need to be taken seriously but I think churches need to develop guidelines, in community, on how they might be incorporated.

6. *Contextual forecasting.* Larger corporations often attempt to broadly scan how the larger context in which they do business is likely to change. Typically they scan economic, demographic, technological, political and cultural trends. From this they paint a picture of how they believe their context is likely to change in the next five to ten years. One of the few Christian organisations I have found using this method is the American Bible Society.

7. *Scenario forecasting.* All of the tools we have briefly reviewed in this kit have merit. But I firmly believe the most valuable tool for larger organisations, that have the resources to do a good job, is scenario forecasting. Essentially scenario forecasting draws heavily on good contextual forecasting. It always incorporates intuitive leaps in the writing of the scenarios. Typically, what you do in scenario forecasting is to write three to four possible stories about the future—all based on good data. Then you ask your staff to play through each scenario as though it was the future. Unlike contextual forecasting you don't bet the farm on a single scenario. You train your staff at how they would deal with change in each one of the scenarios so that they learn to think and plan 'contingently'. When I was working at the Weyerhaeuser Corporation New Business Research Division some years ago I hired science fiction author Frank Herbert to write three scenarios ten years in the future. The new business staff found it very helpful to explore how they would start new businesses in each of those possible futures.[8]

One of the colleagues I consulted with in futures research when I worked with Weyerhaeuser was Peter Schwartz who was employed at the Stanford Research Institute at the time. In his recent book, *The Art of the Longview*, Peter Schwartz makes a compelling case for using scenario forecasting as an important tool for catching waves of change instead of getting battered by them.

Working with Royal Dutch-Shell in 1983, Peter Schwartz developed a possible but improbable scenario for the implosion of the Soviet Union and its economy. In this scenario Schwartz concluded, 'To continue to keep any semblance of a standard of living, the Soviet Union had only two alternatives: Either to muddle through or open up.'[9]

Schwartz reported that by helping the leaders of Shell to play through this scenario they were able to catch the huge wave that swept through the Soviet Union and profit by change that swamped many of their competitors' boats because they never seriously considered the implausible would become a reality.[10]

Surfing with Shakespeare—a user's guide for Christian leaders

Given the available tools for anticipating change, which ones should Christian leaders consider using? How can we learn to catch the waves instead of getting pounded by them? Interested?

Preparing a new generation to surf with Shakespeare—leadership opportunities

Those of us who are parents, grandparents, pastors, educators and youth workers have a special responsibility to equip the young for life in a very demanding future. But most of us are unwittingly preparing the young to live in the world we grew up in instead of the third millennium. As a direct consequence of this crisis of foresight I believe many of our approaches to parenting, youth ministries and education are wrong. I believe we are often doing exactly the opposite of what we should be doing to equip our young people to live, thrive and serve God in a new millennium.

As we will discuss in the next four chapters, tomorrow's McWorld global society is likely to be a much more complex and demanding environment than the one we grew up in. To live and thrive in that world I am convinced our young people are going to need to be much more high initiating self-starters. They are going to need to become very skilled in solving serious problems. And to survive in tomorrow's globalised economy many of them will probably become entrepreneurs.[11]

Now stop and think about how many well-intended parents are raising their children today. Many are waiting on their young hand and foot and raising them in highly indulgent environments. This is not solely an American phenomenon. In Australia they call it 'over parenting'. The worst thing that we can do for young people is to rob them of initiative. I believe young people raised on the farm fifty years ago where they had serious responsibility at an early age were better equipped to live in the third millennium than most young people today.

How do we typically carry out youth ministry in our middle-class congregations? Employ a guy with a sports car to run activity driven programmes to entertain the young people and keep them busy, distracted and out of trouble. Doing for the young again. Secondary-school age students are perfectly capable of planning and running their own activities.

Planting a seed in a leadership empowerment with the young

Andy Hickford, when a youth pastor at Stopsley Baptist Church in Luton, England, took the critical risk of reinventing the entire youth programme to enable young people to run their own activities and develop their sense of initiative. One new thrust was to

send three secondary school students to the church's MAD
project in Ethiopia. He didn't send them to get stretched by a
global experience as many congregations do. He sent them to
Ethiopia with a major adult assignment. Their assignment was
to film a professional video documentary of the mission project. In preparation, these three students learned to storyboard,
script and use the video equipment.

When they arrived in the village they developed a story for
their documentary around the life of one child. They filmed it,
edited it and put music behind it. When they returned to
Luton, England they weren't just three secondary-school kids
waiting for adults at church to tell them what to do. They
began travelling to churches all over the region showing their
video and challenging older adults to get involved in ministry
to those in need in Ethiopia.

Planting a seed in futures education

Very few schools, colleges or theological
schools intentionally prepare students for life in
a world that will be very different from the one
their parents graduated into. One of the few
exceptions are MBA programmes which are
taught at some of America's more progressive
business schools. 'Long accused of training managers to fight
the last business war, America's B-schools are now consciously preparing students for the challenges that lie ahead.'[12]
Attending these schools is reportedly like playing Nintendo
on speed.

One of the courses offered at MIT-Sloan School of
Business is 'Inventing the Organisations for the twenty-first
century'. In this course students are invited not only to study
what has been done in the past and what is being done
today in the world of business, but to create new models for
the future. This is a model I would highly recommend

for adaptation in Christian colleges and seminaries.[13]

Creating a futures watch process for a new generation

Steve Hayner, President of Intervarsity Christian Fellowship in the US, has asked Mustard Seed Associates to develop and test a futures watch process with three different regions of IVCF that could provide the basis for creating a nationwide futures watch process for Intervarsity. The purpose of this process is to enable campus ministry leaders to help students identify some of the new opportunities and challenges that are likely to be waiting for them in the third millennium. Then before they graduate they can begin exploring how, as Christians, they will creatively respond to these new challenges.

Preparing our local churches to surf with Shakespeare—leadership opportunities

Creating a futures watch process for the local church

I recommend that local congregations develop a very simple futures watch process using simple trend extrapolation before they do their planning process. In this process they seek to answer two very straightforward questions:

1. How is the community in which your church is planted likely to change in the next ten years?

2. How is your congregation and your funding base likely to change in the next ten years?

How is your community likely to change in the next ten years?

To answer the first question I simply ask church leaders to draw a circle around the community they are ministering in and then ask: how is the population in this community likely to change in the next ten years? Who is moving out? Who is moving in? How is your community likely to change by age, race and economic level in the next ten years? What are their needs likely to be and how will you have to change your approaches to evangelism and ministry to address those needs?

For instance, while working with a Presbyterian church in Southern California I asked them to identify one population that was likely to move into their community in growing numbers in the next ten years. One of the leaders responded, 'We are going to have a huge increase in the number of single-parent mums.' So I asked, 'What are the special needs of single parents?' Someone responded, 'Child care, emotional and economic support systems.' Before the day was over they were beginning to proactively create a new course for single parents to help address the needs of this population as it became a growing presence in their community.

Planting a seed in housing for the young
How is your congregation likely to change demographically in the next ten years?

In preparation for doing a millennium 3 creativity workshop with a Baptist church in Vancouver BC, we asked the pastor to provide us with a demographic profile of their congregation. The profile revealed that a third of the church was over sixty-five and there were virtually no forty and fifty year olds. The rest of the congregation consisted of a very transitional group of young people who were attending the University of British Columbia and Regent College. In our research we discovered why so many of the young move away. Housing prices in the community started at $500,000 and went up from there.

I asked the pastor to research how much flats cost. To his surprise, flats in small blocks were selling for only $100,000 each. So during our creativity workshop, leaders came up with the creative idea of purchasing three or four blocks of flats, transforming them into condos and then selling individual flats to younger members so that there will be someone to lead the church into a new millennium.

One of the greatest benefits of learning to surf with Shakespeare is that it gives lead time to get creative. Christine and I have had the opportunity, through Mustard Seed Associates, to be part of a team led by Steve Gaukroger to design curriculum for Spring Harvest 1999, a training course for some 80,000 British Christians. Peter Meadows had the task of taking all the input and actually drafting curriculum to help prepare British churches and believers to create new responses to the challenges of tomorrow's world.

Preparing mission organisations to surf with Shakespeare—leaders' opportunity

Creating a futures watch process for Christian mission organisations

I realise that most Christian organisations typically have very little budget to spend on research, particularly research on future trends. Therefore I recommend that leaders find among their constituents those who are already tracking information about the future on the Internet. Ask four to eight of these supporters to become an on-line ad hoc futures watch group. I would suggest that these organisations use contextual forecasting and scenario forecasting.

Contextual forecasting

Have your futures watch group collect a broad spectrum of

information on demographic, economic, technological, political and religious trends and then combine their information once a year and develop two contextual forecasts for the next ten years. It is essential that the major trends identified are based on responsible sources and don't rely on speculative predictions about the future.

Tearfund UK takes contextual forecasting seriously

Doug Balfour, the CEO of Tearfund UK, initiated a process called the Jordan Project. One aspect of the project was to do a contextual forecasting process in which they asked two questions:

1. How is the context in which we work with the poor in Africa, Asia and Latin America likely to change in the next ten years?
2. How is the Church in the United Kingdom and our donor support base likely to change in the next ten years?

In answering the second question they found that their donor base was aging (an issue for many Christian agencies). In response, Tearfund added a new programme to find ways to reach the under-thirties.

Scenario forecasting

One of the limitations of contextual forecasting is that you tend to place all your weight on one possible projection for the future which may not always be accurate. The advantage of using scenario forecasting is that it enables your leadership team to think contingently about two to four possible futures before they embark on strategic planning. In this process I recommend that you use the information gathered in the contextual forecasting phase by your futures watch group to write two to four possible scenarios about the future.

Open Doors taking scenario forecasting seriously

Open Doors invited my wife and me to meet at their international offices in Holland to help them do some scenario forecasting. One of the scenario exercises focused on their work with the underground church in China. We invited their leadership team to play through two very different scenarios for China's economic future. In the first scenario, using some material from a World Bank book entitled *China 2020*, we presented an optimistic scenario that China's economy will continue to grow at 8-9% for the next ten years.

We asked Open Doors leaders to identify the possible impact of a high growth economy for those in the underground church. On the positive side they stated that greater economic growth would probably encourage a greater openness to the outside world. But growing prosperity could be as corrupting, they pointed out, for vital Christianity in China as it has been in Eastern Europe after the Wall came down. Therefore, Open Door leaders responded by proposing to design training materials to prepare members to deal with growing materialism.

The second scenario focused on a future in which the Chinese economy goes into a meltdown. Here the leaders predicted that Chinese society would become much more repressive towards the Church. They also predicted that the church would experience more severe hunger and deprivation. Their response was to explore how to create micro-enterprise projects to enable the hidden Church to support themselves.

Bringing it home

The Church desperately needs leaders who lead with foresight, rather than simply trying to survive a ride on the wild side or recover from a ride on the wet side. We need leaders who learn to both anticipate and creatively respond to waves of change—to be proactive instead of reactive.

Preview of coming attractions

In the next four chapters I am going to take you on some trips back to the future. I will offer you my attempt at a contextual forecast that describes different ways globalisation could impact your life, family, congregation and those with whom we share this planet. Remember we can approach the future with confidence because we know the end from the beginning—the mustard seed wins the day.

Questions for discussion and action

1. Why is it important for Christian leaders to learn to take the future seriously?
2. How can we discern God's activity in the change that fills our world?
3. What are some specific ways you could use these tools to anticipate how change is likely to impact your life, family, church and your community?
4. Anticipate one new likely area of change in the community in which you minister and create one new way to respond. What are the potential benefits of forecasting?

Notes

1   Act 3, Scene 3, *Julius Caesar*, *The Complete Works of William Shakespeare* (The Cambridge Text established by John Dover Wilson for the Cambridge University Press, London: Octopus Books Ltd, 1980), p.853.

2 Wayne Burkan, 'Developing Your Wide-Angle Vision', *The Futurist*, March 1998, p.35.

3 Tom Sine, *Wild Hope* (Word Books: Waco, Texas, 1991; Monarch: Tunbridge Wells, Kent, 1993).

4 William A. Sherden, *The Fortune Sellers: The Big Business of Buying and Selling Predictions* (Jon Wiley and Sons, Inc: New York, 1998), pp.219-222.

5 Richard Kew and Roger White, *Toward 2015: A Church Odyssey* (Cowley Publications: Cambridge, 1997), p.38.

6 William A. Sherden, *op. cit.*, p.14.

7 *WORKSHOP REPORT: Human Relational Concepts for the Emergence of Africa as a Global Power in 2050*, Beeson Divinity School, 5-7 February, 1997, p.6.

8 Frank Herbert, *A Future 2000, The Best of All Worlds*, 1974, p.2.

9 Peter Schwartz, *The Art of the Longview: Planning for the Future in an Uncertain World* (Currency Doubleday: New York, 1991), pp.53-54.

10 *Ibid.*

11 Suzy Parker, 'Age of Profits: Gen-x Goal: Be Your Own Boss', *The Christian Science Monitor*, 2 March, 1998, pp.1, 4.

12 Mary Lord, 'Preparing managers for the twenty-first century', *US News and World Report*, 2 March, 1998, p.72.

13 *Ibid.*, p.72.

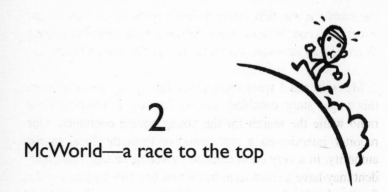

2
McWorld—a race to the top

> In Queensland's far north the sky, the water, the reef and the
> clouds mingle the blues in a dazzling cocktail. From a boat it is
> one of the wonders of the world—the black-blue of the distant
> deep and the azure blue of the shallows. There's cobalt in the sky,
> and below the water's staggeringly beautiful world of coral and
> fish.[1]

Thomas and Eileen Lonergan were on holiday after three
years of Peace Corps service in Fiji, enjoying the incredible
coral and fish of Australia's Great Barrier Reef. They had
decided to treat themselves to one last holiday before they
returned home to Baton Rouge, Louisiana, and started their
family. Since they were experienced scuba divers, they signed
on with the party on the dive boat, the Outer Edge, on one
warm sunny morning in late January. Their fellow divers
reported that Tom and Eileen were thoroughly enjoying the
unique beauty of the reef as the day wore on.

> But take away the boat, the Lonergans would have been utterly
> alone; beauty would have melted to fear. Maybe they saw the
> MV Outer Edge motoring back to port. The crew was serving

savouries, the bar was busy and in the jumble on the decks no one noticed the Americans' unattended bags.[2]

Incredibly, it was fifty hours before anyone noticed the young American couple had not returned with the dive boat. Belatedly, an intensive search began for Thomas and Eileen.

My wife and I were visiting her family in Australia when this tragic story unfolded. On 29 January I listened to the radio while the search for the young couple continued. One reporter interviewed a representative from the local tourist authority. In a very cool, detached voice he stated: 'This incident may have a short-term impact on the dive business and a few tourists might ask questions, but it certainly will not detrimentally impact the local tourist economy. There is absolutely no reason for anyone to be concerned about the economic impact of this isolated incident.'

It's the economy, stupid!

During this entire interview there was absolutely no mention of the tragic human loss or the pain to the family who were waiting for word regarding their loved ones. The focus of the interview was singularly on the economic impact to the local tourist industry. Let me hasten to add there were other interviews that did focus on the human dimension. But this interview could have taken place anywhere in the world because economic impacts are increasingly seen ultimately as our most important concern.

In Woody Allen's nostalgic film, *Radio Days*, we are witnesses to the recreation of another human tragedy that took place in the forties. I was in primary school at the time and can still vividly remember listening to this drama on the radio. A little girl in Texas fell down a deep well. Emergency crews were repeatedly frustrated over a number of hours attempting to rescue her. I was impressed at how the whole nation seemed to come to a complete halt, transfixed by this harrowing crisis.

We became like one very large extended family with our ears glued to the radio, praying and waiting until we finally heard the word. After many long hours they dug a parallel tunnel and successfully rescued the child. When we got that good news, the whole nation joined in a collective sigh of relief. It is difficult for me to imagine that scene taking place in America today.

The point is that over the last fifty years society has changed dramatically in terms of our shared understanding of what's important and what's of value. Increasingly, the overwhelming message from modern culture about what's important couldn't be clearer: 'It's the economy, stupid!' Like the spokesman for the tourist industry Down Under, many of us in Western societies tend to see economic concerns as the ultimate concerns. As we will show in this chapter, this is no accident. Many of us, including people of keen biblical faith, have been influenced by modern culture to define what is important and what is of value in largely economic terms too.

Finding a focus

 The aim of this chapter is to ask, 'How is economic globalisation likely to change our common future and particularly our view of what is important and of value?' In this 'contextual forecast' we will begin identifying some of the possible up sides and down sides of economic globalisation. We will also try to understand the future to which the architects of McWorld promise to take us and the vehicle they will use to transport us there. Finally, we will

ask, 'What impact is economic globalisation likely to have on our lives and communities of faith as we race into a new millennium and how should we prepare to serve God in that world?'

A race to the top—looking backwards

I remember when San Francisco went through two huge convulsions of celebration at the end of World War 2. Mayhem reigned on Market Street at the end of both our war with Germany and that with Japan. The sense of hope for our common future as the war ended was almost palpable. As a sixth grader I was invited to enter a city-wide poster contest to help promote the economic development of our former enemy, Japan, in 1946. My poster read, 'HELP JAPAN TO HELP HERSELF'. To my astonishment, my poster won first place and in the ensuing years the United States did indeed help Japan and Germany and our former allies to help themselves.

Before the First World War there had been an active attempt to create a global economic order. But the great depression of the 1920s and 1930s brought this move towards globalisation to an abrupt halt. On 8 December 1941, when the United States entered World War 2, the United States and Great Britain were essentially the only capitalist countries in the world. The rest of the world was divided between fascists, communists, a few monarchies and a number of colonial regimes.

As a direct result of America helping former enemies to help themselves, Japan and Germany not only became economic dynamos, they became partners in a burgeoning free-market alliance. With the unexpected end of the cold war all the centrally planned economies ended up in the dustbin of history and virtually every nation chose to join the global capitalist race to the top.

Globalisation—determining the shape of the world to come

 It is the contention of this book that the number-one force that will shape the future of our lives, families, congregations and that larger world is globalisation. Someone has written, 'For better or worse we have girded our planet in a global electronic nervous system of satellites and fax machines from which there is no exit.' It is through that global electronic system that we have witnessed the creation of a new one world economic order.

Kenichi Ohame, a leading Japanese economist, offers a description of this borderless new one world economic order. 'With the emergence of "electronic highways" all corporate players can "plug" into the global marketplace freed of government interference to participate in a new open transnational economy.'[3]

The strongest advocates for a new global economic order, like Ohame, are well intended economic and political leaders who want what is best for our planetary community. They have been schooled in a worldview that defines what is best largely in terms of economic growth and economic efficiency. And they have concluded that the best way to achieve those outcomes is through the creation of a borderless economic order. The creation of the European union and the Euro is certainly an expression of this.

There is no question that for those of us who are middle class to sustain life and help the poor achieve a decent way of life we need to expand our economies. I am not as sure as the architects of McWorld that the best ways to expand our economies is to create a one world economic order. Where I have a particular problem with their advocacy is that from a Christian perspective I will never be able to define what's best or what's ultimate in terms of economic growth and economic efficiency. I believe we need to create some forums in which Christian economists, theologians and historians discuss not only where the globalisation of the economy is likely to take us but what the values are that drive it.

To understand this crusade to create a global economic order it is important to understand that not all the national economies who are joining this race to the top are working from the same economic models. The economies of Europe and Japan are essentially 'stakeholder' economies that have a sense of responsibility not only to those who buy stock but to the workers, the communities in which the firms are based, the larger society and even the producers.

The United States and Britain, on the other hand, operate from 'shareholder' economies where the concern is almost entirely focused on meeting the expectations of those who own shares in the corporation. In this very competitive race to the top the shareholder model is setting the pace because the stakeholder model is considerably more expensive.

Those economists, like Ohame, who are strong advocates for economic globalisation promise that this rocketship will transport us to a new future of unbelievable affluence for all peoples. And the advocates of the shareholder model are arguing that their model is the most efficient. In any case virtually all of the world's nations have joined in this brutally competitive economic race to the top because economic growth and efficiency are seen as the ultimate good. Leaders of most nations seem to be convinced that high economic growth increases stability at home and political power abroad. So like it or not we are all along for the ride.

All that is required from us is to trust our lives and futures to the twin rockets of free enterprise and free trade. We are told that if we allow the market to have complete freedom and we support complete free trade where everyone is able to fish in everyone else's pond, the global economy will enter a long boom that will lift all boats. But as I write we are in the midst of a global economic crisis that is raising serious questions for some as to whether the perils of creating a global economic order outweigh the benefits. However, short of a total meltdown, I don't think there is any way we are likely to get off this course.

Globalisation—conspiracy or consensus?

Not everyone is excited about the creation of a borderless world economy. Pat Buchanan sees the creation of a 'one world economic order' in the most sinister terms. In his book, *The Great Betrayal*, he seeks to rally those on the right to oppose free trade to protect America's economic power, American jobs and American nationalism. Some on the extreme right believe that globalisation is being engineered by some conspiratorial élite of Zionist bankers.

There are those on the left who also talk in the darkest tones about a global conspiracy being directed by wealthy corporations. They are at work aggressively opposing NAFTA, free trade and the work of the World Trade Organisation. But contrary to the inflamed opinions of both the right and left I haven't found any evidence of a global conspiracy being orchestrated by a small élite of corporate CEOs or European financiers. In fact everything I have seen convinces me that no one seems to be in the driver's seat of this run away global economy. I find the prospect of a ride on the wild side with no one at the wheel even more terrifying than a small sinister élite calling the shots because no one has any idea of where this ride will take us including the most ardent advocates of economic globalisation

William Greider characterised this powerful movement towards economic globalisation as a race and a revolution:

The present economic revolution, like revolutions of the past, is fuelled by invention and human ingenuity and a universal aspiration to build and accumulate. But it is also driven by a palpable sense of insecurity. No one can be said to control the energies of unfettered capital, not important governments or financiers, nor dictators or democrats. And, in the race to the future, no one dares fall a step behind, not nations or major corporations. Even the most effective leaders of business and finance share in this uncertainty, knowing as they do that the uncompromising dynamics can someday turn on the revolutionaries themselves.[4]

I will show that while there is certainly no conspiracy there is a growing consensus among the advocates of globalisation about what is important and what is of value. Not surprisingly these values come directly from the aspirations of the values of modern culture. As we will see, those aspirations and values are, in many ways, in direct conflict with those undergirding a biblical faith.

While a number of economists see economic globalisation as simply the creation of an unregulated transnational economy for the free exchange of goods and services, other authors are convinced that there is more to it than that. For instance, in *Jihad vs McWorld* Benjamin Barber contends that the fabricators of McWorld are also intent on creating an entire new global culture that reflects its core values.

Barber writes:

McWorld is a product of popular culture driven by expansionist commerce. Its template is American, its form style . . . It is about culture as a commodity, apparel as ideology. Its symbols are Harley-Davidson motorcycles and Cadillac motorcars hoisted from the roadways, where they once represented a mode of transportation, to the marquees of global market cafés like Harley-Davidson's and the Hard Rock where they become icons of a lifestyle . . . Music, videos, theater books, and theme parks—the

new churches of a commercial civilization in which the malls and
public squares . . . are all constructed around image exports creating a common world taste around common logos, advertising slo-
gans, stars, songs, brand names, jingles and trademarks.[5]

In other words, Barber is arguing that the way we are creating
global free exchange of goods and services is not a value free
or a culturally neutral activity. Quite the contrary. McWorld is
driven, as we will show, by the aspirations and values of
modernity and is aggressively at work creating a one world
consumer culture where the shopping malls are replacing the
Church as the centres of religious devotion and all of life is
reduced to a commodity.

The best of times—the worst of times

The best of times

As my wife and I left a wharf-side restaurant in Seattle we
were greeted with a huge display of luxury yachts open for
inspection. And at a recent home exhibition in the north-west
of the USA, it seemed like every second display boasted lavish baths large enough to test a kayak in. If you drive up in the
hills above Microsoft you will see gigantic multi-million dollar homes with large hot tubs that would rival the baths of
ancient Rome. The amazing thing to me is that these luxury
items have been, until recently, selling like hot cakes.

In Seattle, hundreds of middle-class people boarded the
Microsoft rocket in the eighties and have joined the ranks of
the Microsoft millionaires in the nineties. I have met those in
the financial districts of London who have also benefited
handsomely from the recent McWorld lift-off. Millions of
people in the middle class have seen their consumer choices
expand dramatically in the past ten years with the globalisation of trade. Even those in poorer countries have benefited
from economic globalisation.

'I arrived!' shouted Martha Fuñes. In the last ten years Martha and nine of her relatives have risen from a hand-to-mouth existence in a run-down border town to the American middle class. Her new car, new suburban home and more affluent lifestyle all come from Martha and her relatives boxing computers for Dell for an exploding global market.[6] Martha and her family are representative of numbers of people who are celebrating their move into a new 'global' neighbourhood and directly benefiting economically from this race to the top.

We are all being rocketed, at breath-taking speed, into a new 'global' neighbourhood of mega-mergers, digital entertainment and consumer cornucopia. Borders are melting, and distance is dying as five billion of us now shop at the same macro-mall and stare transfixed at the same electronic images. *The New York Times* heralded this extraordinary period of global economic growth as the 'best of times'.[7] The advocates for a McWorld future insist we haven't seen anything yet.

The future of the long boom

Futurist Peter Schwartz paints a very vivid scenario of the better future of the long boom to which economic globalisation promises to transport us:

> We are watching the beginnings of a global economic boom on a scale never experienced before. We have entered a period of sustained growth that could eventually double the world's economy every dozen years and bring prosperity for—quite literally—billions of people on the planet. We are riding the early waves of a 25-year run of a greatly expanding economy that will do much to solve seemingly intractable problems like poverty and to ease tensions throughout the world. And we will do it without blowing the lid off the environment. These two metatrends—fundamental technological change and a new ethos of openness—will transform our world into the beginnings of a global civilisa-

tion . . . that will blossom through the coming century.[8]

Opportunities for Christian leaders

How can those in leadership prepare us to deal with both the opportunities and the challenges of the long boom?

1. In our lives and families, some of us who are middle class might begin to climb the same escalator used by the Microsoft millionaires. We would be able to be more economically secure, send our young to the finest universities and purchase goods out of reach before. And we would have more money to give to the Church. But a number of the Microsoft millionaires will tell you that one of the costs of that climb to the top was that they weren't around to see their kids grow up. Pastors working with those who have joined the ranks of the very affluent report that they have often become more preoccupied with issues of status, materialism and influence than issues of vital faith. Therefore, to get people ready for the future of the long boom those in leadership will need to develop educational materials to enable Christians to deal with the seductions of the consumer culture and to learn to put first things first in their lives.

2. In our churches, if members earned better incomes they would have more financial resources to give to the Church and worthy causes. But during the seven-year boom in the United States, giving did increase but not nearly as rapidly as the rise in salaries of church members. Congregational leaders, in this scenario, would also need to offer courses that would enable members to become responsible stewards of their increased affluence.

3. One of the most promising aspects of the long boom scenario is that increased economic growth could mean that more of those on the margins in our country and abroad would have

a possible opportunity to provide the essentials of life for their families. It doesn't happen automatically however. Therefore in the long boom scenario the more affluent churches need to form partnerships with poorer congregations in their own country and overseas to create small-scale businesses and credit unions so the poor don't miss this opportunity to create a decent way of life for their families.

4. One of the most concerning consequences of a high global growth scenario is that it will dramatically increase the rate at which we use and degrade environmental resources. Therefore, in this scenario Christian leaders will need to invest much more emphasis on caring for the creation in partnership with organisations like The Evangelical Environmental Network.[9]

The worst of times

'Is it time for investors to sober up?' asks *The New York Times*. 'Wall Street analysts agree that profits will decline a few percentage points in the third quarter [of 1998], ending an almost seven-year run of intoxicating profit gains. The bigger question is what happens next. Will this just be a brief headache or . . . turn into a real hangover?'[10]

As I was doing final editing on this manuscript, an editorial in *The Economist* seriously questioned the buoyant optimism that is lifting the American economy after overcoming a recession scare. They are convinced the boom can't last. 'The most striking evidence of why this cannot last is that total household savings turned negative in September for the first time in 60 years. Companies have also been borrowing heavily to finance capital investment. As a result, the combined private savings rate [the gap between total private income and spending] has fallen to levels below anything ever seen in America before.'[11] Sooner or later we know that what goes up must come down and I don't think most Western Christians are prepared to deal with a serious recession.

Report from the trenches

Tim Dearborn, at World Vision US, explained to me that the global economic meltdown is having a devastating impact on the lives and families of many of our poorest neighbours. In a number of cities in the poorer countries of Asia—Thailand, Indonesia and Malaysia—unemployment is soaring and families are having extreme difficulty in keeping their children fed. As a consequence more and more children are being forced into the international child prostitution trade and more people are accepting sweat-shop jobs with very low pay and brutal working conditions.

Dearborn said the only ones who are somewhat better off in this depression are the rural poor who use their land to grow food for their families instead of cash crops for global trade. Reportedly those braving the Russian meltdown have had their most savage winter in years as a result of the economic crisis and severe shortfall in food production.

The slow melt down

Working on this manuscript before anyone else caught the 'Asian flu', I wrote: 'One of my concerns is that as we all become much more tightly hardwired together in a single one world economy we also become much more vulnerable. If Russia, China or Brazil experience a major depression none of us will be spared the pain.' Since I penned those words Russia's economy has completely imploded. China's economy is rapidly slowing and they are making every effort to avoid the crippling contagion. As I write, Brazil is attempting to avoid contracting the Asian flu and spreading the global recession to the Americas.

There are conflicting opinions as to whether this global

meltdown, which started in Asia, will engulf North America and Europe. What is clear is that it is going to at the very least slow the rate of economic growth if not lead to a recession in all our countries. Michael Mandel writing for *Business Week* stated, 'Today, it's clear that both globalisation and technological change are creating new risks. The increased interconnectedness of the global economy means that economic or financial disturbances in Asia or Russia can be transmitted much faster and more powerfully to the rest of the world.'[12]

John Heilemann, an editor for *WIRED* who is an enthusiastic booster for economic globalisation, shares the same concern about our economies becoming more tightly wired together. 'The invention of superhighways made transportation better and safer overall. But it also increased the risks of spectacular smash-ups. I think the development of modern financial markets and greater interconnectedness is very much like the development of the superhighway.'[13] A total global meltdown could give us all a firsthand experience of what it would be like to be in a 'spectacular smash-up' and discover just how vulnerable we are likely to be in a new, more volatile, global economic order.

'There is no international body able to play the role of global regulator, and an inability by the United States and other powers to impose changes on the often-reluctant governments and banks in nations at risk'[14] was the diagnosis of *The New York Times* as we headed into a possible global smash-up. As the crisis has worsened global financial leaders are working feverishly to construct a new global architecture. But it is still years away and a number doubt we will ever develop the universal ground rules essential to avoid these kind of smash-ups.

Getting ready for the millennium bug

Also on the horizon as I write is the coming collision with the millennium bug. As we cross the threshold into the year 2000 we will discover how serious the breakdown is going to be as a result of a failure to make all computers compliant. There are some religious extremists who are linking the Y2K bug to their pet end times theories, selling their homes and stockpiling food and guns in mountain hideaways. Frankly, this kind of hysteria isn't terribly helpful and the survivalist movement causes people to become self-involved in times of crisis instead of concerned for the needs of others. This kind of fear-mongering might cause more of a crisis than the bug itself.

Having said that, I believe the coming collision with the Y2K bug needs to be taken very seriously. If you know when an earthquake is coming (and we do) common sense dictates you get ready. I have encouraged a number of Christian organisations that I work with to develop a broad range of contingency plans so they are prepared to deal with worse case scenarios. Two of the most helpful sources I have found on the subject are the Joseph Project at: www.josephproject2000.org and the year 2000 information centre at: www.year2000.com. I was among those who urged Intervarsity Christian Fellowship to postpone Urbana since it was scheduled to take place as we entered the year 2000. I was concerned about the risk of transporting some 20,000 college students from all over North America at a time when it wasn't clear how many airlines would be compliant.

In any case, as we cross the threshold into a new millennium we will all discover together how bad the Y2K crisis is going to be. It is certain to have a major impact on the economy. If we aren't in recession by then, the year 2000 bug could well push us over the edge.

Opportunity for Christian leaders

 Christian leaders have a responsibility to prepare their members not only for the possibility of the long boom but also for the possibility of the slow meltdown. Regardless of whether those of us in North America and Europe catch the Asian flu, we are all going to be impacted by the millennium bug and we know that sooner or later we will experience an economic recession. So we need to get people ready, like Joseph prepared Egypt for seven bad years, while increasing our trust in God. Leaders have the opportunity:

1. To prepare individuals and families to get ready for a more volatile economic future in which we will all be more vulnerable. I suggest that you encourage people to reduce their exposure by reducing their debt load as much as possible, increasing their savings and planting gardens (where possible) to increase food self-reliance. It is essential that Christians in hard times be encouraged to put their faith in God and learn to work together in the body to help others;

2. To enable local churches to design programmes of mutual care and co-operation (like starting food co-ops) in advance of hard times, so Christians are able not only to help one another but also those in need in their communities;

3. To enable those who work with the poor to develop a buffer of emergency food and medical supplies against hard times because the poor are always hit hardest by recessions or natural disasters. Urban ministries also need to encourage the poor to use their backyards and roof tops to increase their food self-reliance. And we need to create a range of partnerships between middle class and urban churches, in this scenario too, to work together to address the needs of our poorest neighbours during a time of economic crisis;

4. To get your people and Christian organisations ready for the coming of the Y2K bug crisis. I believe it is always prudent, like those of Mormon faith, to have some food and water set by for any kind of a disaster. This could help us, in a time of crisis, to focus beyond our own survival and help others in need. I urge all Christian organisations to develop carefully thought out contingency plans to be able to deal with the possible fall-out of this crisis.

Welcome to the great McWorld auction

Regardless of whether we enter a future of the slow meltdown or resume the future of the long boom, we are going to see continued rapid globalisation of every aspect of God's world and our lives. We are racing into a McWorld future in which everything from jobs to small businesses to our own bodies are up for auction. Economists assure us it is just good common business sense to assign everything a price.

British author Charles Handy explores where this business of assigning a price to everything might take us. 'If people want to sell their kidneys, or their bodies for sex, why shouldn't they, as long as there are willing buyers? In this rhetoric the value of anything is in its price. It gets tempting, this commodification of everything. It reduces everything to a convenient common denominator. One can even, technically, demonstrate that the marginal productivity of some members of society is too low to allow them to purchase the cost of living. Should they then Perish?' Handy concludes: 'A society which was a grand auction block would not be a society worth having. It might even be far less economically successful than its proponents imagine. We should not be over-impressed by the early energies released by deregulation. Everything cannot be for sale.'[15]

But as we will see the architects of McWorld are intent on

creating a new global economy of free enterprise and free trade in which everything is up for auction and everything is for sale. Let's look at where this great auction could take us.

The great job auction

Impoverished photographers who live in the ramshackle Mexican border town of Juarez convey a very different picture of life for those employed in the new global factories than the story of Martha Fuñes that we just mentioned. Multinational corporations have come here to Juarez for the same reason they have gone to Vietnam and Thailand: very cheap labour. They pay their workers a bit more than Mexican factories in the area but many of the people don't make enough to pay for child care let alone have the resources to move out of the squalour that has them trapped. The photographic exhibit, on display in the United States, shows pictures of the cardboard shanty towns with no electricity, heat or water.[16]

One of the essential conditions of economic globalisation is that all businesses should have unlimited access to the global labour pool to produce their goods as efficiently as possible. This viewpoint insists that the employer has no responsibility to either the worker who loses his job in a car plant in Flint or to pay a living wage to a worker who replaces him in Juarez. Their singular responsibility is to show their shareholders a profit. They insist it is up to the free market to sort out the future for those in Flint whose jobs went south. And it is up to the free market to set the wages of workers in Juarez even if the going wage is not enough to provide a decent way of life for their families.

Even the middle class are being impacted by the great job auction. Computer programmers in Bangalore, India, are willing to work for a tenth to a fifth of what their counterpart in San Jose is paid. And their work arrives via the internet twenty-four hours a day.[17]

Pat Buchanan on the right and Richard Gephart on the left are both challenging the contentions of prominent free-trade economists that this global job auction will have very little impact on workers in major industrialised nations like the United States. They both tilt in the direction of protectionist policies.[18]

I personally find it difficult to imagine an alternative to this global free-trade rocketship on which we are all riding. Protectionism does seem to be fraught with difficulties. However, a member of the European Parliament proposes one alternative I find intriguing. He urges that we 'reject the concept of global free trade and replace it with regional free trade. That does not mean closing off regions of the world from trading with the rest of the world. It means allowing each region to decide whether and when they want to enter into a bilateral agreement with other regions for mutual economic benefit. We must not simply open our markets to any and every product regardless of whether it benefits our economy, destroys our employment, or destabilises our society.'[19]

Planting a seed in Juarez

There are a number of firms like The Gap and Levis that have taken the initiative to pay those who make the garments a living wage even if it is more than the prevailing market wage. *Forbes Magazine* grudgingly acknowledged the successful work of Roman Catholic Sister Susan Mika in her advocacy for the working poor in Juarez who are employed in this McWorld industrial park. Sister Susan, working through a shareholder's group, persuaded General Motors to construct 7,000 basic homes for their workers who had been living in wooden or cardboard shacks with no plumbing.[20] There are thousands of others, like Sister Susan, who are working as a part of God's mustard seed movement to challenge those in positions of power to do justice.

The great small business auction

We are rapidly moving into a future in which the family farm, the small retailer and the corner café are rapidly becoming artifacts of a bygone past. They are all on the auction block too because small is inefficient. Economists assure us that we have all benefited from the gradual disappearance of the family farm.

Undeniably the major superstores' huge purchasing power can offer the consumer a lower price than the local shop. But belatedly many are discovering, as the local shop disappears, that they provided our communities with much more than consumer goods. They offered services and a presence in our communities that the huge superstores will never replace. As they disappear we are finding our communities are disappearing too. And the new shopping options appearing on the internet may even gobble up the super stores.

Destruction of local communities and families

Wendell Berry, a Christian ecologist, decries the destruction of local communities and families in the name of economic efficiency and centralisation of economic power. 'The danger of the ideal of competition is that it neither proposes or implies any limits. It proposes simply to lower costs at any cost, and to raise profits at any cost. It doesn't hesitate at the destruction of the life of a family or the life of a community.'[21] We are witnessing for the first time in history the fashioning of a highly centralised global economy in which a handful of economic Godzillas will increasingly establish their domination. As these monoliths mate they create even larger offspring. And while this will mean high dividends for shareholders I believe it will often come at a very high price to families and local communities.

'Did someone say McDonalds?'

Ronald McDonald has accomplished what neither Napoleon nor Hitler were ever able to achieve. Ronald and the invading armies of McDonalds have made it all the way to Moscow and become a visible bastion of this new economic order. 'The scale of the global MAC ATTACK is impressive,' reports *The Economist*. They plan to open at least 3,200 new outlets a year until the year 2000. Michael Quinlan, Chairman of McDonald's board, declared, 'I am open to any course that helps McDonald dominate every market.'[22] In the McWorld business auction domination is the name of the game as huge corporations all over McWorld are seeking to establish their absolute supremacy in this new one world market.

Many regional family-run restaurants and cafés all over the world are being replaced with a globally standardised diet of Big Macs, KFC chicken strips and Pizza Hut's latest pizza hit. In Sylvester Stalone's film *Demolition Man*, set in the year 2032, they have fun parodying pop-culture today. They celebrate the fact that only one restaurant survived the franchise wars and established total global domination. And now everyone dines exclusively at Taco Bell. Now there is a better future we can all get excited about!

Dominating the global food supply

There are a handful of corporations that are just as intent on dominating global food distributions as McDonalds is to dominate the fast food market. One of the leaders in this race is Conagra, an agribusiness colossus based in the US that aspires to dominate the global food business within the next ten years. While most people have never heard of Conagra, many Americans consume their products seven days a week. They produce everything from Armour and Butterball meat products to Wesson Oil and Peter Pan Peanut butter. They control a huge share of US fertiliser, grain and frozen food production.[23]

While Conagra is committed to dominating the global food distribution network, Monsanto is committed to dominating the genetic seed stock for the world food supply. They are busy creating new genetically engineered plants that have their own built-in pesticides to increase agricultural production. Their goal is to persuade farmers to switch to these genetically engineered seeds to increase their profits. Since Monsanto holds the patents on these designer seeds, farmers can't use seed from their own harvest for planting next year's planting. They will be forced to become totally dependent on Monsanto. Europeans are adamantly opposed to what they call 'frankenplants'. But in the United States the food industry has got a law passed making it illegal to inform people they are eating genetically engineered potatoes or drinking genetically engineered milk.[24]

This all began with a Supreme Court Decision. 'In 1980, in a historic five to four decision, the Supreme Court ruled that new life forms created in the laboratory could be patented. That decision was the harbinger of a whole new age.'[25] Since that historic vote, not only have corporations been involved in a genetic gold rush to patent new life forms created in the lab, they have been patenting plant, animal and even human genetic material from all over the planet for their private economic gain. Some have labelled this multi-billion dollar a year business 'bio-piracy' because the people from whose regions this genetic material is 'prospected' often derive very little of the economic benefit.[26]

Will we all feel more secure when a handful of corporations control the global seed stock and the food distribution networks? Is this an inevitable future or are there ways in which individuals can find access to other alternatives? The problem is not only the control but the safety of our food supply in a McWorld future.

Food efficiency versus food safety

Globalising the food supply has brought us an extravagant selection of foods from all over the world. Raspberries in the winter from Guatemala, grapes from Chile, prawns from Thailand, mangos from Mexico. But even this has a downside. Thousands of Americans became ill last year from a parasite that was also imported with the raspberries.[27] As we are dramatically increasing the amount of food we import in the US we are actually cutting back funding for inspectors to reduce the drag on the US economy in this global race to the top.

One of the benefits of allowing the food giants to take greater control of food production is that it has reduced costs. But unfortunately we are discovering that cost reduction in the efficient production of our food is sometimes coming at a very high price in food safety. Mad Cow Disease is one of the outcomes of cutting feed costs in Britain by putting animal waste into the feed. The recent outbreak of a particularly virulent strain of E.coli which killed 250 Americans and made thousands of others seriously ill thus far isn't an accident. It is a direct consequence of ranchers trying to produce beef more efficiently.

The World Health Report tells us that ranchers, in recent years, wanting to protect the quality of their cattle, routinely give them sub-therapeutic doses of antibiotics. This inadvertently created a virulent strain of E.coli which has become very dangerous to humans because it is extremely resistant to antibiotics.[28] This is only one of a growing list of concerns about the efficiently produced food supply.

Planting a seed in Community Supported Agriculture

There is a movement called Community Supported Agriculture that is giving small family farms some hope for the future while providing a safer and better quality of food for members. There are roughly 600 CSA farms all over the United States. Essentially what members in these food co-operatives do is pay farmers to grow a year-round selection of fruits and vegetables for their families.

Michael Docter started a CSA farm in Hadley, Massachusetts. Shares in the farm cost $350-$450 a year. 'We serve nearly 600 families,' he explained. 'The size of the share is so large that two or three households often buy them together.'[29] Families know their food is safe. They annually grow over 200,000 pounds of produce on sixty acres at or below supermarket prices. 'The farm annually gives away half of what they grow to emergency food pantries, shelters and programmes for the elderly in their community.'[30]

Christine and I are, as a Christian stewardship goal, attempting to grow the majority of our fruit and vegetables on one urban plot. We presently grow sixty per cent of our vegetables but our fruit trees have a lot of growing to do. Based on this research we are beginning to purchase more organically grown food too.

The great creation auction

Since the leaders of McWorld view economic growth and efficiency as the greatest good then creation is viewed as simply a resource to be used in the cause of accelerating economic growth. This has fostered a reductionistic view of God's creation where it is seen as nothing but an economic resource.

The long boom—the environmental price tag

Our expansive and growing appetites are already responsible for over-harvesting many of the earth's forests and fish stocks as well as seriously eroding some of our best agricultural land. In the future we are likely to see growing conflicts over competition for shrinking fresh water resources. Some even predict a new oil crisis because of the tremendous amount of fossil fuels required to fuel this race to the top. Few nations have adequate resources to clean up the toxic, chemical and nuclear waste that is a by-product of a half century of rapid growth and development let alone the pollution that will be generated by the next half century of growth.

The summer of 1998 was the hottest on record and this, plus dramatic changes in global weather, has heightened public concern about pollution and climate change. Ironically the insurance companies are the ones who are raising the greatest concern about global warming. The reason for their sudden fit of conscience is that they are getting hammered by huge losses due to unprecedented weather-related claims in the last eight years.

If the long boom scenario resumes it will dramatically escalate the rate at which we auction off our planetary resources and pollute our environment. Rarely do economists ever factor the cost of environmental degradation into their equations. Short-term decisions often have long-term costs. Do we really believe that if we continue to use dwindling resources to produce a short-term gain there won't be long-term costs to our children and grandchildren? Do we really believe that somehow the invisible hand of the market will take care of the problem?

Considering growing the economy on purpose

Not only is the next generation and God's creation imperiled by our short-term and often short-sighted economic policies but so are the world's poor. Reportedly it takes 12.2 acres of land to supply the needs of an average American. In the Netherlands the basic needs are met with the resources of 8 acres and in India only a single acre is required. If the implicit promise of McWorld was realised and all the world's people achieved an American lifestyle it would take three planets the size of ours to support the present world's population.

Stuart Hart, who writes for the *Harvard Business Review*, wants to persuade corporate leaders to develop a sustainable approach to economic growth in which the goal is to enable all the world's people to achieve a decent way of life for themselves and their kids so they don't totally lose out in this devil-take-the-hindmost race to the top. Hart points out that our poorest neighbours simply aren't able to compete with us in this great earth auction.

> Owing in part to the rapid expansion of the market economy, existence in the survival economy is becoming increasingly precarious. Extractive industries and infrastructure development have, in many cases, degraded the ecosystems upon which their survival economy depends.
>
> Rural populations are driven further into poverty as they compete for scarce natural resources. Women and children now on average spend four to six hours per day searching for fuel wood and four to six hours a week drawing and carrying water . . . Worldwide, the number of such 'environmental refugees' from the survival economy may be as high as 500 million today and the figure is growing.[31]

Planting a seed in BMW

Hart cites how a German 'take back' law required car manufacturers to take back their cars at the end of their useful life. Innovators like BMW now design cars for easy disassembly and profitable recycling. Hart concludes, 'In the coming decade, companies will be challenged to develop clean technologies and implement strategies that drastically reduce the environmental burden in the developing world while simultaneously increasing its wealth and standard of living.'[32]

Planting a seed in Belize

While the Christian Environmental Association was in Belize negotiating for a small property they planned to use as an environmental study centre, they learned that Coke was also there bidding on 8,000 acres of rain forest. Apparently in the great earth auction it is cheaper for Coke to produce Minute Maid Orange Juice by clear cutting the rain forest in Belize than to grow it in Florida. Obviously this provides short-term benefits for their shareholders but comes at a very high price when you consider the long-term impact on the rain forest and future generations. The young Christians who head up the Christian Environmental Association decided to challenge Coke in a bidding war. To their own amazement they outbid Coke for this 8,000-acre parcel. They have set up the Eden Conservancy to preserve this huge section of rain forest in perpetuity. They did this because they believed that the Bible taught this huge section of rainforest was more than a commodity to be auctioned off like so many used cars. As we have seen, the values implicit in McWorld are at a number of points in conflict with the values implicit in a biblical faith.

Opportunity for Christian leaders

 Christian leaders not only have the opportunity to get ready for the long boom or the slow meltdown scenarios but to enable people to contend with the great earth auction that is going to be a part of our McWorld future:

1. We need to create an international Christian forum to talk about the future of economic globalisation in terms of the values that are driving it and the consequences of economic centralisation on families, local communities and the environment.

2. We need to expand our sense of Christian responsibility not only to include efforts to care for individuals and families who are poor or middle class but also, in the face of globalisation, to work to strengthen the local communities and local businesses in those communities of which they are a part.

3. We need to enable people, where possible, to grow more of their own food or join agricultural co-operatives to have a more reliable food supply.

4. We need to promote economic growth that seeks to promote a decent way of life for our poorest neighbours while caring for God's good creation.

Re-defining the ultimate

As we rush into a new millennium we are entering a future changing at a blinding speed. Certainly one of the primary forces that is directing the course of that change is globalisation. In many different ways most of us have benefited from

globalisation. McWorld promises us that if we can successfully navigate through this time of troubles we can look forward
to the future of the long boom. We need leaders with foresight
who can help the Church prepare for times of both economic
crisis and times of economic bounty.

But we also need leaders who are skilled at making sense
not only of change but also of the values that are driving
change. Many people, including Christians, treat our current
form of free enterprise and economic globalisation as though
it is values neutral or values free. As we have seen, the architects of McWorld are not only intent on changing the course
of international trade and economics but redefining what is
ultimate.

As I attempted to illustrate in the opening story about the
young couple who perished in the Great Barrier Reef, the
tourist representative seemed singularly concerned about the
economic impacts of this tragedy as if the ultimate concerns
are always economic. The clear message from many of the
well-intended advocates of economic globalisation of what is
ultimate is: 'It's the economy, stupid!'

When the cold war abruptly ended, Francis Fukuyma wrote
in his celebrated article 'The End Of History' that we're witnessing the end of history as the nations of the world join in
the capitalist race to the top. Fukuyma asserts, 'The laws of
economic efficiency and growth have replaced the divine
plan.'[33] Have 'the laws of economic efficiency and growth'
indeed 'replaced the divine plan'? Lester Thurow, an MIT
economist, states, 'To flourish, human societies need a vision
of something better.'[34] Is the ultimate vision of 'something
better' to be defined primarily in terms of economic growth,
centralisation and efficiency or is there something more?

Our present form of free enterprise not only isn't value
free, it has implicit within it a set of assumptions as to how
the world works that are a product of the Enlightenment and

modernity. Many of the advocates of this new global order define the ultimate primarily in economic terms. It appears that we are travelling into a future in which everything in God's good creation, including human beings, are reduced to a commodity and assigned a price.

Jane Collier, a British economist, calls this set of assumptions undergirding the modern economic enterprise: 'economism'. According to the *Oxford English Dictionary*, 'Economism imposes the primacy of economic causes or factors as the main source of cultural meanings and values.' As an economist and a Catholic, Collier is very concerned at the way in which the values of the marketplace increasingly seem to be shaping the values of human culture.[35] Deep down I think most of us are not keen to see our lives and God's creation reduced to its economic value. 'Economism' is not the source of ultimate value and McWorld is not our real home. As followers of Jesus Christ aren't we sojourners in search of a better homeland?

Questions for discussion and action

1. What has brought about the rapid economic globalisation of our planet and what are the twin rockets of globalisation that promise to transport us to a more affluent new future?
2. Describe both the up sides and down sides of the long boom scenario and how the Church needs to get ready.
3. Describe both the up sides and down sides of the slow meltdown scenario and how the Church needs to get ready.
4. How is the great auction likely to impact our lives, congregations, the poor we work with and the creation we care for, and what can we as Christians do to make a difference?

Notes

1 Paul MacGeough, 'Depths of Despair', *Sydney Morning Herald*, 31 January, 1998, p.35.

2 *Ibid.*

3 Kinichi Ohame, *The Borderless World* (Collins: New York, 1990). Kinichi Ohame, 'The Rise of the Region State', *Foreign Affairs*, spring, 1993, pp.77- 80.

4 William Greider, *One World Ready or Not: The Manic Logic of Global Capitalism* (Simon and Schuster: New York, 1997), p.12.

5 Benjamin R. Barber, *Jihad vs McWorld* (Times Books: New York, 1995), p.17.

6 James L. Tyson, 'Behind Those Boxes, a Boom', *The Christian Science Work and Money*, 26 May, 1998, p.11.

7 Peter D. Sutherland and John W. Sewell, 'Gather The Nations To Promote Globalisation', *The New York Times*, 8 February, 1998.

8 Peter Schwartz and Peter Leyden, 'The Long Boom', *WIRED*, July1997, p.116.

9 Glenn Pascall, 'Starving for time', *Seattle Times*, 5 July, 1998, p.B5.

10 Jonathan Fuerbringer, 'Growling but for How Long?' *The New York Times*, 9 October, 1998, p.C1.

11 'The World's Forgotten Danger', *The Economist*, 14 November, 1998, pp.17-18.

12 Michael J. Mandel, 'The New Economy: For Better or Worse', *Business Week*, 19 October, 1998, p.42.

13 John Heilemann, 'The Netizen: The Integrationist vs. The Separatists', *WIRED*, July 1997, p.186.

14 Jeff Gerth and Richard W. Stevenson, 'Poor Oversight Said to Imperil World Banking', *The New York Times*, 22 December, 1997, p.1.

15 Charles Handy, 'The Invisible Fist', *The Economist*, 15

February, 1997, pp.3-4.

16 Vicki Goldberg, 'Images of an Economy Devouring the Poor', *The New York Times*, 22 March, 1998, p.44.

17 Jeremy Brecher, 'Globalisation: The Race to the Bottom', presented at The Community Church, 9 April,1995, p.3.

18 Eyal Press, 'The Free Trade Faith: Can We Trust the Economists?' *Lingua Franca, The Review of Academic Life*, December/January 1998, pp.30-38.

19 James Goldsmith, 'The Winners and the Losers', Jerry Mander and Edward Goldsmith, ed., *The Case Against The Global Economy: And For a Turn Toward the Local* (Sierra Club Books: San Francisco, 1996), p.178.

20 Jose Aguayo, 'St. Benedict And The Labor Unions,' *Forbes Magazine*, 9 February, 1998, p.64.

21 Wendell Berry, *What Are People For?* (North Point Press: San Francisco, 1990), p.131.

22 'McWorld', *The Economist*, 29 June, 1996, pp.61, 62.

23 Barnaby J. Feder, 'Cultivating Conagra', *The New York Times*, 30 October, 1997, pp.C1 and C12.

24 Michael Pollan, 'Playing God in the Garden', *The New York Times Magazine*, 25 October, 1998, pp.44-51.

25 Tom Sine, *The Mustard Seed Conspiracy* (Word Books: Waco, Texas, 1981), p.60.

26 Marilyn Berlin Snell, 'Bioprospecting or Biopiracy?', *UTNE Reader*, March-April 1996, p.83 and Andrew Kimbrell, 'High-Tech Piracy', *UTNE Reader*, March-April 1996, pp.84-46.

27 'U.S. Food-Safety System swamped by Booming Global Imports', *The New York Times*, 29 September, 1997, pp. A1 and A8.

28 The World Health Report 1996: Fighting disease, Fostering development, Report of the Director-General, World Health Organisation, Geneva, 1996, p.20.

29 Harriet Webster, 'Stop, Shop and Share', *Parade*

Magazine, 15 September, 1996, p.21.

30 *Ibid.* p.21.

31 Stuart I. Hart, 'Strategies for a Sustainable World', *Harvard Business Review*, January-February 1997, pp.68-69.

32 *Ibid.* pp.75-76.

33 Robert H. Nelson, *Reaching For Heaven On Earth; The Theological Meaning Of Economics* (Rowan and Littlefield, Publishers: Savage, MD, 1991), p.2.

34 Lester Thurow, *The Future of Capitalism: How Today's Economic Forces Shape Tomorrow's World* (William Morrow and Company: New York, 1996), p.17.

35 Jane Collier, 'Contemporary Cultures and The Role Of Economics', Hugh Montefiore, editor, *The Gospel And Contemporary Culture* (Mowbray Publishers: London, 1992), p.103.

3

A trek into a cyber-
future: Re-wiring our
communities and
politics for
millennium 3

A small black box strapped to Steve's head completely covered the left lens on his glasses. Through this micro-technolo-
gy he was actually videoing Morey Safer who was interview-
ing him on *Sixty Minutes*. While *Sixty Minutes* was being
broadcast on network television this MIT student was broad-
casting the interview at the same time on his own WEB page
and storing it in his own data bank. The unit strapped to his
head also contains a small computer screen that he constantly
monitors with his left eye while viewing his immediate sur-
roundings with his right eye. In other words he lives constantly on-line regardless of whether he is in class or at a party. He
also has a state of the art five-key entry pad strapped to his
left hand so he is able to access data every waking moment.

Morey Safer asked the obvious question, 'Why do you
want to be constantly on-line?' The student responded,
'Because I am immediately in contact with the entire world
and I have unlimited access to information. Ask me any question.' Safer asked him what were the lifetime statistics for
Mickey Mantle. Immediately Steve's left hand went to work
and he reported starting to receive a number of hits on his

screen. Within moments he was sharing, in detail, the lifetime statistics for Mickey Mantle. But as he parroted the stats it became immediately evident he had absolutely no idea that Mickey Mantle was a baseball star.

This very unusual interview gives us a glimpse into cyber-future where many of our children and grandchildren will actually be wearing computers as part of their wardrobe. We are racing into a future in which we, like Steve, are going to be much more tightly wired into a global electronic communi-ty than we ever imagined.

Waking up to a new one world electronic order

In the last chapter we awakened to discover that we are all a part of a one world economic race to the top in which we are increasingly being influenced to define what is important and of value in terms of economic efficiency and economic growth. As we saw, what has made the globalisation of the economy possible is the creation of a global electronic ner-vous system. Even as I write, the final satellites are being placed in orbit so that all peoples are permanently linked together in a single interactive system in which information is rapidly becoming the most prized commodity.

Finding the focus

This new electronic nervous system is much more than simply a conduit for planetary commerce. Being connected together into a single economic order and a single electronic grid is radically changing how we relate to one another in community and how we govern our-selves politically. The aim of this chapter is to anticipate some of the new challenges and opportunities that McWorld and this cyber-connection are likely to raise for the ways we relate to one another and function politically. We will specifically identify the implications of these challenges for people of faith and those in leadership.

Welcome to cyber-future

Net Goddesses, Newbies, Cyber-Surfers, Cyber-Punks, Muders, Stalkers, Flamers, Zippy Wavers, WEB-Treckies, Internet Geeks, Intranet Techheads and Virtual Freaks are residents in the new cyber-future to which we are being transported via cyber-space. Frankly, as one who is 'pre-digital' I feel a bit apprehensive about the Internet, community in cyber-space and some of my new neighbours. But I am also fascinated at some of the new opportunities it affords as well as the challenges it raises.

In London you purchase your morning cappuccino at the Cyberia Cafe for £2.35 and for an additional 50 pence purchase half an hour's access to the Internet on one of their ten computers. By 2010 every Japanese home will be connected to the new sophisticated interactive fiber-optic system. While there are still a few bare spots in central Africa and Mongolia that are not hard-wired into this global network of satellites, fiber optics and personal computers it is only a question of time.[1]

A remarkable number of people are actually homesteading in cyber-space starting a broad range of Geo-Cities. You can travel to virtual Vienna and enjoy classical music, or reside in any one of twenty-nine cyber-cities where you can live, love and put down roots.[2] While travelling in Britain I learned of a new cyber-community being planted on an imaginary island in the Hebrides where 'residents' from Johannesburg to New York City co-operate in land-use planning for their community as well as creating a culture and activities on their imaginary island in keeping with local customs and tastes.

While few of us will ever homestead in cyber-space, the Net affords a wonderful opportunity for all of us to get to know our neighbours all over the world. The Internet could be a tool to help us all get to know people from other cultural, religious and political backgrounds in order to foster mutual understanding and respect.

The Net also provides a tremendous new educational resource to mission organisations working with the world's poor. Within five years many remote areas that have no access to books, schools or libraries today could be hooked up through the Net. In other words it would be possible to start schools where none exist—fully recognising that there are also some risks to getting wired in.[3] Nicholas Negroponte of The Media Lab predicts that people in the Two Thirds world might use the capacity of the Net to leap-frog into the twenty-first century.[4] Specifically how is our getting connected to one another through this cyber-technology likely to impact our lives and alter how we relate to one another?

Cyber-community and McWorld: the good, the bad and the predatory

Belinda made her daily mile-long trek to her campus minister's office at the State University of Alabama in Birmingham. The campus minister told me she showed up like clockwork every day during lunch hour to use his computer. When I asked what this unusual ritual was all about he suggested I ask Belinda. I caught her racing back out of the door. She immediately responded, 'Oh there's no mystery, I need to pick up my daily Email—mostly from women on my dorm floor back on campus.' I said, 'You walk a mile every day to the campus ministry office to use the computer to communicate with your friends back on campus on your dorm floor?' 'Absolutely! Don't you think it's important to keep up with friends?' She completely misunderstood the basis of my mystification. When I was a college student, light years before the advent of computers or Email, we simply wandered down the hall and talked to our friends. It seemed so simple.

I have seen the future and it looks like Finland

How could this remarkable new technology alter our lives and particularly the lives of our children as we race into a cyber-space future together? One way to answer this question is to watch what is happening in Finland. Finland leads all other nations in hooking into the global Net. Almost a third of all Finns have cellular phones. There are sixty-two Internet host computers for every one thousand Finns—twice the numbers in the US. Some speculate the reason for this high level of Finnish connection is the long cold nights. Whatever the reason, if we want to observe where this wave might take us in the future we should watch the impact life on the Net is having on the lives and communities on the front edge of this wave in Finland.[5]

Computer wearables for a new generation

Another way to anticipate where this wave might take us is to pay attention to the emergence of new technologies and explore where these waves of change might go. One of the ongoing developments in technological innovation is miniaturisation of various computer and communications technology like Steve was using in the opening story. This has led to the introduction of 'wearable technology' and the earliest manifestation of a new community of cyborgs of technologically augmented humans.

These first crude models wear an assortment of computers, sensors, video cameras and headgear strapped to their bodies. Some of the wearables are nothing more than a whacky fashion statement. But most actually enable the wearer to be constantly hardwired into cyber-space. One laser device actually projects onto the back of a person's retina and projects a transparent computer screen three feet in front of the subject.

Within a few years we will be able to purchase wardrobe items with built-in technological devices. It is only a question of time until those interested in serious human augmentation create ways to do surgical implants. These new human augmentation technologies also hold tremendous promise for medical research but they raise a host of new ethical issues as they are embraced by a new generation.[6]

Cyber-community—opportunities and perils

With many of our young people already heavily involved with TV, MTV, video games and now the Net, how do we prepare them for both the opportunities and risks of life in cyber-space? One of the major waves of the future is that a number of people are turning to the Net and cyber-space to find community. 'Relationships can be complicated in cyber-space because the very technology that draws most people together also keeps them apart. Over time, the safe sense of distance that initially seems so liberating to newcomers on the Net can become an obstacle to deepening bonds of friendship, romance and community.' David Hughes of the Old Colorado City Electronic Cottage declares, 'You can't lead a total life on-line.'[7]

But some seem to be satisfied not only with a 'vicarious community' but in a real sense with a vicarious way of life—living on line through the lives of others. Some are 'lurkers' who, like voyeurs, simply watch and don't enter in. Some are 'stalkers' who fixate on certain people on the Net and habitually harass them. 'Flamers' are those who come on-line enraged, drunk or stoned and are simply abusive and hostile. Too often people who don't have much of a social life become addicted to the virtual community of the Net—even sneaking on-line during work.[8]

Glenn Cartwright at McGill University in Canada raises questions about the impact of these new technologies on the development of human identity and personal relationships. He voiced concern that some will, through the Net, develop their own parallel reality in which they appropriate a new identity, perhaps change genders, or live through a more attractive virtual body. Obviously, for some their parallel identity might become preferable to their real identity.

Cartwright not only discusses the obvious dangers of living out a virtual identity but he suggests it could create a host of 'de-centred' persons who could become dangerously self-destructive. It is possible that individuals could also develop 'distributed' identities or multiple identities that could impair their ability to function in the present reality. He concludes: 'The twenty-first century may well be the century of technologically induced disaffection, characterised by an increased sense of loneliness, alienation, powerlessness and disembodiment.'[9]

I have had a number of church youth workers tell me that one of the most addictive aspects of cyber-space is on-line sex. One worker told me how, as a fifth grader, he had made a copy of the key to his dad's computer room and unbeknown to his parents spent several very impressionable years trying to satisfy childhood curiosity by taking in the swill available on the Net. Douglas Groothius' book *The Soul in Cyber-Space* does an excellent job of highlighting these dangers.[10]

Perhaps of even greater concern are the growing numbers of paedophiles who deliberately stalk the young on the Net, sometimes posing as children themselves to develop trusting friendships. In 1996, sixteen men from the United States, Finland, Canada and Australia who were a part of an on-line paedophile group called the 'Orchid Club' were indicted in the US for their illicit activities. 'Its members shared home-made pictures, recounted sexual experiences with children and even chatted electronically as two of the men molested a ten-year-old girl.'[11]

The 1996 Telecommunications Act was passed in the US to try and help protect children from these on-line predators. But since there is such a huge and expanding world-wide market for all kinds of pornographic material I am not convinced that this is going to reduce the flow or protect the young. We need some new creative approaches to prepare the young to live in a highly connected, seductive future.

Coming soon—the brave new world of virtual reality

We are not far away from creating virtual reality chambers in our labs, offices, schools and homes. These may not fully achieve the 'touchy feely' environments of *Brave New World*, but they will create stunningly life-like three-dimensional worlds that will be very convincing. Imagine the educational applications of such virtual reality chambers.

Students will never go to sleep in history class again. You will be able to transport them back in time to the landing at Normandy at the climax of World War 2 where they will liter-ally be in the centre of the action. You will be able to take them out in space three-dimensionally and lead them on a tour of Mars. And in a science class you will be able to transport them down into molecular structures—three-dimensionally. Imagine the possibility for the arts of creating richly textured environments that have never existed before. We are already seeing the creation of virtual reality entertainment centres all over the US. But you can be sure that the same folks bringing hard core sex and violence to the Internet, stage and screen have plans to bring us virtual sex and virtual violence. We are rapidly entering a new one world cyber-age.

Neil Postman expresses concern that this new cyber-age

totally lacks a transcendent narrative to provide moral under-pinnings for our technological innovation or strong social institutions to steer it. Furthermore he predicts, 'Symbols that draw their meaning from traditional religious or national con-texts must therefore be made impotent as quickly as possi-ble—that is drained of sacred or even serious connotations. The elevation of one god requires the demotion of another. "Thou shalt have no other gods before me" applies as well to technological divinity as any other.'[12] This will be a growing challenge to the Church in the twenty-first century.

Planting a seed in Bible gateway

Gospel Communications has created a WEB site called Bible Gateway that not only offers a broad spectrum of translations of the Bible but has designed it so that users can do topical searches for material. They also provide on-line devotionals and a selec-tion of Christian magazines.

Planting a seed in a wired centre for global mission

Bill O'Brien had the foresight to see the potential of the Internet for world mission. He has created a new Global Centre for strategic mission planning at Beeson Divinity School at Samford University. Essentially, what O'Brien has done is to cre-ate a very sophisticated computer data base linked into World Bank and United Nations data bases to enable mission strate-gists from all over the world to monitor global trend informa-tion in helping them in their missions strategising [wrobrien@samford.edu].

Opportunity for Christian leaders

Christian leaders have an opportunity to not only use the emerging new technologies but to enable local churches to develop guidelines for the stewardship of these new technologies before they arrive. Christian leaders have the opportunity:

1. To create new ways that the new cyber-technology including virtual reality can be used to advance the cause of the kingdom;

2. To design guidelines in churches for the stewardship of the emerging technologies before they are in our homes and our young are already locked in;

3. To establish forums where people of Christian faith can discuss and strategise how to deal with the growing range of new ethical issues that these technologies are creating, particularly regarding the issue of the changing character of human comity;

4. To create innovative ways to use the new technologies to empower the poor in our own communities and abroad.

Politics of McWorld—the good, the bad and the conspiratorial

Not only is the globalisation of communications and the economy dramatically changing the ways we relate to one another but it is also decisively changing how we function politically. First, one of the immediate benefits of using the Net to create a global economic order is that it has motivated world leaders to work for political stability because conflict and war are very expensive and get in the way of doing business. The architects of McWorld are a major force for peace and stability in our world.

Satellite communications, cellular phones, Xerox and fax machines are creating de-facto open societies and totalitarian states can no longer control access to information. This, of course, encourages openness and challenges the repressive rule in countries intent on controlling their citizens. A number of people advocate using the Internet to create a direct form of representative government. There is no question that the Internet can be used to create a more participatory civil society in which citizens not only have more input within their own communities and countries but even in the shaping of global policy.

Planting a seed through Internet activism

A Nobel Peace Prize is the unexpected result of Robert Muller, President of the Vietnam Vets of America Foundation, launching a world wide campaign to ban land-mines using the Internet. Jody Williams, the activist who ran the process, demonstrated how a small group could shape international policy using Email.[13]

Eclipse of the nation state

The twentieth century has been called the century of the state. In the twenty-first century we will witness the declining influence of the state: first because economic globalisation is rapidly eclipsing the influence of individual nations; secondly because we are seeing many of our Western nations undergoing a process of devolution in which politics is being shifted back to more responsive local governments.

The widespread movement towards privatisation is one expression of this movement. In the past five years the United States has experienced a revolution of devolution, shifting programmes and controls from the federal government back to state and local governments. In Britain Tony Blair has been a keen advocate of a devolution of greater power to Scotland, Wales, Northern Ireland and throughout England as well.

'Devolution is occurring in some new ways, too. Regional co-operation across old national borders (some of them are evaporating as the EU integrates) may in time engender a new set of economics-driven loyalties that weaken the pull of old nation states . . . but without necessarily breaking them up.'[14] In many nations power is indeed shifting back to the grass roots, eroding the power of central governments everywhere.

One of the places where both those on the political left and right often come together is in favouring the development of strong local communities where people have much greater control of their own destinies. These community associations have the potential not only to stand up to the totalitarian inclinations of the state but also to the growing centralising tendencies of McWorld. And through the Internet, communities with common cause are beginning to have important influence beyond their national borders on global policies such as human rights and religious liberty abuses as well as concern for the care of creation.

Indigenous people recovering their voice

Another expression of the movement towards the decentralisation of power is a world-wide movement of indigenous peoples who have often been denied a voice to have a greater say in their own future. From the Maori in New Zealand to the Aboriginals in Australia and native peoples in Canada and the United States, indigenous people are calling for just treatment in the lands of their ancestors.

Planting a seed for reconciliation

 Ray Minniecon is an Aboriginal Christian leader who has been one of the leaders of a movement for reconciliation in Australia. Groups of Aboriginal and European (Australian) Christians will visit and pray over massacre sites together, praying for God's forgiveness, reconciliation and healing. Aboriginal Christian leaders have also found a sincere welcoming of indigenous leaders in Canada and Hawaii who are also struggling with land claim issues. The Internet has become a vital link between them in their common struggle for justice.

There has been little similar effort by Christians in America to deal with the history of our crimes against Native Americans or to recognise that much of our prosperity today is a direct by-product of our appropriation of native lands. I pray that one day we can see this same widespread quest for reconciliation become a part of the Church in America. Regrettably not all the concerns for national and tribal identity in our world today are positive.

Jihad vs McWorld—unleashing the furies

We are witnessing a growth of fragmentation, civil conflict and the rise of alienated ethnic, nationalist and extremist groups all over the world. The most destructive expressions of this fragmentation can be seen in ethnic cleansing in Bosnia, terrorist activities in Algeria and militia groups in the US.

Benjamin Barber states that one of the major causes in the rise of extremist groups is almost a visceral reaction to the homogenising, modernising and colonising inclinations of McWorld which threaten to take away people's sense of identity and control.[15] What I believe is happening is that these alienated groups often create for themselves distorted conspiratorial views of what has gone wrong. They then convince themselves that these challenges can only be addressed by the adoption of the most extreme measures.

For instance, right-wing hate groups are becoming more visible and vocal in Germany, France and America. 'This is a global phenomenon with its strongest influence now in Europe, from the Balkans to Russia,' says James Hooper, editor of *Fascism Watch*. 'They are much better organised than in the US, and unlike the US, they have a formal expression through the parties of [Jean-Marie] Le Pen in France, [Gianfranco] Fini in Italy, and especially [Jorge] Haider in Austria.'[16] These groups are successfully using the Internet and WEB pages to market their message. They also produce CDs featuring their own brand of racist rock.

Five years ago white supremacist, Nazi or militia groups in the US might have been able to get thirty people together in a garage to ventilate their conspiratorial fears and show off their fire power. Today a very small hate group can reach millions of potential new disciples on the Internet. Extremist groups in America have enjoyed a twenty per cent increase by going on-line and targeting a broader audience.

What is of particular concern in America is that leaders of many of these right-wing militia and white supremacist groups have totally bought into some of the end times conspiracy theories espoused by some leaders on the religious right. They are reportedly stockpiling weapons so that they are ready to go to war in the year 2000 against the American government which they are convinced is in league with European socialists to collectivise us for a one world anti-Christ takeover.[17] I predict that if terrorism does increase, those who are intent on protecting the emerging global economy will take decisive, repressive action to try to quell the threat.

McWorld versus the nation state

McWorld's sole interest is in creating a borderless market for free trade. There is growing evidence that McWorld is, in a number of different ways, eclipsing the influence of the state while showing little concern for the common good. 'McWorld forges global markets rooted in consumption and profits, leaving to an untrustworthy, if not altogether fictitious invisible hand issues of public interest and common good once nurtured by democratic citizeneries and their watchful governments'[18] charges Benjamin Barber. The traditional conservators of freedom: constitutions and bills of rights will be replaced, he claims, by 'new temples of liberty'— 'McDonalds and Kentucky Fried Chicken.'[19]

Instead of constitutional principles guiding our political course I believe we will see market efficiency becoming the new arbiter of justice. I am very concerned that a growing number of citizens will seriously confuse expanding consumer choice ushered in by McWorld with political liberty and constitutional freedom. There are different levels at which the globalisation of the economy is already beginning to seriously erode national sovereignty and undermine popular consensus, from a fire in a toy factory in Bangkok to decisions made regarding the rules of international trade in Belgium.

The worst industrial fire in the history of capitalism took place in the Kader Toy Factory on the outskirts of Bangkok in 1993. It left 188 dead and 469 injured. Young workers were trapped on upper floors with no fire escapes and their fate was sealed. Scattered among the dead in this macabre scene were soot-covered dolls—Bugs Bunny, Bart Simpson and Big Bird.

The government in Thailand sought to force the Kader Toy Company to install minimum safety equipment including fire escapes and a sprinkler system when they rebuilt their factory. Corporate leaders stated that in a globalised economy they had no intention of building safer factories in Thailand when they could open new factories in Burma or China without those concerns. The government of Thailand backed off from enforcing its own legislation in this area since this tragic accident and the number of work related accidents in Thailand has tripled.[20]

Citizens versus the World Trade Organisation

Of even more concern is the new reality that citizens are losing their ability, through legislation, to determine the quality of life in their own communities. Increasingly, as those of us within countries pass legislation to protect workers, food supplies or care for the environment these laws can be set aside by those who direct global trade.[21]

Through a series of world trade agreements the World Trade Organisation has been given sweeping powers over domestic politics of nations like Britain, Canada and the United States. Ralph Nader charges that:

> under the new system, many decisions that affect billions of people are no longer to be made by local and national governments but instead, if challenged by any WTO member nation, would be deferred to a group of unelected bureaucrats . . . The bureaucrats can decide whether or not people in California can prevent the destruction of their last virgin forests or determine if carcinogenic pesticides can be banned from their food; or whether European countries have the right to ban the use of dangerous biotech hormones in their meat.
>
> Moreover, once the secret tribunals issue their edicts, no external appeals are possible; worldwide conformity is required. A country must make its laws conform or else face perpetual trade sanctions. At risk is the very basis of democracy and accountable decision making that is the necessary undergirding of any citizen struggle for sustainable, adequate living standards and health, safety and environmental protections.[22]

McWorld—the best government money can buy

In the last chapter we witnessed the creation of huge economic behemoths which have announced that they are intent on global domination of the international marketplace. We need to realise that this growing economic domination inevitably means growing political clout. Because of their singular concern for their shareholder's investment these corporate heads are not only under the gun to expand their economic influence but to politically protect their huge global investments as well.

It is important to remember that of the one hundred largest economies in the world today, fifty-one are corporations. General Motors is bigger than Denmark, Ford than South Africa, and Toyota than Norway. Wal-Mart by itself is larger than 161 countries.[23] We are likely to see a continuation of mega-mergers between corporations, banks and other financial institutions which makes shareholders happy but will also mean these humungus corporate institutions seek to expand their political influence in all of our societies.

The wealthy élite of these corporations have inordinate influence in all our nations. William Domhoff, in his book *Who Rules America Now?*, persuasively argues that a relatively small affluent élite is significantly over-represented on interlocking boards and foundations and exerts a very high level of influence over government policy.[24] One person one vote is largely becoming a fiction in the era of growing big money politics.

The cost of being elected to political office in America has soared in the last five years. It costs $10 – $20 million to successfully run for a seat in the US Senate. In 1995 both Bill Clinton and Bob Dole set a new record raising roughly $25 million each. In that same year major presidential candidates also set a new record raising over $110 million in private money.[25] Scarcely a week goes by when we don't hear new allegations about the illegal ways that both democrats and republicans have sought to raise these huge amounts to insure their grip on power. Charles Lewis, in his important book *The Buying of the President*, documents how we have increasingly become a people whose government is run by wealthy special interests.[26] American humourist Will Rogers once observed 'that we have the best government that money can buy.'

McMedia shaping political opinion

Those who are running McWorld have a very big stake in using every facet of the new international order not only to move their products but also to shape our political views and our personal preferences. Very small groups of powerful corporate interests control virtually all the news and entertainment industry. They are also rapidly becoming the gate-keepers on the Internet so they will even control the information that private citizens are able to access.

> The flow of information world-wide is controlled by an ever shrinking number of transnational media corporations led by seven giants: Time-Warner, Disney, Telecommunications Inc (TCI), Bertelsmann, General Electric, Viacom and Rupert Murdoch's News Corporation . . . Between them these media giants . . . have pretty well taken over the whole global mind-scape and 'developed' it into a theme park – a jolly, terrifyingly homogenised Las Vegas of the mind. What does freedom of speech mean in this kind of mental environment?[27]

These 'opinion makers' have become very skilled at manipulating public opinion. Particularly troubling is the enormous amount of information that corporate interests are constantly collecting about us. There are serious discussions on how to use this information to create 'narrow cast' commercials targeted at us, and people with our profile, not only to change our consumer preferences but also alter our political opinions.

Robert Kaplan notes that 'Material possessions not only focus people toward private and away from communal life but also encourage docility. The more possessions one has, the more compromises one will make to protect them.'[28]

Steven Miller raises yet another concern regarding that larger world of McMedia and the human future:

> As advertising and marketing become increasingly integrated into every aspect of our media-mediated culture, we will be fed an endless diet of advertorials, infomercials, and advernews—all carefully purged of anything that might annoy potential sponsors, anger important market segments, provoke public controversy, or lead us to question the overall process into which we have been drawn.[29]

Perhaps one of the reasons there seems to be so little concern about the growing influence of the economic sector over our lives and politics is due to our changing attitude towards the state and the free market. Many Americans have enormous and growing distrust of the state and a swelling confidence in the free market. In fact there are those who would turn our schools, social service institutions and prisons over to 'free market' solutions. Based on the track record of for profit HMOs some of us aren't that enthusiastic. Other Westerners while not sharing this high distrust of the state do seem to share some of the optimism towards the free market. It might be helpful to put this discussion of trust in the state versus trust in the free market in a historical frame for a moment.

Utopian state versus Utopian free market

At the threshold of the last century also there were competing notions regarding the nature of the better future to which we should aspire and the vehicle we should rely on to transport us there—the state or the free market. These discussions bear remarkable similarity to some of our conversations today. Intriguingly, both of these views found their expression in two very different streams of nineteenth century literature.

Looking back on the potential of the state

In 1887 Edward Bellamy, a Christian and a journalist was so deeply moved by the inequities and suffering he witnessed every day in Boston that he had chronic problems sleeping at night. His distress motivated him to write a book, *Looking Backward* that caused something of a social revolution throughout America.

Bellamy's hero, Julian West, goes to sleep in 1877, over-sleeps a bit and wakes up in Boston in the year 2000. He wakes up to a Boston transformed. No longer is the city filled with entrenched poverty and suffering. No longer are families living under bridges, children being orphaned and running the streets. He wakes to an egalitarian modern society where all work has dignity, everyone has opportunity and all people are treated with respect.

In response to this compelling utopian vision people all over America started hundreds of 'Bellamy groups' which set to work attempting to transform their own communities. The instrument that Bellamy chose to transport society to this humane new future was the state—the government. Bellamy was not only a Christian with a very sensitive social con-science but a nationalist and a patriot. He truly believed that the government was capable of fashioning a more egalitarian, just and compassionate society. This view is one expression of a stream of social Darwinism that has been shaped by the ideas of democratic liberalism which has impacted many Western countries.

As we reach the end of the twentieth century, political con-servatives, the religious right and particularly libertarians have become very hostile towards the state in the United

States in a way that is incomprehensible in Europe or Down Under. They are convinced that the government has absolutely no capacity to achieve anything positive in terms of promoting social change. They are particularly hostile to the utopianism and so-called 'social-engineering' of those on the left and would have little sympathy for Edward Bellamy's vision of society transformed through the humane efforts of the state.[30]

Looking back on the potential of the free market

Horatio Alger, a graduate of Harvard Divinity School, was also very much aware of the plight of the young and vulnerable in our urban communities at the end of the nineteenth century. In 1867 he wrote a book called *Ragged Dick*. In this book, and a series of others including *Mark The Matchboy*, we are shown a different hopeful vision for the future. Alger's was an individualistic not a corporate vision. It certainly wasn't the vision of a new egalitarian order where everyone had opportunity and dignity. In his utopian novel, Alger tells how a little urchin named Ragged Dick overcomes poverty and scorn to become successful and prosperous 'through a little luck and a little pluck'. Then through the mythic success of Ragged Dick he is able to become a protector and mentor for Mark The Matchboy and start him on the upwardly mobile quest for a life of prosperity and the upscaling of his income and social status.

While Bellamy's vision emphasises a form of social Darwinism in which the state was seen as the agent that could enable society to achieve the common good, Horatio Alger was an advocate of something much more akin to economic Darwinism. He believed the market was a more certain agent than the state to deliver us to a better future. He believed we could trust the marketplace to determine winners and losers. He espoused a belief which, in our globalised economy, has almost been elevated, by some, to the state of religious dogma. He believed that if we all pursue our own economic self-interest it will not only improve our lives economically but will automatically improve the condition of those around us.[31]

What those who are devoted to this viewpoint don't seem to recognise is that their vision is no less utopian than that on the other end of the political spectrum. Nor are they able to clearly explain the rationale behind their optimism that if we create a completely free market it will raise all boats and create a future of unbelievable affluence and prosperity.

Political centralisation versus economic centralisation

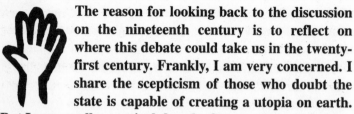 **The reason for looking back to the discussion on the nineteenth century is to reflect on where this debate could take us in the twenty-first century. Frankly, I am very concerned. I share the scepticism of those who doubt the state is capable of creating a utopia on earth. But I am equally sceptical that the free market can fashion the utopia the apostles of McWorld promise us. Since the rise of the nation state we have repeatedly seen the disastrous results of the centralisation of political power. We are at the threshold of witnessing the unprecedented centralisation of global economic power. Do we have less to fear from the centralisation of economic power than we experienced from the centralisation of political power?**

In his book *The Spirit of Democratic Capitalism* Michael Novak states that the free market is designed 'to defend efficiency, productivity, inventiveness and prosperity. It is also a defense of the free conscience—free not only in the realm of the spirit, and not only in politics but also in the economic decisions of everyday life. It is a defense of the pluralist order of democratic capitalism against unitary and commanded order of socialism.'[32] While democracy does indeed create an environment that encourages free-market capitalism there is growing evidence that the reverse doesn't appear to be true.

Rob van Drimmelen points out that the Oxford Declaration on Christianity and Economics advocates that all people should have adequate decision-making opportunities for the decisions that affect their lives. As we have seen, the United States, Great Britain and a number of other nations are experiencing a devolution of power where more and more decision-making is moving from the central government to local municipalities and therefore into the hands of average people.

But as we have also seen, the momentum of McWorld is rapidly moving in the opposite direction. More and more political influence is moving away from local and even national centres of decision making to global economic centres in which the average person has no input at all. Donald Hay states that the 'internationalization of the world economy tends to shift political and economic decision making centers away from local levels'.[33]

Free market advocates have no trouble vividly describing the totalitarian character of centrally planned political systems. But it seems to be much more difficult for them to realise that the creation of a global capitalist economic system could have some of the same tendencies. In his book *After 1989: Morals Revolution and Civil Society* Ralf Dahrendorf warns that 'liberty is often at risk. The new economism of capitalists is no less illiberal than the old one of the Marxists.'[34]

I don't know if Dahrendorf is right. But I believe we need to create an international forum in which Christians from all our nations can come together and have a thoughtful discussion about the future of economic globalisation and the way it could shape our common future.

Opportunities for leaders

In light of this survey on the changing character of politics, leaders have the opportunity:

1. To create an international Christian forum to discuss how economic globalisation and the centralising of economic power could impact our lives and communities in the future;

2. To create ways to activate Christians on the Internet to become a part of transnational groups of believers committed to unmasking those powers that threaten people's lives and freedoms;

3. To participate in creating civil societies where those haven't existed before to give people more influence over their lives and families;

4. To become advocates for the free flow of information and to reduce the influence of powerful élites on the political forum in all our countries.

Questions for discussion and action

1. In what creative ways can we use the new technologies to advance the purposes of God?

2. What guidelines could be helpful in enabling Christians to steward more responsibly the existing technologies as well as the emerging ones?

3. What are some of the new ethical issues raised by the creation of new cyber-communities?

4. How is economic globalisation likely to change the character of politics and how should people of Christian faith respond?

Notes

1   James O. Jackson, 'It's a Wired, Wired World', Special Issue, *Time,* Spring 1995, p.80.

2   Kristin Spence, 'Geo-Cities: Homesteading on the Electronic Frontier', *WIRED,* March 1997, p.175.

3   Nicholas Negroponte, 'The Third Shall Be First', *WIRED,* January 1998, p.96.

4   *Ibid.,* p.96.

5   Youssef Ibrahim, 'Finland: An Unlikely Home Base For Universal Use of Technology', *The New York Times*, 20 January, 1997, p.1.

6   Thomas A. Bass, 'Dress Code', *WIRED,* April 1998, pp.163-187.

7   Jill Smolowe, 'Intimate Strangers', Special Issue, *Time,* Spring 1995, p.21.

8   *Ibid.,* 'Live Wires', p.43.

9   Glen F. Cartwright, 'Virtual or Real?', *The Futurist*, March-April 1994, pp.22-26

10 Douglas Groothius, *The Soul in Cyber-Space* (Baker Books: Grand Rapids, Mi., 1997).

11 Tim Golden, '16 Indicted On Charges Of Internet Pornography', *The New York Times,* 17 July, 1996, p.A8.

12 Neil Postman, *Technopoly: The Surrender of Culture to Technology* (Vintage Books: New York, 1993), pp.83 and 165.

13 'A Lesson for ministry outreach from Nobel Prize winner', *Cyberchurch Update and Analysis: Christian Commentary on Today's Technology*, Vol. 4, No. 1, p.4.

14 'Devolution can be salvation', *The Economist*, 20 September, 1997, p.53.

15 Benjamin Barber, *Jihad vs McWorld* (Times Books: New York, 1995), p.3.

16 Robert Marquand, 'Hate Groups Market to the

Mainstream', *The Christian Science Monitor*, 6 March, 1998, p.4.

17 Kevin Sack, 'Hate Groups in US Are Growing, Report Says', *The New York Times*, 5 March, 1998, p.A10.

18 Benjamin Barber, *Jihad vs McWorld* (Times Books: New York, 1995), pp.6-7.

19 *Ibid.*

20 William Greider, *One World, Ready Or Not: The Manic Logic of Capitalism* (Simon and Schuster: New York, 1997), pp. 337-345.

21 Roger C. Altman, 'The Force Is With Us, Global Markets Wield Awesome Power', *The Seattle Post Intelligencer*, 8 March, 1998, p.E1.

22 Ralph Nader and Lori Wallach, 'GATT, NAFTA, and the Subversion of the Democratic Process', Jerry Mander and Edward Goldsmith, *The Case Against the Global Economy: And For a Turn Toward Local Control* (Sierra Club Books: San Francisco, 1996), pp. 93-94.

23 John Cavanagh, 'Global Economic Apartheid', Presentation at Takoma Park Maryland, 19 September, 1996, p.1.

24 G. William Donhoff, *Who Rules America Now?: A View for the '80s* (Vintage: New York, 1987), p.33.

25 Statement of Charles Lewis, Chairman and Executive Director, The Center For Public Integrity, National Press Club's 'Newsmaker Luncheon', 23 April, 1996, p.3.

26 *Ibid.*, pp.1-4.

27 Kalle Lasn, 'Communications Cartel', *Adbusters*, Winter 1998, No. 24, pp.20-21.

28 Robert D. Kaplan, 'Was Democracy Just a Moment?', *Atlantic Monthly*, December 1997, p.76.

29 Steven E. Miller, *Civilizing Cyberspace: Policy Power and the Information Superhighway* (Addison-Wesley Publishing: New York, 1995), p.384.

30 Edward Bellamy, *Looking Backward* (Penguin Books: New York, 1982).

31 Horatio Alger, *Ragged Dick* and *Mark The Matchboy* (Colliers Books: New York, 1962).

32 Michael Novak, *The Spirit of Democratic Capitalism* (Simon and Schuster: New York, 1982), p.112.

33 Rob van Drimmelen, 'The Oxford Declaration as a Contribution to the Ecumenical Debate', Herbert Schlossberg, Vinay Samuel and Ron J. Sider, *Christianity and Economics in the Post-Cold War Era* (William B. Eerdmans Publishing Company: Grand Rapids, Mi., 1994), p.140.

34 Mitchell Cohen, 'No More Systems: A Leading Sociologist Thinks the New Capitalism Has Some of the Dangers of the Old Marxism', *The New York Times Book Review*, p.21.

4

McWorld—a race to the bottom for the West

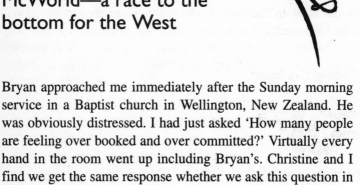

Bryan approached me immediately after the Sunday morning service in a Baptist church in Wellington, New Zealand. He was obviously distressed. I had just asked 'How many people are feeling over booked and over committed?' Virtually every hand in the room went up including Bryan's. Christine and I find we get the same response whether we ask this question in a house church in London or a Presbyterian church in Philadelphia. People in all our western countries seem to be feeling mounting pressures on their lives and families.

Bryan, a forty-two-year-old engineer with a wife and three children told us his story. He explained that two months previously his employer had offered him a promotion. Since it provided an opportunity for advancement and a small increase in pay, he took it. The condition for the promotion was that he not only worked harder but longer. His new position required him to increase his work hours from fifty to seventy hours a week. He suddenly woke up to the fact that he has very little time left over to spend with his wife and three children. He has also belatedly realised he needed to resign his responsibility on the church council and counts himself fortunate when he can make it to church once in a while.

Bryan also told how in order to increase productivity he is under pressure from management to persuade his new staff to ratchet up their hours at work from fifty to seventy hours a week to increase productivity—without an increase in pay. Bryan said, 'I am feeling very guilty both for the impossible situation I have created for myself and my family, and for the pressure I am supposed to put on my staff.'

Do you know what Bryan and his family are going through? Are you among those who never seem to have enough time in the day or enough pennies in the purse to make ends meet as we race into a McWorld future?

Finding the focus

 In the last chapter we saw how our global society is being wired together into a new cyber-community in which our political influence is both growing and diminishing at the same time. In this chapter we will identify some of the specific hidden costs of economic globalisation for those of us on the middle rungs, particularly our young. The aim of this chapter is to enable those in leadership to help their members and their children to get ready for both the new opportunities and challenges that are likely to confront them in a new millennium.

Welcome to the McWorld macro-mall

'World consumption has expanded at an unprecedented pace over the twentieth century, with private and public consumption . . . reaching $24 trillion in 1998, twice the level of 1975 and six times that of 1950.'[2] One of the most remarkable achievements is the rate at which McWorld has literally created a global macro-mall where the wealthy and those of us on the middle rungs have been presented an incredible and expanding array of consumer choice.

Without leaving home we can shop on-line purchasing digital TVs from Korea, Parma hams from Italy or elegant jewellery from Tiffanys in New York. Until the economy slowed those on the middle rungs were consuming as never before. For example, home sales in the US reached a thirty-five year high.[3]

McWorld wants more of your life and cash

Expanding our appetites for MORE

We have experienced seven years of incredible economic growth in the United States, Canada and Britain. Not only the wealthy but many of us in the middle class have benefited from this long boom. What will be required to enable this new one world economic order to resume the level of growth that shareholders all over the world have come to expect? There simply won't be enough growth in developing markets to make it happen. What it will require is for all of us, particularly our children and grandchildren, to dramatically increase our appetite for MORE.

In his provocative book *The End of Work*, Jeremy Rifkin recalls how in the 1920s corporations began designing a strategy to motivate us all to want MORE. They invented a market strategy to create a permanent class of 'dissatisfied consumers'. Until then most people were quite content if they were able to meet their essential human needs. Once they reached that point their levels of consumption levelled off. People being satisfied with enough has always been a serious problem for those who want to promote a high level of economic growth.

Economist John Kenneth Gailbraith stated that the new

mission of business therefore was to 'create the wants it seeks to satisfy'.[4] The only way it is possible to create new wants is to persuade people to seriously change their values. Over the past seventy years the corporate world has succeeded brilliantly in persuading us to change our values and our wants and the Church hardly seemed to notice.

In recent years marketers have discovered a very effective way to persuade us to increase our appetites for MORE. They have sought to convince us that in addition to the basic human needs of air, water, food and shelter from the elements we all have a fifth human need—the need for novelty. 'The need throughout our life for a continuous variety in external stimulation of our eyes, ears, sense or organs and all our nervous network.'[5] By far the majority of us, including people of faith, seem to have bought this propaganda. In this constant quest for novelty we have accepted McWorld's constant claim that yesterday's luxuries become today's necessities.

It isn't surprising that we succumb. Over any twenty-four-hour period we are assaulted with an average of 3,000 messages that seek to persuade us we are inadequate if we don't purchase the newest novelty.[6] Before a child enters first grade they will be exposed to over 30,000 advertisements not only to give them an appetite for novelty but to decisively shape their world view. The message of the McWorld 'consumer church' couldn't be clearer, 'The ultimate meaning of human existence is getting all this stuff.'[7]

Spending MORE in the McWorld macro-mall

It isn't enough to persuade us to expand our appetite for MORE. The pied pipers of McWorld are constantly fashioning new novel ways to convince people to spend MORE too. Coming soon—'shoppertainment' to a mega-mall near you.

Listen to this testimony of a satisfied shopper: 'I've just survived twelve straight hours of . . . "shoppertainment" . . . I
rescued comrades from deep space via virtual reality . . . stood
eyeball to eyeball with live bobcats, lizards, and badgers . . .
got jostled into pulp in a flight simulator . . . participated in a
movie rather than merely watching one . . . destroyed fake
temples . . . rode fake jet skis, and a skate board on a fake
obstacle course.'[8]

The news from the Ontario Mills Mall in Southern
California couldn't be better for those who bring us McWorld
and their shareholders. The typical mall-goer spends three
hours of their time and $167 for a visit. Reportedly that is a
$100 more per head than you currently spend at an old fash-
ioned mall.[9] I don't know about you but I can hardly wait until
they build one in our neighbourhood.

McWorld has even found a way to move their macro-malls
into cyberspace. Their new on-line free-for-all auction welcomes the grasping and the brutal. 'Not so fast, TR, you over-
weight lardo.' That not very polite message appeared recently
on On Sale, an Internet Web site that auctions everything from
computer gear to Omaha steaks. Civility takes a back seat to
acquisitiveness as Net-surfers wrangle over everything.
'People are bidding on nose hair trimmers,' says a bewildered
Kirk Loevner, president and chief executive of Internet
Shopping Network. 'It's just bizarre.'[10] Increasingly all of our
lives are being drawn into McWorld's to auction everything in
sight and there is evidence that it is already changing our
notion of what is important and of value.

Flash—MORE doesn't happiness make

But there is also growing evidence that even though we are
consuming much MORE from all over our shrinking global
village it isn't making us happier. Just the contrary. 60% of
successful professionals report that they are suffering from

chronic stress and depression. 48% of top corporate executives report that their lives are empty and meaningless. For the past twenty-five years the American Index of Social Health has tracked the well-being of Americans. While the Gross Domestic Product has risen continually for the past twenty-five years the Social Health index is fully 52% lower than it was in 1973.[11] Is the long boom future to which McWorld promises to transport us really going to satisfy our deepest human longings?

High cost of MORE on family life

Australian commentator Bob Santamaria insists it isn't an accident that families are feeling more pressured. He contends that the global economy has declared war on the family. He points out that the take-home salary of the average production worker in the US is lower than it was twenty-five years ago:

> At first, American families believing this was only a temporary phenomenon, adapted. High consumption levels were maintained. This was possible because family income was 'stretched' on the one hand by the depletion of savings, by the increase in borrowing—particularly through the growth of consumer credit—and partly by the de facto conscription of married women into the work force. Marriages were postponed. Birth rates were lower. Household savings declined. Families went into debt.[12]

Let's look at how much this race to the top is costing average families.

High cost of buying MORE than you can afford

One of the immediate consequences of persuading those on the middle rungs to continually ratchet up their levels of consumption in the global macro-mall is that we aren't saving nearly as much as we used to for a rainy day. In the US savings have fallen from 8% to an all-time low of about 3%.

Total household debt in America has soared to $5.4 trillion dollars. The share of disposable income that households must pay simply to service their debts has risen 18%.[13]

The average consumer debt load per household was $38,734 in 1990. It rose to $50,529 in 1995 and is projected to reach over $65,000 by the year 2000.[14] In 1996 1.1 million Americans declared personal bankruptcy. That was a 29% jump from 1995 and new records are still being set.[15] On the one hand financial institutions want to continue making it easy for people, including those who aren't good risks, to secure credit and receive bank cards and at the same time they want to make it much tougher for them to file for bankruptcy protection.[16] These financial corporations refuse to take any responsibility for their heavy handed marketing techniques. And the young who are most vulnerable are being swamped with credit cards as are many who are in continual economic crisis.

McWorld wants more of our time

In this increasingly competitive global economy McWorld not only wants more of our money but also our time. We find that employers from Liverpool to Los Angeles expect their employees, like Bryan, to work longer and harder. In 1977 less than half of families relied on dual incomes. Today it has dramatically increased to two thirds and is still climbing. Some women are working simply to help pay the bills and keep their heads above water. Some are working to be able to buy extras.[17]

For a number of years not only the American poor but the American middle class has been losing ground economically. The level of income has not kept pace with the rate of infla-tion. But for the first time in years American income for a typical household rose in 1997 by 1.2%. 'After years of salary stagnation in the early 1990s the American household was better off for the second straight year in a row—though admittedly, it was still 3% worse off than it had been in 1989' according to *The Economist*.[18] What isn't clear is whether the recent upturn is a clear indication of middle-class incomes finally leaving a long period of chronic stagnation or whether it can be explained by people taking on additional part-time work.

Juliet Schor in her book *The Overworked American*, tells us that middle-income dual-earner families with two children were spending 6,500 hours at work in 1995, up from 5,000 hours in 1969.[19] One of the new reasons families are still seeing the number of hours spent at work increase is because employers are pressuring their employees to spend more time on the job.

We now also have a new phenomenon according to *Money Magazine*: the four-income family.

> Just about every American knows that the one-earner Ozzie and Harriet family doesn't live here any more. Today, however, a growing rank of the middle class is realising that the two-career couple of the '70s and '80s is giving way to the four income household of the '90s.
>
> Simply put, it can now take four—or more—jobs to provide the level of comfort and financial security that one income delivered only a few decades ago. As a result many Americans are working 55 or more hours a week. Since 1980, the number of Americans who hold more than one job has grown by 54% to more than 7 million, or almost 6% of the labor force according to the US Bureau of Labor Statistics.[20]

'The economy is creating tens of thousands of new jobs, that's the good news,' says a man looking up from his newspaper. 'So what's the bad news?' he is asked. 'To support a family you'll need three.'[21] The poor and the young are the ones who are having particular difficulty in making it economically on only one McJob.

Bottom-line people in Western countries are spending more time at work so they have significantly less time left over for other things—including things of faith. The Harris Poll reports that the average American spent forty-one hours per week at work in 1973. In 1997 that had increased ten hours to fifty-one hours a week.[22] As we gallop into a new century, McWorld will insist that we spend even more of our waking hours at work. That means we will have less time for family and friends, less time to pray and study Scripture and less time to volunteer to address the mounting needs of the poor in our societies.[23]

McWorld wants more of the life and money of the young

Branding the young

'You must get kids branded by age 5 if you want to have them as faithful consumers of your product,' admonished a market-ing executive in a corporate training session. The footage of this training session was included in a very compelling docu-mentary on consumerism called 'Affluenza' aired on PBS.[24] 'What I wanna, wanna, really wanna be' sings Cyndy, a four year old, as she is getting ready for Sunday school in her home in Birmingham, England. The Spice Girls seem to be the first popular music group to sell four, five and six year olds 'girl power' and brand them with their label.[25] A primary school teacher in the north of England told me that students ridicule classmates who aren't wearing acceptable corporate logos on their clothing.

In North America corporations have created a fund-raising gimmick to get into schools and literally brand kids with their corporate logos. The programme that started several years ago is called: 'Tattoo You Too!' Appealing to the current tattoo craze, corporations offer schools a certain amount of money for each child they can brand with a temporary tattoo, like the Nike 'swoosh' or a grinning Joe Camel, on their arm. 'The companies . . . are pleased with the response. Brad Randolph, industry insider, said, 'This is wonderful. It delights me to see that so many people's lives are enriched by such an innovative programme.'[26]

Generation Y programmed to want MORE

Generation Y is the front edge of what demographers call the Baby Boomlets. The Baby Boomers, 77 million strong born from 1946 to 1964, have been very busy having kids. While the generation that followed them, the Baby Buster generation born between 1964 and 1983, contains only 55 million the Baby Boomlets contains 72 million very active young people.[27]

Madison Avenue has dubbed the 27 million thirteen to nineteen year olds, who are the front edge of this population, generation Y. Marketers describe them as 'America's most free-spending, jobless and unskilled laborers who finance their role of arbiters of cool with ever greater amounts of disposable cash.' Robert Williams, executive director at the Rand Youth Poll, stated, 'They have a higher incremental allowance from their parents, and with growth in the service economy, they're able to secure jobs easily and at rising minimum wages. They're exposed to so many different products on TV, in the mall and through their friends. It's a generation who grew up with excess as a norm.'[28]

In addition to marketing their wares to this generation through the media, Internet and the mall, corporations are also gaining a firm foothold in our schools. For example, tobacco companies are providing educational materials on smoking for school use. Many educators justify the slow

McDonaldisation of the school on the grounds that it saves money.

Since 1996 Dr Astin has been taking a survey snapshot of freshers at college. In the early seventies about 70% of young people went to college to develop a meaningful philosophy of life. Today 75% of freshers in McWorld go to college to be very well off financially, and developing a meaningful philosophy of life has dropped to 40%. While working with a Baptist campus ministry in Tennessee I asked a junior what his major was and he told me right up front he was a 'pre-wealth major'. More and more of our young people, including Christian young people, really believe the ultimate goal of life is to get ahead economically.[29] While some are doing smashingly in this boom economy many others will not.

Western young and the race to the bottom

While unemployment among young adults in parts of Europe is as high as 40% there is little shortage of work for young people in Britain and the United States. But much of it is McJobs or temp. positions. And the temp. agencies not only do not offer benefits or health care, you can't even get sick. If you get sick you get sacked.

However, it is a different story for young people with degrees in business and computer science. They are in high demand. Norm Ewert, a professor of economics at Wheaton College, said he has never seen such a demand for college grads in those fields. They are starting out as economically comfortable as some of their poorer cousins are starting out economically insecure. But many of our young people are hitting the economy at a very difficult time. Virtually no one in our churches, Christian colleges or campus ministries is preparing them for the new economic realities they are likely to face in a new millennium.

Recently when I spoke at Biola University I ran into a disturbing number of students not only graduating with debts but debts ranging from $20,000 to $60,000. For those who want to get involved in mission it will be out of the question for at least a decade. We are running into more and more young people from Britain and New Zealand who are beginning to graduate from college with debts too.

The relationship of what young people earn to what they can buy has changed drastically since I graduated from a Christian college in 1958. The total annual cost then for tuition, fees, books, room and board was $700 a year. I had no problem working as a janitor during the summer to pay that amount. In the intervening forty years the educational costs have soared to more than twenty times what I paid. But the summer jobs today pay roughly only two or three times what we earned in the late fifties. As a consequence it is impossible for the young today to earn enough from a summer job to pay their annual college costs.

The relationship to what the young earn to what they are able to afford in housing has also dramatically changed since I was a young man. The first house I bought in 1961 was a four-bedroom, two bathroom in Portland, Oregon. It had a huge front porch and a full basement that had been totally restored. An older couple had added a modern kitchen and bathroom, rewired, replumbed and then painted this beautiful old bungalow inside and out. The total price was $14,500. My monthly payment was only a $100 a month. I had no trouble making that monthly payment on a welfare level salary of $4,800 a year working for Cascade College from where I had graduated.

Today the same house would probably sell for close to $400,000—more than twenty times what I paid. But two young people today with good incomes would have serious difficulty even qualifying for a loan on that size of mortgage.

As my wife and I work with young couples in Great Britain, New Zealand, Australia, Canada and the United States, we find more and more of them are spending more than 50% of their income on rent or mortgage.

In America where there is no government health coverage, over 40 million are uninsured. I am discovering that many of these are young people. They are betting they won't need health coverage and when they are wrong, the leading cause of foreclosure is medical bills. In other words, today's young in many of our Western countries, certainly America, will never have the economic lifestyles in which they were raised.

The decline in generational income is documented in the book *The State of Working America 1996-1997*. 'The average income of families headed by someone under 25 declined at an annual rate of 2.4% from 1979 to 1989 and 1.8% from 1989 to 1995. These young families in 1994 had $6,148 less income to spend in real dollars than their 1967 counter parts had when they were starting out.'[30] In fact there is growing concern because many of these young people have so little left over for savings that they will have very little resources on which to retire. This means that the under thirty-fives are likely to have significantly less time and money left over to contribute to the work of the kingdom than older generations.

Coming soon—a new blended, borderless generation

Blending of the West

This generation will also be the most racially blended, border-less generation we have ever seen. Birmingham England, Auckland New Zealand and Los Angeles California are cities that are examples of the kind of blended future into which all Western countries are heading. However, the United States of America is well on the way to becoming the first truly universal nation. Non-Hispanic whites made up 73.1% of the population in 1996. That proportion is likely to fall to 52.8% by 2050 and it won't be very long after this that the United States becomes the first predominantly non-white Western nation.[31] And generation Y is the front edge of this demographic wave. We need to prepare the young and the Church for a blended future.

McWorld celebrating the creation of a borderless youth market

The marketers of McWorld are celebrating that for the first time in history they have created a borderless youth market in which they can sell their Nikes, Marilyn Manson MTVs and Coke anywhere on the globe. *Shampoo Planet* is a book by Douglas Coupland that describes this generation as the first borderless generation. The reason for their brilliant success in evangelising this borderless youth is that marketers have found ways not just to sell the young their products but actually to change their values so they want to buy their products. 'These kids have the same interests whether they're in New York, London, L.A. or a small town in Indiana,' says Jeanine Misdom, a youth marketing consultant.

This class of young consumers is being heavily conditioned to acquire appetites for identical McWorld products that transcend local customs, values or tastes. Marketers gleefully report that 'they are all increasingly prone to the same influences in music, food and fashion—easily transported across national boundaries through CDs, MTV, Hollywood and multi-national franchises. The Internet has only hastened the shift.'[32]

What isn't generally realised is that we are going backwards not forwards in world evangelisation. Peter Brierley of the Christian Research Association reports that 28% of the world's people identify themselves as some brand of Christian: Protestant, Catholic or Orthodox. Because population growth is outstripping our best efforts it will decline to 27% in 2010 and continue to decline after that.[33] The people who are doing a brilliant job at world 'evangelisation' are the marketers of McWorld who are persuading the young everywhere to change their values so they will all buy the same soda, watch the same MTV videos, and wear the same clothing.

As my wife and I travel in Britain, Australia and New Zealand it is astonishing to see the success McWorld is having in blaring American pop culture into every corner of the world. The golden Arches are everywhere. Billboards scream the latest Hollywood hit. American cultural colonisation for a new borderless youth market is relentless.

Gail Griffith writing about this troubling global phenomenon wonders aloud:

> When policy analysts in the coming century look back on this final decade of the twentieth century, they will wonder how our leaders could have so underestimated the impact of popular culture on the rapid pace of social and cultural change around the globe. How could we have missed the clues—some measured in decibels—as the younger generation came to embrace wholesale the values espoused in Western pop culture?[34]

McWorld—greying of the middle class

Cutting Back Support For the Middle Class

Not only does McWorld want more of our time and money and that of our young, this new globalised economy is bringing pressure on governments in the United States, Canada, Britain, Australia and New Zealand to reduce their funding for programmes that serve the middle class. In this brutally competitive race to the top, all Western nations are cutting back their programmes which serve the middle class. This means we will all be forced to use more of our shrinking discretionary time and money to provide for more of the costs of education, health care and retirement.

As we have seen, governments throughout the West are shifting more of the cost of public education back on the middle class. Therefore, it is reasonable to predict that the Western young will continue to graduate with serious debt burdens.

Commonwealth countries still have government financed health-care programmes for all their citizens but these are on the chopping block as well.

> In Britain an aging population, more expensive and sophisticated treatment and the Conservative Government's systematic cost-cutting have stretched the health service's budget to the breaking point. Last year Dr Sandy Macara, the medical association's president, compared the health service to the Titanic, and said it would need billions more pounds in Government financing to keep it from sinking.[35]

Contending with the challenges of the greying of the West

What is hitting both the health and pension systems hard in all industrialised countries is the rapid greying of the population. In America and most industrialised countries the boomer population is by far the largest generational grouping. In the US there are 77 million boomers. The most terrifying word in the boomer vocabulary is 'bi-focal'. They live in absolute terror of moving into the 'bi-focal' phase of life. Really the aging of the boomer generation is going to be a terror for all of us.

The boomer population will begin retiring in 2010 which will make the problems in our national pension acute. By the time the last boomer retires in 2030 it could be calamitous. Politicians are trying to avoid the issue because trying to fix it could prove unbelievably expensive. Martha Phillips, executive director of the Concord Coalition, offers one forecast of how bad it could become in the United States. She states the trustees for the social security system are now predicting a $233 billion shortfall in 2030 between projected benefits paid and income to the fund. Covering this deficit in the present system would require 38% in FICA taxes dedicated to Social Security.

In 2013 Social Security's annual expenditure will begin to exceed the annual tax income. Martha Phillips says that if we wait this long 'there will be only three choices, none attractive: raise taxes, reduce government spending, or borrow approximately $7 trillion between 2013 and 2033.[36]

None of our Western pension systems will be able to survive the onslaught of the greying of the boomers without major alterations. And younger generations could get stuck with the bill. As with health-care cutbacks, I think we will see Western governments encouraging their citizens to assume increasing responsibility for creating their own private retirement schemes. Which will have an additional negative impact on people's discretionary time and money.

In his 1996 sci-fi novel *Holy Fire*, Bruce Sterling envisions a future world ruled by an all-powerful gerontocracy. They appropriate most of the world's wealth to design ever more expensive life-extension technologies. We already live in a world in which those over forty-five control the lion's share of the world's wealth. They are thoroughly enjoying spending it on romantic cruises, luxury cars and haute cuisine.

You can be sure that boomers, the so-called 'youth generation', will not go easily into the night. They are already setting records in turning to hormones, nutritional supplements and plastic surgery to hold back the aging process. Nutritional and lifestyle research has demonstrated that individuals can achieve modest gains in life extension by taking better care of themselves. And the boomers are going for it.

Recent breakthroughs in cellular research indicate that it could be possible to actually reset the aging clock. Essentially the aging process is brought on by the failure of human cells to keep dividing. This leads to the onset of disease and eventually death. Biologists at the Geron Corporation in Menlo Park, California and the University of Texas Southwestern Medical School altered human cells in a way that enabled them to break the limit of their natural life span. This technique could not only lead to the extension of human life but the growing of new tissues, arteries or even new retinal cells for a person afflicted with blindness.[37]

You can imagine how excited many boomers are by this news. But imagine the economic chaos it will mean for health-care and pension systems that are totally inadequate for the challenges of existing mortality rates. The science fiction scenario might turn out to be more on target than the author intended.

Those of us on the middle rungs of the ladder are undoubtedly going to benefit if the long boom resumes in terms of our affluence. But I am afraid that it could come at a fairly high price for many of us, particularly the young. Numbers of them will get busier, more locked into the consumer culture, more in debt and stray further from their spiritual moorings. For these folk the race to the top may well be a race to the bottom.

Planting a seed through video decoding

Teaching a Fuller Seminary class in leadership development, I invited students to view three different videos from three different generations to unpack the cultural values implicit in each film. First we viewed *The Wizard of Oz* that was from the 'silent generation' (over 60s). The students did an excellent job of unpacking the values of Oz—the importance of looking good and 'there's no place like home'. The film we watched from the boomer generation was the Beatles' *Yellow Submarine*. This largely gen X group were able to identify the sixties' values of love, peace and tranquility—but they expressed frank hatred for them. The final film was from their generation, *Lawn Mower Man I*, and they loved this very dark fantasy—even though they identified the values of power, destruction and ego that were displayed in the film. It proved very useful for all of us to decode the messages that come at us through popular media so that we can deal with them.

Seeds of hope in Seattle

One of the reasons Americans are running up such large debt loads is the excessive amount many of us spend at Christmas. Reportedly half of all Americans were still paying for Christmas spending for 1996 in 1997 and fully 28% were still paying off those bills in October of 1997. Scott Jones in Seattle was concerned at how much his family spent not only at Christmas but throughout the year. But as an orthopaedic surgeon he was also concerned at the amount of time he spent at work. Scott decided to cut his schedule back to three-quarter time and he and his family decided to stop spending money on Christmas consumerism. The Jones family found resources, like the *Alternative Celebration Catalogue*, which helped them learn to do alternative gift-giving at Christmas and throughout the year so they made gifts for those they cared about.[38] For instance, one Christmas I gave my two grown-up sons a family history including video recordings of both of my parents sharing their stories about growing up in the twenties and thirties, getting married and starting their families.

Seeds of hope in New Zealand

The major debt most families struggle with is the mortgage and for many Christian young, as we saw, it is becoming a huge burden. Two Baptist churches in Whakatane, New Zealand came up with a very creative way for the body of Christ in their community to work together to set members free, not only from the mortgage trap but also so they have more of their lives back to invest in mission to those in need.

The seeds of the Liberty Trust were sown in 1988. Essentially everyone who joins this co-operative contributes NZ$10 weekly per NZ$25,000 of their unpaid mortgage. As the fund grows a ballot is held to determine who receives an interest-free loan for their balance. Contributions to the fund continue until their interest-free mortgages are paid off. The average waiting time to win an interest-free loan is eight years. Over that time a family would typically invest about NZ$20,000 in the fund but when their turn comes they wind up saving roughly NZ$100,000 in interest. To date they have given out fifty interest-free mortgages.[39] For information you can contact John Bartley at <jbartley@wave.co.nz>. There are no end of creative ways we can help the people of God join the mustard seed conspiracy if we use our imagination.

A Christian disconnection between materialism and faith

William J. Bennett, former US Secretary of Education, raises serious questions about whether this economic race to the top is able to satisfy our deepest longings or whether it is destructive of our lives and spirit:

> More than ever before, thanks largely to mass marketing, to television, and to the unbridled and omnipresent market capitalism,

we are constantly pushing our children and adults to buy things—things they don't need. As a result we are not living at the center. We are misreading the essential human condition, because if we are actually moral and spiritual beings . . . then we ought to act in ways which are consonant with that reality.

Tony Campolo shares similar concerns, 'I believe we will be likely to find that capitalism's corrosive materialism will destroy us every bit as much as the materialism of Leninist Communism.'[40]

I think they are both right. I think in some fundamental ways this race to the top is actually a race to the bottom. While Christians may on occasion rail at consumerism and materialism, research shows there is almost no connection between our religious faith and how we steward our resources. In 1995 in fact, the Pew Charitable Trust funded a study of American Protestants. 'Most striking were Protestant attitudes about materialism and television,' said Chris Smith, Professor of Religious Studies at the University of North Carolina, in Chapel Hill. While respondents consistently decried materialism and consumerism, they also defined problems in such a way that excluded their own behaviour.[41]

Robert Wuthnow, in his book *God And Mammon In America*, found very much the same result. There appears to be a major disconnection between people's religious beliefs and how they use money. It is an expression of Western dualism and reflects a frank failure of the Churches of virtually all traditions to enable believers to develop a biblical view of stewardship. Wuthnow writes

If a single word had to be used to describe the relationship between religion and money however, it would be compartmentalisation . . . There is a kind of mental or emotional gloss to contemporary religious teachings about money that prevents them from having much impact on how people actually lead their lives.[42]

Opportunities for Christian leaders

Christian leaders have the opportunity to prepare their middle-class members and their young to live in a future in which the promoters of McWorld are going to want more of our time and money. These marketers know that the only way they can increase our appetite for MORE is to persuade us to change what we value. Therefore, Christian leaders have an opportunity:

1. To recognise that we are in a battle for the hearts and minds of a new generation that is powerfully attracted to sirens of the McWorld macro-mall. We will need to create whole new approaches to evangelism that recognise and counter the seductions of this borderless consumer culture;

2. To enable our church members and particularly their young people to recognise that we are also in a contest with a secularism we seldom discuss. We need to institute courses in our churches to help people decode the messages, reduce their consumption and get out of debt as quickly as possible so they have more of their lives to invest in the work of the gospel. As part of this initiative we will need to help them seriously to re-evaluate their life priorities in the light of faith and to create communities of resistance to enable people to resist the seductions of McWorld and discover in Scripture an alternative to the aspirations and addictions of modern culture;

3. To enable Christians to fundamentally reinvent their timestyles and lifestyles so that they can resist the pressures of modern culture and create a more festive way of life in which they are able to free up more time and money to invest in the work of God's kingdom;

4. To enable the Christian young to develop a plan, before they graduate, of how to put God's purposes first in deciding where they work and how long for as well as how they stew-

ard their time and money;

5. To reexamine the expectations of local churches on their members to insure that the expectations of time use in the local churches are clearly essential to the nurturing of faith and the advance of mission into the communities;

6. To persuade Christian organisations that they can no longer simply ask constituents for their leftovers and expect giving to be constant or to grow. To expand giving in the third millennium I am convinced that the only way forward is to conduct serious stewardship education that challenges the seductions of our consumer culture and offers creative alternatives;

7. To enable churches and Christian organisations to get ready for the rapid greying of our societies in Europe, North America and Down Under. Create ways to use the growing volunteer capability of greying boomers while preparing for the economic impact of their reduced economic support for the Church after 2010.

Questions for discussion and action

1. In what specific ways are you over-committed and over-booked and in what creative ways can you reduce the pressure?

2. In what specific ways are the messages of McWorld influencing you and your young people to increase your appetite for more? In what ways can you counter these messages?

3. How could the local church create a curriculum to enable members to steward all their lives to put first things first?

4. How can we help the Christian young to develop a life plan after graduation that enables them to create a less expensive way of life so they have more time and resources left over to make a difference for God's kingdom?

5. How can we enable the growing number of senior citizens in our society to reorder their lives to use the remainder of their lives to put God's purposes first?

6. What resources should churches and Christian organisations design to help Christians counter the messages of the consumer culture and learn to steward their lives in a way that more authentically reflects the aspirations of God's mustard seed instead of the addictions of McWorld?

Notes

1 Richard Neville, 'The Business of Being Human', *Good Weekend*, 23 August, 1997, p.48.

2 The Human Development Report 1988, UNDP, United Nations, Overview, p.1.

3 Christine Dugas, '1998 Pace Could Reach 35-Year High', *USA Today*, 30 June, 1998, p.1.

4 Jeremy Rifkin, *The End of Work: The Decline of the Global Labor Force and the Dawn of the Post-Market Era* (G. P. Putmans: New York, 1995), pp.20-21.

5 Stuart Ewen, 'Waste a Lot, Want a Lot: Our All Consuming Quest For Style', *UTNE Reader*, September-October 1989.

6 'The Goods Life: How Much Stuff is Enough?' *Sierra Magazine*, July-August 1997, p.20.

7 Brian Swimme, 'How Do Our Kids Get So Caught Up In Consumerism', *Enough*, Published By the Center for a New American Dream, Vol. 1, No. 2 Fall 1997, pp.1-5.

8 Daniel B. Wood, 'Shop Trek: The Next Generation', *The Christian Science Monitor*, 24 December, 1997, p.3.

9 Daniel B. Wood, *Ibid*., p.3.

10 Julie Pitta, 'Competitive shopping', *Forbes,* 9 February, 1998, p.92.

11 Andy Dappen, 'When Less Means More', *Hemispheres,*

November 1997, p.155.

12 Bob Santamaria, 'The global economy—at war with the family', *Humanity* (a New Zealand Publication), July 1998, p.6.

13 Maria Fiorni Ramirez, 'Americans at Debt's Door', *The New York Times*, 14 October, 1997, p.A19.

14 Saul Hansell, 'We Like You. We Care About You. Now Pay Up.' *The New York Times*, 26 January, 1997, p.F2.

15 Damon Darlin, 'The newest American entitlement', *Forbes,* 8 September, 1997, p.113.

16 *Ibid.,* p.113.

17 Tamar Lewin, 'Men Assuming Bigger Share At Home, New Survey Shows', *The New York Times*, 15 April, 1998, p.A16.

18 'Better off, but not much', *The Economist*, 4 October, 1997, p.35.

19 Shelley Donald Coolidge, 'Less Leisure: Work and Spend Cycle Makes Company Slaves', *The Christian Science Monitor*, 4 April, 1995, p.9.

20 'Here Comes the Four-Income Family', *Money Magazine*, February 1995, p.1.

21 'American economy: Backlash against McJobs', *The Economist*, 19 October, 1996, p.10.

22 The Harris Poll No. 31, Table 2, 'Work Hours Per Week', 7 July, 1997, p.3.

23 Shelley Donald Coolidge, 'Work and Spend Cycle Makes Company Slaves', *Christian Science Monitor*, 4 April, 1995, p.9.

24 'Affluenza, Warning: Materialism May Be Hazardous to Your Health', *UTNE Reader*, September-October 1997, p.19.

25 Richard C. Moraise with Katherine Bruce, 'What I wanna, wanna, really wannabe', *Forbes,* 22 September, 1997, pp.186-190.

26 'Branding', *Adbusters,* spring 1997, p.39.

27 Brad Edmondson, 'The Next Baby Boom', *American Demographics*, September 1995.

28 Nicole Rosenthal, 'The Boom Tube', *Media Week*, 18 May, 1998, p.44.

29 'A Long Way From Flower Power', *The Economist*, 17 January, 1998, p.26.

30 Lawrence Mishel, Jared Bernstein, John Schmidt, *The State of Working America 1996-1997* (M. E. Sharpe: New York, 1997), p.47.

31 Katharine Q. Seelye, 'Future U.S.: Grayer and More Hispanic', *The New York Times*, 27 March, 1997, p.A18.

32 Nicole Rosenthal, 'The Boom Tube', *MEDIAWEEK,* 18 May, 1998, p.44.

33 Peter Brierley, *Future Church: A Global Analysis of the Christian Community to the year 2010* (Monarch Books: Crowborough, England, 1998), p.33.

34 Gail Griffith, '10,000 Maniacs Found in Southeast Asia', *The Christian Science Monitor*, 8 April, 1994, p.23.

35 Sarah Lyall, 'For British Health System, Bleak Prognosis', *The New York Times*, 30 January, 1997, p.A6.

36 Martha Phillips, Letter to the Editor, *The New Republic*, 22 June, 1998, pp.40-41.

37 Nicholas Wade, 'Cell Unlocked: Longevity's New Lease on Life', *The New York Times*, 18 January, 1998, p.WK1.

38 Ann Scott Tyson, 'Christmas Without Shopping', *The Christian Science Monitor*, 11 December, 1997, pp.1, 9.

39 John Bartley, 'Interest Free=Set Free! Economics and the Kingdom', *New Zealand Baptist*, December, 1997, p.6.

40 John Paarlberg, 'Questioning Capitalism', *The City Gate, The Reformed Church of America*, September 1997, p.1.

41 Robert Marquand, 'Protestant Ranks Become More Secular', *Christian Science Monitor*, 19 December, 1995, p.4.

42 Robert Wuthnow, *God and Mammon In America* (Maxwell McMillan: New York, 1994), pp.150-151.

5

McWorld—a race to the bottom for the world's poor

A gigantic orange sun began its descent into Lake Victoria as John Otieno stood patiently in line at the back door of the Euro Fish Factory. John, his wife Beatrice and their four children lived on the edge of Lake Victoria in Uganda. He had just completed twelve hours of hard work on a road construction project moving boulders and preparing the road bed. In a good month when work is regular he makes $80. In addition to caring for her young children Beatrice works in a community garden plot to grow vegetables for her family's diet. She also does odd jobs for neighbours which brings in another $10 to $15 a month to help the family income.

The Otienos live on the edge of an urban slum in a small two-room hut that costs them $25 a month. A single light bulb suspended from the ceiling costs them $7 a month and kerosene for their cooking stove another $8 to $10 a month. They spend an additional $3 to $4 a month to purchase water from a neighbourhood standpipe. In other words this family spends roughly half their meagre income for shelter and utility costs leaving very little left over for food, medicine and the education of their two oldest children who are in a state-run school.

They attend a local Anglican Church and have been praying for God's help to make ends meet. But in the last three
years their situation seems to be steadily getting worse. One
of the major changes for them is a serious decline in the quality of their diet. Until three years ago they budgeted their funds
to buy fresh fish twice a week from local fishermen. This
enabled Beatrice to supplement their sparse rice and vegetable
diet with a little protein. But globalisation has changed all that
for the Otienos and thousands of their neighbours who live
near Lake Victoria.

The local fishermen used to sell their Nile Perch fillets for
$1 a kilogram (2.20 lbs). But in the past three years the price
of fish has increased more than four-fold and the Otienos and
many others can no longer afford to buy it. They are very concerned about how to provide an adequate diet for their four
children.

The reason fish prices have soared beyond reach is no mystery. After the 1986 take-over of Uganda by the forces of
Yoweri Museveni the new leader developed some very close
relationships with European investors. A number of these
investors live in areas of Northern Europe in which, over the
past four decades, fish supplies have been seriously depleted
by over-fishing. When these investors learned of the bountiful
resources in Lake Victoria they entered into an agreement
with the Ugandan government to build fish factories on the
edge of the Lake. Reportedly they are buying, processing and
flying 200 tons of fish a week from Lake Victoria to dinner
tables in Europe.

John stands in line at one of these fish factories with his
neighbours to buy the bones and fish heads since they can no
longer afford the fish harvested by their own fishermen from
their own lake. One of the cardinal doctrines of the new religion of free trade is that everyone on the planet has to be

allowed to fish in everyone else's pond. The advocates of this doctrine insist that if everyone is allowed to own the banks, phone systems and harvest the fish in other people's countries eventually it will work out to everyone's benefit.

It is difficult to understand how this will work. For example, America's preference for white chicken meat has produced a glut of chicken legs which US producers can't sell in the US. So they are dumping them at very low prices in Haiti and other countries. This practice is threatening to destroy the local poultry industry in Haiti because they can't compete with these very low give away prices. How will this kind of globalisation ever work out for the Otienos in Uganda or for the chicken growers in Haiti?

Finding a focus

 In the last chapter we examined the specific ways in which the growing globalisation is likely to impact the lives of those of us on the middle rungs and the new challenges and opportunities it presents to the Church. In this chapter we will focus specifically on how those on the lower economic rungs of our global society like the Otienos are likely to be impacted by globalisation. We will specifically try to identify new needs, challenges and opportunities that are likely to confront the global and Western poor as we rush into a new century and identify the implications for a Christian response.

Starting with the good news

There is a great deal of good news we need to celebrate regarding the global poor. Child mortality has been steadily improving since 1960. As a result, life expectancy is rising in almost every country on earth. Immunisation is on the threshold of eliminating diseases like smallpox and polio. Per capita global income is also beginning to rise in most countries and global population growth is beginning to slow. God has been influencing people, churches and organisations all over the world to help our poorest neighbours to help themselves. Over and over again it is often the small mustard-seed projects that are most effective in enabling those on the margins to see their local economies improve and their lives and communities transformed.

One of the positive aspects of globalisation is that the United Nations and a number of Christian organisations are beginning to find new partnerships with corporations to enable poorer communities to participate in the global economic lift-off. World Vision is one of the first to experiment in these new forms of collaboration with corporations.

It is important to stress from the outset that those who are spearheading the globalising of the economy have no interest in seeing anyone excluded from global economic growth. There is growing evidence that recent global economic growth has benefited many poor and marginalised people in the Two Thirds world. However, millions of those who benefited from the lift-off in Asia are struggling for their very survival again as most of Asia is suffering through a massive meltdown. But in spite of the global lift-off many of the world's poor are being left behind. We will see that the global race to the top seems to favour those with assets and it is a tough race for those without.

A rising tide lifts all boats?

'A rising tide lifts all boats,' they say. But America's soaring stockmarket has inevitably benefited the rich, who own more shares . . . The richest 1% of Americans—who earn over

$225,000 a year or have assets of more than $3m have enjoyed an increase in their shares of 70% since 1993. This has helped raise their net wealth by 43%.[1] The leaders of McWorld continue to insist that this race to the top will indeed raise all boats. But the evidence consistently shows that the shareholders who have benefited most from this global lift-off are the very wealthy.

Forbes magazine does an annual snapshot of those who are thoroughly enjoying this race to the top. When they started this annual feature in 1982 there were 13 billionaires in the US. In 1997 there were 170. Over the same period the cost of admittance to what they call the Forbes Four Hundred has quintupled in net worth to over $475 million each. 'If wealth isn't compounding . . . it is certainly growing at a faster clip than any other time in history. Last year on average Bill Gates' net wealth grew by an astounding $400 million every week. Michael Dell's net worth increased five fold, to $5.5 billion.'[2]

Michael Jordan takes over $65 million to the bank every year. CEOs are bringing home outrageously high salary packages that often seem to have little relationship to job performance. Glenn Pascall reports that 'thanks to stock options, chief executive officers at the 1,000 largest companies receive compensation equal to 336 times the average employee according to the latest *Business Week* survey. That's up from 240 times a decade ago. The survey found no link between CEO pay and performance.'[3]

What we are witnessing is the creation of a two-tier society in our Western countries. The very wealthy new élite from Britain, the United States and Australia increasingly live in gated communities of extravagant affluence. They often take holidays in the same luxury resorts in France, Mexico and the Caribbean. Reportedly they have more in common with one another than with those in their countries of origin. When they share a bit of their wealth in philanthropy, typically they give to the arts and medical research that directly benefits their own select community. What is particularly troubling is not only the enormous disparity between the global rich and poor but the race to the top seems to be widening that gap.

358 billionaires now 'control assets greater than the combined incomes of countries with 45% of the world's people'.[4] The World Bank predicts that the gap between richer and poorer nations will continue to widen in the next ten years and there is little real hope of moving towards convergence any time in the near future.[5]

The United Nations development programme is particularly concerned about the long-term consequences of this troubling trend. They state that thirty years ago the poorest 20% of the world's population earned 2.3% of the world's income. Now they earn only 1.4% and that amount is still declining. At the same time the richest 20% increased their share of global income from 70% to 80%.[6] The point is that the race to the top seems to be dramatically expanding the wealth of the richest 20%, while at the same time it is shrinking the resource base of the poorest 20%.

Joining the race to the bottom in Haiti

Louie Enel returned home late one humid evening with his head down. He had just come back from the rice merchant in Cayes with bad news. Seven months earlier he had sold half his rice crop to the merchant to make enough money to buy beans, oil, salt and sugar to feed his family for the rest of the year. He thought he had saved enough rice back to make it until the next harvest. But rats destroyed a third of the rice.

The merchant offered to sell Louie some of his rice back to him—at ten times the price he had been paid for it. Louie had no other option. But the purchase came at a very high price. He had to sell the family milk goat in order to purchase enough rice to keep his family fed for the next three months. After that he didn't know what he would do to try and make ends meet.

Louie and Lorraine and their family are typical of many in the bottom 20% of our planetary community who are being passed over by the global economic lift-off. While global population is indeed beginning to level off, that isn't the entire story. Population growth is still soaring among the world's poorest inhabitants. Today we share the planet with 6 billion neighbours. By 2050 that could reach between 9.5 and 9.8 billion.[7]

For instance, the population of Africa is expected to double by 2020—however the AIDS epidemic could change that forecast. The future of many in the poorer regions of Africa are seriously imperiled because they simply don't have the resources to join the race to the top. And for too many of the poorest nations on that continent, as elsewhere in the Third World, population growth is exceeding both economic growth and food production.

Debt, unemployment and lack of education greasing the skids

The global debt crisis makes it virtually impossible for many of the poorer countries to ever join the race to the top because such a high percentage of their income has to go to pay for the interest on their loans. For example, Nicaragua and Algeria are using over 50% of their export income to service interest on their debts. Recently the Anglicans held their worldwide communion in which one of the major issues was debt among the poorer countries. 'The Lambeth Conference has demanded action on international debt and economic justice, not only from governments and banks, but also from churches. The resolution asks bishops to take money from their own budgets to help pay international development and to co-operate with other faiths in advocacy programs.'[8]

Today's high unemployment rates in the Two Thirds World are escalating as the Asian crisis threatens to go global. It is projected that the global economy has to come up with some 2 billion new jobs by 2020 to meet the burgeoning population of young people who will be entering the workforce in these poorer countries. However, job creation isn't enough. We must make a major effort not only to educate young men but also the young women so that they are qualifed to work in tomorrow's world. This is a major opportunity for those involved in mission.

One of the other formidable problems confronting the global poor is that population growth is outstripping the carrying capacity of the environment in countries like Haiti and Bangladesh. A growing number of these regions will be in peril. Every missions initiative in the twenty-first century must include a component to care for creation.

 **The message from the twenty-first century is loud and clear. The poor are totally unable to play in this game without assets. We must all make a much greater investment to help the poor to help themselves. But the globalisation of the economy is not only happening in a way that benefits those with resources but it is influencing many governments to sharply reduce their investment in economic aid to enable the global poor to join the lift-off.**

McWorld—reducing the drag: cutting assistance to the global poor

As the industrial nations join this brutally competitive race to the top they are doing everything they can to reduce the drag on their economies to be more competitive including reducing humanitarian aid to the poor.[9] David Beckmann, president of Bread For the World, stated, 'The trend in cutting back foreign aid is global. But the United States is the leader of the trend, which will mean increased hardship for poor people in poor countries.'[10] The religious right in the US has consistently supported legislation to cut back humanitarian aid to the world's poor without explaining how this advances a pro-life, pro family agenda. In other words, since many of the world's governments are cutting back their humanitarian aid to the growing ranks of global poor it will mean that the Church, voluntary organisations and the private sector will need to do much more.

What will it take to raise all boats?

As we saw in the opening story, economic globalisation that is lifting the boats of European investors is swamping the boats of poor Ugandans. The reason? Those with financial means can always outbid the poor, even for resources in their own country. The world's poor are simply not playing on a level field because they have virtually no assets with which to participate in this very competitive contest.

As we saw in the story from Haiti the poor aren't even playing on a level field in their own country or in doing business with their own people. Louie Enel has absolutely no leverage to improve his family's lot economically. But the rice merchant is fully enjoying the race to the top because he has leverage. While Louie is having serious difficulty feeding his children and there is no way he can afford to send them to school it is a very different story for the rice merchant and his family. His six children are very well fed and they go to a private church-related school. Indirectly, Enel's family is helping to make a more secure future for the rice merchant's children.

You see, the very greed that makes the free market economy work so brilliantly in efficiently producing goods and services is what undermines its capacity to work justly on behalf of the poor and the marginalised. You can count on anyone who achieves wealth and power to use it to acquire more wealth and power—often at the expense of those who are at an economic disadvantage. That's the name of the game. There is no way that the free market and free trade will ever improve the lot of the marginalised unless people of faith and people of compassion make it happen.

Enabling the global poor to enjoy a taste of the McWorld banquet

Plowing the Sea is an important book that makes a compelling case that the standard economic prescriptions of McWorld simply are not adequate to the real world challenges of poor countries. How can a poor nation join this race to the top? The standard economic prescription is simple: Educate your people, reduce inflation, open your economy to free trade and investment and watch your gross domestic product soar.

But from Bangkok to Barranquilla, the poor still declare that it isn't that simple. Thailand's economy took off like a rocket only to wind up with huge trade deficits, a currency devaluation and a clamp down by the IMF and now major recession. In Peru the economy is growing. The wealthy are doing well. But unemployment is high and the gap between rich and poor is growing while inflation rates are dropping.

Essentially the authors of *Plowing the Sea* argue that the standard prescriptions aren't adequate. There must be a commitment to radical change at the micro-economic as well as macro-economic level. Corporate executives, politicians and Church leaders must create a broad spectrum of micro-economic opportunities down in the bowels of the economy. Poorer countries must fundamentally re-evaluate how they operate economically if they are to have any hope of their people benefiting rather than being victimised by the globalisation of the economy.

Too many Andean companies are trapped into being suppliers of inexpensive commodities. Since these companies compete on price and quantity instead of quality and innovation, they pay meagre wages and keep living standards for their workers depressed. Many Andean countries are also trapped in a dead-end form of economic growth. They are becoming increasingly dependent on the export of natural resources to make their economy grow. Then the more highly industrialised countries use those resources to produce higher margin goods—which they sell back to the nations from which the resources came.

Clearly the global race to the top will, for many of our poorer neighbours, become a race to the bottom if people of compassion don't take massive action. The global poor need education and economic opportunity that enables them to achieve a decent way of life. Poorer nations need to create regional micro-enterprise ventures that are more innovative in transforming their own resources into higher quality economic goods. In light of the escalating challenges and declining government programmes it is essential that Christians wake up to the biblical call to bring justice to our most vulnerable neighbours. The people of God have a unique opportunity, that we dare not pass up, to partner with churches in poorer communities to increase educational and economic opportunity as an expression of the inbreaking of God's new order.

Opportunities for Christian leaders

In response to the mounting challenges facing the growing numbers of the global poor, the debt crisis, the decreasing governmental aid and failure of the global economy to include many of our poorest neighbours, those in leadership have new opportunities:

1. To enable those working in mission with the poor to assist them in developing strong local and regional

economies that include the poorest residents while helping them to work for the spiritual and cultural transformation of their communities, plus the care of creation, in a way that much more clearly reflects the values of the mustard seed than those of McWorld;

2. To encourage local communities, where possible, to develop a high level of self-reliance in the production of basic foods to reduce vulnerability to the ups and downs of the global economy;

3. To enable us to address the needs of the most vulnerable including: education for the poor, especially for girl children (to promote community development and improve the quality of family life); land reform projects to help landless families to secure a way to support themselves now and in their retirement years; empowerment programmes for abandoned children to help them grow spiritually, educationally and in all their relationships;

4. To fashion a range of new co-operatives and partnerships to maximise the impact of our efforts to see the transformation of communities of need. These partnerships need first of all to include churches in these communities partnering with churches abroad. We need to create new opportunities for Christian relief and development agencies to partner with church planting agencies to work for the common goal of community transformation. But we also need to experiment with mission organisations collaborating with UN agencies, corporations, environmental organisations as well as national governments.[11]

Planting a seed in a coffee co-operative

 Thousands of people shouted and praised God as the prayer meeting around the old truck loaded with bags of coffee beans concluded. It was a bright spring morning and people had come from all directions to the market square in Plaissance de Sud in Haiti. The week before, thousands of people from this rural Haitian community had pooled their resources to purchase the truck so they could take their own coffee beans to market.

The buyer in Port au Prince had already quoted a price for their first truck load. By-passing the middle man increased their income by 250%. This additional income would mean that thousands of families who, like the Enels, were constantly on the edge of survival would be able to feed their children, send them to school and have enough economic leverage to start a small business selling small items like home-made soap in the market.

This story actually began seven years earlier when leaders from the valley invited World Concern to partner with them and their churches to improve the quality of community life. We turned the development project back over to the valley leaders after we had helped them attain their initial goals three years earlier. This was the second phase and they had every reason to celebrate the success of this co-operative mustard seed venture.

Planting a seed of hope in Mozambique

Mike Morris is a Christian leader in Great Britain who has taken initiative to challenge the Church to address the tremendous debt load that is making it impossible for many poorer nations to participate fully in the global economic lift-off. He is bringing together support from a number of Christian groups to secure the resources to pay off the debt of smaller Third World countries for the year 2000 as a part of a celebration of God's jubilee when all debts will be forgiven.[12] Part of the terms to pay off the debt for a small nation like Mozambique would be that the debtor nation contribute $2 million to local NGOs for every $8 million they save in annual debt servicing. These faith based organisations would use this money to carry out programmes in education, community health and infrastructure reform.

Planting a seed for global awareness

A group of twenty-year-olds in the UK have started a unique ministry called CREDS to raise awareness in churches regarding the growing global plight of the poor and our Christian responsibility. They promote fair traded products such as coffee, tea, nuts and crafts that are produced under just working conditions.

McWorld and the future of the Western poor

Stacey Jackson gave Carol Johnson a huge tearful hug as the judge read his ruling in the Chicago municipal court. Stacey and Carol had been on a three-year journey together. It all started when Stacey, aged twenty-nine, was arrested for possession of crack cocaine. At the time she had a twelve-year-old daughter, a nine-year-old son and she was pregnant. The court ordered her into drug treatment at Leland House and her children were placed in foster care with their grandmother. That is where Stacey first met Carol, who was a volunteer to Leland House from Jesus People USA. Carol became her mentor and friend and saw her through a lot of ups and downs.

Carol reported to the judge that Stacey had attended ninety meetings, over three years, of Narcotics Anonymous. She was clean of any drug use which was periodically checked by random drug testing. She had successfully completed a course in parenting training. And she had also taken a course in basic computer training while she was at Leland House. During this rehab time Stacey recommitted her life to Jesus Christ. Carol noticed a profound change in her attitude. At one point Stacey confided to Carol, 'Without the Lord in my heart I know I wouldn't be alive today!' Also, Stacey's church has begun to take an active role in helping her get her life back together.

So when the judge ruled that Stacey Jackson had completed all the conditions to return her children to her custody there was a lot of hugging and celebrating. Stacey got a job working at a burger franchise at an entry level income of under $7 an hour. But like a lot of single mums coming off welfare she is at an absolute loss as to how she can make that income stretch to cover basic living costs. The least expensive rental she can find for herself and her three children is a two-bedroom flat for $900 a month, right on the edge of a high crime and drug area. She and the baby share a room. Her daughter has the other bedroom and her son sleeps in the living room. It is not a neighbourhood she wants to live in but she simply can't afford anything better.

As Stacey prepared to move she looked at her budget and it dawned on her that on her entry level salary after she had paid rent, utilities and bought food and clothes from charity shops there simply wasn't any money left for other things like medical insurance, food stamps or child care. She has no idea who will watch her baby daughter and look after her other two children when they get home from school at 2.30 in the afternoon.

Stacey is one of millions in many Western countries who are making every effort to get their noses above water but are a long way from enjoying the bounty of the McWorld lift-off. Not only the global poor but also the Western poor are discovering that for too many the race to the top is in reality a race to the bottom. The growing threat of a global recession could devastate many of the Western poor who are barely hanging on by their fingernails.

Counting the heads of the Western poor

The globalisation of the economy has created a new class of millionaires in Poland, Bulgaria, Romania and throughout Russia. But millions of Russians are finding their living conditions plummeting as their economy is in free fall. In Holland, Germany, Denmark and other European societies the middle class is living very comfortably in the main. But these countries too are experiencing high levels of unemployment particularly among the young and immigrant groups.

Down Under there are very high rates of unemployment among Aboriginals in Australia and Pacific Islanders and Maoris in New Zealand. Many of the unemployed have become chronically dependent on government welfare. In

Britain, like America, there is less unemployment but many, like Stacey, are trying to make ends meet on poorly paid jobs and are not having a lot of success.

Nowhere is the gap wider between rich and poor than in America. According to a United Nations survey the United States has the highest rate of child poverty of eighteen industrialised nations. In 1996 36.5 million Americans including Stacey Jackson didn't earn enough to rise above official poverty thresholds. That is 13.7% of the population. One child in five is born into poverty in America but closer to 40% of American children experience poverty at some time in their lives.[13]

While employment among African Americans has slowly been increasing, that isn't the case for black teenagers. Only 14.5% of white teens are unemployed, but the Department of Labor's Bureau of Labor Statistics reports that 32.7% of all black teenagers are out of work. Some of these young people have graduated from schools where they didn't learn basic literacy skills which has obviously hindered their ability to participate in a highly technological society.[14] The poorest of the poor in America are still native Americans who experience more than 30% unemployment and a third of those who worked earned less than $10,000 a year in 1995.[15]

The US Census Bureau states that recent research indicates the gap between our richest and poorest citizens is wider than it has been any time since the end of World War 2. From 1964 to 1994 they reported that the income of the wealthiest 20% of Americans jumped 44% after being adjusted for inflation. During the same period the bottom 20% only saw a 7% increase which actually resulted in a reduction of purchasing power during this period.[16] The economic lift-off is not raising all boats in America either.

Assessing the future of the working poor

The Annie Casey Foundation reported a dramatic increase in the number of children living in poverty where one or more parents worked. Between 1989 and 1994 that figure swelled by 30% with 5.6 million children—more than a third of all poor children in America—living in working poor families.[17] What is of particular concern is that while the race to the top has seen a steady improvement in real GNP, worker productivity and rapid creation of new jobs between 1989 and 1995, the number of children starting out poor and with serious disadvantages in America is growing.

During the late sixties a bread-winner could work full time at an entry level job and earn enough to support a three-person family above the poverty line. By 1995 someone working full time at an entry level job fell 30% below the three-person poverty line. Many of the new jobs that have been created in the last few boom years simply don't pay a living wage.

One of the reasons for the widening gap between rich and poor in a number of our Western countries is the way this new McWorld economy is designed. John Challenger, who heads up a Chicago-based outplacement firm, says 'The advent of free trade and deregulation is causing American companies to increasingly view the world as their playing field. We see the jobs that require no skills as jobs that can go overseas.'[18]

One of the major reasons that the working poor don't seem to become any more competitive in the global market-place is that they simply don't have access to the educational opportunities that can help them break out of the basement. Like the global poor they aren't playing on a level field and therefore they have very little leverage to improve their situation.

In America the children of the poor and working poor are at a particular disadvantage because of the way in which we fund state schooling. Jonathan Kozol, in his very disturbing book *Savage Inequalities*, describes in vivid detail how we have inadvertently kept millions of children locked in poverty by creating a very discriminatory state schooling system where quality is largely determined by the local tax base.

Schools in some poorer urban districts can scarcely afford text books let alone the new computer learning tools abundantly available in wealthier districts. Recent legislation in the US to do away with affirmative action programmes will make it even harder for kids from the poorer communities to ever get out of situations of entrenched poverty because their opportunities are shrinking.

Since in a McWorld economy the primary commitment is to maximising benefits to shareholders, there is an inherent bias to keep labour costs as low as possible. We are in serious danger in the West, especially in the United States, of creating a permanent under-class that will be largely excluded from the opportunity to participate in the affluence of the McWorld lift-off.

McWorld—reducing the drag: cutting back assistance to the Western poor

In order to reduce the drag on their Western countries in this very competitive race to the top, governments are not only cutting back aid to the poor in the Two Thirds World but assistance to the poor and marginalised in their own countries as well. The United States, Great Britain, Australia, New Zealand, the UK and even Sweden are cutting back their social benefit programmes for the poor to reduce the drag on their national economies. For example, Austria has recently attacked its welfare programme because it gobbles up 28% of Austria's GDP today and if it continues at the present rate it will consume a huge 40% of the GDP by 2020.[19]

Of course the United States has made the most draconian cut-back in its social welfare programmes, limiting mothers with children to two consecutive years or five years over life and these funds are now administered at the state level.[20] Some people leaving welfare are finding jobs but many of those, like Stacey, can only find entry level McJobs that don't pay enough for mums coming off welfare to afford child care, health insurance or in many communities even pay rent.

New York State tracked those coming off welfare from July 1996 to March 1997 and discovered that only 29% found full-time or part-time jobs in the first few months after they were cut from welfare. Early evidence seems to indicate that this kind of welfare while helping some out of chronic dependency, is driving other Americans into another kind of chronic poverty that is the lot of the working poor in the United States.[21]

Having been a social worker, I know first hand that it just doesn't work in all cases to cut back social welfare and tell people to go to work. It isn't that simple. 28 million Americans can't read and write. Many of them are products of those woefully inadequate urban schools. There is no way those people can fill out an employment form at McDonalds or KFC let alone find a job that would hire the illiterate. Many more have no work experience or job skills. Millions of others are addicted to alcohol and drugs or are emotionally disabled and there is no way they can join the work force without serious rehabilitation first.

McWorld—cutting back funding to the caring edge

The cut-backs aren't just in direct assistance to the poor they are also in governmental funds to help voluntary agencies that are supposed to pick up the slack from government cut-backs. Catholic charities across the country predict that they will receive $200 million less from Washington for social services by 2002. The Lutheran Social Services organisation will be set back at least $200 million by the same date and the Salvation Army expects a $50 million cut-back.[22]

Here again the race to the top could for many of the poorest residents in our Western countries become a race to the bottom if people of compassion don't find ways to join with others in creating genuine opportunities for the excluded. The Bible convinces me that we Christians will face the judgement of God for the callous way so many of us ignore the plight of the poor and vulnerable who live in our communities and our world.

Listen to God's warning to the children of Israel regarding the sins of Sodom: 'Now this is the sin of your sister Sodom: She and her daughters were arrogant, overfed and unconcerned; they did not help the poor and the needy' (Ezekiel 16:49). We will be without excuse when we find ourselves reciting those words, 'When did we see you hungry, naked, alone or in prison and didn't respond?' In light of the mounting challenges it is essential that our middle-class congregations don't fail to partner with churches in communities of poverty to increase educational and economic opportunity in the twenty-first century as a witness for God's love for the poor.

Opportunities for Christian leaders

Christian leaders in the Western Church have the opportunity:
1. To focus on community restoration, which certainly includes the economic dimension, but also the transformation of the spirituality and relationships in that community so that they would reflect the values of the mustard seed rather than McWorld;
2. To facilitate churches in suburban and small towns as well as urban congregations to provide inexpensive child care for single mums coming off welfare or for families of the working poor;

3. We will need many more churches and Christian agencies to start literacy and job-training programmes (such as training in computer education) to enable the young and the poor to secure jobs that pay a living wage;

4. We will need to learn from micro-loans and micro-enterprise projects in the Third World how to help the poor to start small businesses to break out of poverty. We will also need to enable the poor to become more self-reliant through urban agriculture projects and even the possible development of fish ponds and small livestock projects;

5. We will need to develop whole new collaborative relationships between urban and suburban churches, between urban ministries, government agencies and corporations.

6. Finally, we will need to develop new economic crisis capabilities to deal with sudden need among the poor during times of economic crisis in our volatile McWorld future.

Planting a seed in Liverpool

A friend encouraged Tracy to visit a Christian ministry in Liverpool called Training Into Jobs. Tracy left secondary school three years early but had never been able to find work. Like Stacey she had no job skills or work record. She also had very low self-esteem and it took all her courage to visit the Training into Jobs offices since she had experienced many rejections in her efforts to apply for work. The worker at the centre listened to Tracy's story and enrolled her in a training programme in the hospitality industry. Nine months later Tracy not only had her first job in a hotel near her home but she had become a Christian and had taken a course to help her develop her confidence and leadership skills. As a result her church asked her to lead a women's Bible study group. Her entire life has been transformed because some Christians found they simply couldn't ignore any longer the large number of unemployed youth in Liverpool and the seed they planted is bearing good fruit.

Planting a partnership seed in Ohio

A rural Methodist church in Ohio developed a partnership with a Methodist church in an inner-city area in Cleveland. The creative part of the partnership was that the rural church was growing and grafting fruit tree seedlings which they planned to bring to the inner city. The two churches together could plant them in parking strips and back gardens throughout the neighbourhood to take a step in promoting local food self-reliance.

Planting a seed in habitat Belfast

Habitat for Humanity Belfast made history in 1997 when Catholics and Protestants gathered together to dedicate an eleven-house development in the Catholic part of Belfast. Then they prayer-walked to a ground-breaking in the Protestant side of town. This was the culmination of three years of hard work by hundreds of volunteers from both parts of Belfast who are committed to giving peace a chance.

Planting a seed in down payments for urban housing

 Nehemiah Ministries is a creative, black-run national ministry in the US that provides down payments for poor families so they can purchase their own homes. They are creating collaborative ventures with other urban organisations to rapidly expand this form of economic empowerment.

Planting a seed in national advocacy for the poor

 On June 1, Call to Renewal convened a day long 'Capitol Preach-in' to bring the message of God's concern for the poor to the US Congress. Hosted by Rev. Tony Hall (D-Ohio), a dozen of the best-known preachers in America participated in the event . . . Jim Wallis concluded the day: 'In our discussions of public morality, it is important that we remember that morality is also about how we treat the poor. On June 1, we reminded Congress about what is important and called America to a new moral awakening about its responsibility to our nation's poorest families.'23

The Call to Renewal is an effort in the United States to bring together African American, Hispanic, Catholic, Evangelical and mainline Protestant churches with the government and corporations to promote community economic empowerment and social justice for God's kingdom.

Questions for discussion and action

1. How could this rapid movement into global free trade benefit or penalise the poor?
2. How are the needs of the global and Western poor likely to change as we enter a new millennium?
3. Why are many Western governments cutting back their assistance to the poor at home and abroad?

4. What is our biblical responsibility to the poor and the vulnerable and what are creative new ways your church could become more directly involved in helping the poor to help themselves?

Notes

1 'Rich Pickings', *The Economist*, 6 June, 1998, p.30.
2 Michelle Conlin, 'When billionaires become a dime a dozen', *Forbes,* 13 October, 1997, p.148.
3 Glenn Pascall, 'Starving for time', *The Seattle Times*, 5 July, 1998, p.B5.
4 Barbara Crossette, 'UN Survey Finds World Rich–Poor Gap Widening', *The New York Times*, 15 July, 1996, p.A3.
5 'Disparities In Global Integration', *Finance And Development*, September 1996.
6 'A Global Poverty Trap', *The Economist*, 2 July, 1996, p.34.
7 'World Population Growth', *Global Child Health News and Review*, No. 1, 1995, p.19.
8 Nan Cobbey, *Episcopal Life*, 18 August, 1998.
9 'United States Falls To Fourth In Global Giving', *Bread For The World Newsletter*, August-September, 1996, p.9.
10 *Ibid.,* p.9.
11 Jane Sutton, 'In Peru: the Means to Serve', *World Vision*,

December 1997-January 1998, p.15.

12 http://reports.guardian.co.uk/debt/>.

13 Elia Kacapyr, 'How Hard are Hard Times?', *American Demographics*, February 1998, p.30.

14 Ron Scherer, 'Whose Boat The Economy Isn't Floating: Black Teens And The Unskilled Are Among Those Still Jobless Despite Buoyant Labor Market', *Christian Science Monitor*, 1 August, 1997, pp.1, 5.

15 Michel Marriot, 'Frank Racial Dialogue Thrives On The Web', *The New York Times*, 8 March, 1998, pp.1, 22.

16 Stephen Holmes, 'Income Disparity Between The Poorest And The Richest Rises', *The New York Times*, 20 June, 1996, p.1.

17 Linda Feldmann, 'More Children Of Working Parents Now Live In Poverty,' *Christian Science Monitor*, 4 June, 1996, p.3.

18 William O'Hare and Joseph Schwartz, 'One Step Forward Two Steps Back', *American Demographics*, September 1997, p.53.

19 'Who Remains Left Out of the Economy of the "Roaring '90s"', *Christian Science Monitor*, 1 August, 1997, p.5.

20 'Stakeholder Capitalism: Unhappy Families', *The Economist*, 10 February, 1996.

21 Raymond Hernandez, 'Most Dropped From Welfare Don't Get Jobs', *The New York Times*, 23 March, 1998, pp.1, A16.

22 Milt Freudenheim, 'Charities Say Government Cutbacks Would Jeopardise Their Ability To Help The Poor', *The New York Times*, 5 February, 1996.

23 'Putting the Poor on the Map', *Sojourners,* September-October, 1998, p.56.

6
The incredible shrinking Western Church

Sarah lived in a small flat in Buffalo, New York, barely scrimping by on her social welfare. Her only living relative, her thirty-five-year-old daughter Natalie, was permanently institutionalised because of schizophrenia in a hospital sixty miles away. There was no public transport to the hospital and Sarah didn't own a car. She discovered that Concerned Ecumenical Ministries conducted a senior citizen support programme. Sarah applied and twice a year was shuttled to visit her daughter. One day the phone rang and Sarah got the bad news—the transport she had come to rely on had been cancelled due to a sudden cut-back in funding by the American Baptist Church in that region.

Now let me give you the story behind the story. In 1984 I had the opportunity to lead a two-day consultation with the Executive Council of the American Baptist Church regarding its future. We presented projections that made it clear that the ABC would have to do more to respond to the growing human needs at home and abroad.

Then I showed them demographic projections on how their own denomination was changing. Black and Hispanic churches made up about 30% of the membership and were slowly growing. But white membership was greying and declining at a rate that would seriously undermine giving and the ability of the ABC to even sustain their present level of mission to those in need. It was clear that this was the first time most of these leaders had seen these figures. And they immediately understood the implications for the future of their denomination and its mission. Before we finished the consultation ABC leaders developed a plan to increase church growth and giving to respond to this projected decline.

Almost ten years later I was asked to meet with the Executive Council of the American Baptist Church again. I discovered that no one had followed up on the recommendations the Council had made ten years earlier to get the church growing. Regrettably, my projections proved to be valid. While ethnic membership had grown to over 35%, white membership and giving had declined. As a consequence many districts of the ABC were forced to cut back funding to important ministries including Concerned Ecumenical Ministries in Buffalo which provided that shuttle twice a year for Sarah to visit her daughter.

I have been able to identify very few major denominations or mission organisations that make any effort to anticipate either how the larger context in which they carry out mission is changing or how their demographic and funding changes will impact the ability of the Church to carry out its mission in a new millennium. As we have seen in the early chapters, we are racing into a future that is changing at blinding speed—a future of growing human need in which the Church is going to be called on to do more. But we have also seen how the forces of globalisation are likely to decrease the amount of discretionary time and money members are able to invest in the Church and its mission given our present models of discipleship.

Finding the focus

 The question we want to answer in this chapter is, 'How effectively will the Church be able to address the mounting challenges of the third millennium given changes taking place in attendance and giving patterns within the Western Church?' We will share an overview of these changing patterns in the Church in Britain, Australia, New Zealand, Canada and the United States in order to predict the future of the Western Church and its mission. Finally, we will describe creative ways that those in leadership can take decisive action if the Western Church is even going to sustain its present level of mission between now and 2020. We will begin by looking at the changing character of religion in the future.

Globalisation of religion

As we race into a new global future everything is changing at time-warp speed including the religious character of our global village. First, other world religions that once had geographic boundaries are now going global as Christianity has done. For example, recently when we flew into Auckland, New Zealand we saw the completion of the first Hindu temple. Hinduism and Buddhism are currently the fastest growing religions in Australia. For those living in Western countries it is no longer simply what brand of Christianity to choose. As a result of globalisation individuals now have access to all the historic world religions and an absolute explosion of other alternatives.

In the musical *Sweet Charity* there is an intriguing song entitled the 'Rhythm of Life' in which people are invited to join the Religion of the Month Club. For those interested in shopping around there has never been such an astonishing array of the weird and the wild. Reportedly over 500 new religions a year are created in Southern California alone.[1]

As we enter a very uncertain new global future everyone from George Gallup to *Time* magazine has documented a growing hunger for spirituality throughout the Western world. One thing is clear in the nineties—those cults which require a high threshold of commitment aren't nearly as popular as they were in the sixties. Many people seem to be looking for a post-modern faith that offers a form of spirituality which makes very little demand for serious change in their lives. That is why various New Age religions and scientology are more popular today than the more demanding religious forms of the Moonies or the Hari Krishnas.[2]

One of the examples of the ultimate in low-demand religion is the annual ritual of the Burning Man Festival in Black Rock Canyon, Arizona. From small beginnings in Southern California this ritual burning of a huge male form has attracted huge numbers of participants from many different religious and cultural backgrounds. It is the ultimate example of religion without dogma or demand. Every participant is free to interpret The Burning Man in any way that makes sense to them. One guy in a military helmet with Mickey Mouse ears said, 'When you burn the man, you recognise the past is ashes, and that is significant—everyone recognises that—it's all gone.'[3]

Graham Cray, a lecturer at Cambridge in the UK, is particularly concerned at the extent to which Christians in the West are embracing a form of religious pluralism in which, like people outside the church, they are picking and choosing those elements they want to embrace as true. He is alarmed that this kind of post modern relativism is particularly spreading among young Christians in Europe.

Religion is also rising in pop culture. Touched by an Angel,

Soul Man and Nothing Sacred are beamed into our homes. In America, Christian music is breaking over into the mainstream. Books on religion and spirituality have increased sales by 112% between 1991 and 1996. They are the only form of adult non-fiction whose sales have been rising.[4] A growing number of patients in hospitals are requesting alternative therapies including prayer and spirituality.[5] The question is how can Christians both counter the relatism of post modernity and respond to the growing spiritual hunger in the West?

Back to the future one more time

Remember that we are going backwards not forwards in global evangelisation. 28% of the world's people would identify themselves as Protestant, Catholic or Orthodox today. By the year 2010 that will decrease to 27% and continue to decline from there because the global population is growing more rapidly than the global Church.[6] Human needs at home and abroad are going to be mounting. The question again is, 'How ably will the Church be able to respond to these mounting challenges given the changing demographic and giving patterns in the Western Church?'

Starting with the good news

First the good news from the Church worldwide. Dudley Woodberry, who heads the School of World Mission at Fuller Theological Seminary, states that 'through the efforts of the Lausanne Committee for World Evangelisation AD 2000 and Beyond and the World Evangelical Fellowship, co-ordinated efforts are being made in church planting, especially in the 10-40 window—with considerable church growth.'[7]

Patrick Johnstone, in his new book *The Church is Bigger Than You Think*[8], documents the remarkable growth of the

Church in much of Africa, Latin America and parts of Asia. Through DAWN and the AD2000 movement new churches have been planted in regions with little gospel witness. Johnstone states that while the Bible was translated into only 537 languages at the turn of the last century, by the time we reach the twenty-first century it will have been translated into 2800 languages.[9]

Interdev predicts that 95,000 missionaries will be sent out from non-western countries by the year 2000.[10] *Christianity Today* celebrates the emergence of a new truly global Church where Episcopalians in America recruit leadership from the Anglican Church in Uganda and Australian churches are adopting Korean cell groups to nurture spirituality.[11]

The recent Lambeth Conference for those in the Anglican tradition has signalled a shift in the global axis of the Church. The British/American Church is no longer defining the direction. Anglican bishops from Africa, Asia and Latin America have taken leadership of the Anglican parade much to the dismay of many old-line, liberal bishops in the North who are used to framing the faith and setting the course. I think we will continue to see the leadership of the Church shift to Two-Thirds World leadership in many traditions as we enter a new millennium.

Another one of the hopeful trends is reverse missions. In the future we will see missionaries from Asia, Africa and Latin America bringing a more vital faith to many Western communities. For example, a small vibrant Pentecostal church in Concepcion, Chile sent their pastor as a missionary to an affluent, stiff United Church of Christ congregation in Massachusetts. The pastor said that as he worked with this group of old-line Congregationalists 'we could sense a spiritual hunger'.[12]

Scoping out the future of the Western Church

While there is robust growth in much of the Church in the Two Thirds World, regrettably that isn't true in much of the Western Church. We will describe many positive ways that God is at work in the Western Church. But we will also share some very concerning patterns in church attendance and giving patterns in the West.

In describing the Western Church I will focus principally on English-speaking nations because that is most relevant to the intended readership of this book. These countries include Britain, Australia, New Zealand, Canada and the United States. Let me add that my research and travels in continental Europe suggest that in the main the Church there is in even more serious decline than the Church in English-speaking nations.

As I profile the Church in the English-speaking Western countries I think you will see that the trends in these countries are remarkably similar. A word of caution before we begin. This analysis will not be fully satisfying to those trained in statistics because the data we will be sharing was not all gathered in the same way or organised in a consistently parallel fashion. Therefore it is not offered as a scientific study but rather as an impressionistic examination of the best data I have been able to find. Even so I hope this information will be useful.

A road map for the tour

First we will look at how the changing attendance patterns for the Church in Great Britain, Australia, New Zealand, Canada and the United States will affect its ability to respond to the new challenges of a new millennium. Then we will explore how changing attendance patterns by age are likely to determine the future of the Church in the West. Finally, we will examine how changing giving patterns are also likely to impact the ability of the Western Church to expand its mission thrust to respond to the mounting challenges of tomorrow's world.

Recently I sent an article to a number of Evangelical denominations' magazines. This article was about the future and the Church and cited examples of what God is doing in Australia, New Zealand and Great Britain. One editor from a denominational magazine, that will remain nameless, said he wouldn't be able to use my article. Then he added, 'Why in the world did you mention examples from Great Britain, Australia and New Zealand? They are all part of a post-Christian culture where the Church is no longer vital or growing. What do we possibly have to learn from them?' I have found that his viewpoint is fairly common in the US. But as I will show, in many ways I have found a more vital, creative faith in these countries than I have found in the States.

The future of the Church in Great Britain

In many ways I believe that the Church in Britain is a much healthier Church than the one in North America even though their attendance patterns are lower.

A seed planted for Christian collegiality in the UK

First of all Clive Calver, now head of World Relief in America, collaborated with other leaders in the UK (over twenty years) to create a remarkable informal network of Anglican bishops, Pentecostal pastors, leaders of parachurch agencies working in world mission and the full spectrum of Protestant denominations—Methodists, Baptists and Reformed Church. I have not seen another country in the West in which such a collegiality of Christian leaders are working in common cause for the gospel of Christ together.

In the past twenty years Christians in the UK have spear-headed efforts in church planting and evangelism that out-stripped anything going on in the United States during the same period. Hundreds of new churches were planted from Icthus Fellowship to Revelation House Churches. Tens of thousands of British people came to vital faith in Jesus Christ during this period of Christian expansion and renewal.

Also we have found much more creative approaches to advancing God's kingdom per square mile in the UK than in the US, particularly among the under thirty-fives. This move-ment to plant churches, evangelise neighbours and work with the poor is still going strong in the UK. The only problem is that the established, old-line denominations like the Methodists, Anglicans and Reformed are greying and declin-ing more rapidly than other denominations are able to increase Church growth.

As a consequence adult church attendance in England was 10.2% of the population in 1980. In 1995 it declined to 8.1% and is projected to decline even further to 7.7% by the year 2000.[13]

According to the Christian Research Association the decline has been even steeper for the Church in Scotland and Wales. Imagine what the rate of decline would be if there weren't so many Christians working at expanding the Church. Even more concerning than the steady decline and greying of the Church in Britain is the serious drop in church attendance among the under-thirties.

Attendees in the over-sixty-five group contain 25% more of their age group than English society at large, while attendees in the twenty to twenty-nine age group show about 30% fewer individuals in attendance than the English society at large.[14] Peter Brierley and Heather Wraight at the Christian Research Association track not only demographic change in the United

Kingdom but throughout the larger world. Their Email is 100616.1657@compuserve.com.

As you will see, as we look at the Church in Australia, New Zealand, Canada and the United States there is a consistent pattern. All the old-line denominations are greying and declining and slowly going out of business. The charismatic movement has largely plateaued in all our Western countries. Evangelical and Pentecostal churches are often showing growth but the overall pattern is still one of decline like it is in England and the missing generation is consistently the under-thirty-fives.

The future of the Church in Australia

In the past twenty years in Australia one can also point to a period of energetic growth in church planting and evangelism. A number of new Pentecostal and charismatic churches have been planted during this period. The Sydney Diocese of the Anglican Church is conservative theologically and has also been in the forefront of church planting and evangelism. As a result they have actually grown until lately, unlike most Anglican communions in Britain, Canada and the United States.

A seed planted Down Under for justice

John Smith, a prophetic Australian Christian leader, has started a network of ministries called Care and Communication Concern (CCC), to address the growing urban needs in Melbourne and Newcastle. In one ministry, Hand Break Turn, young men caught stealing cars are trained to rebuild cars by CCC. For graduation, CCC arranges for the young to race their rebuilt cars with the police.

But again it's the same story as in England. The old-line

denominations are greying and declining. And the growth among charismatic Pentecostal and evangelical churches is not enough to offset the overall trend. Peter Kaldor who, with his colleagues at the National Church Life Survey, reports, 'Sample survey data can provide a picture of trends over the past forty years for all denominations including the Catholic Church. During the fifties, over 40% of the population attended church at least once a month. By the nineties this had dropped to around 25% of the population.'[15] Philip Hughes and Peter Bentley state that their research indicates that weekly attendance is only about 10% for adults.[16]

While smaller Pentecostal groups have attracted more under-thirty people than the general Australian population, larger Protestant groups are attracting significantly less than the larger population. Peter Kaldor states, 'Around 40% of mainstream attendees are over sixty years of age. If patterns continue as they are, in twenty years there will be a significant decline in numbers.'[17]

The future of the Church in New Zealand

The charismatic renewal vitalised many traditional denominations in New Zealand like the Presbyterians, Congregationalists and Anglicans. The same winds of the Spirit stimulated a tremendous growth of church planting and evangelism among Pentecostal churches. For example, the New Life Centre in Christchurch planted over a hundred new churches in the seventies and eighties.

Evangelical denominations like the Baptists have also experienced vigorous growth in recent years. Christians in New Zealand respect the indigenous Maori culture more than Christians in the United States do the native American people. Youth For Christ is very active in trying to find new ways to reach a new generation with interest-based clubs and performance-oriented cafés. The Church in New Zealand sends more missionaries overseas percentage wise than any other Western country other than Norway.

During the past two decades there has been a growth in church planting, evangelism and the creation of innovative Christian ministries. Perhaps the most significant development is an umbrella organisation called New Vision New Zealand. Headed by Brian Hathaway it is committed 'to the growth of the kingdom of God by all means possible.'[18]

In spite of all the good things that God is doing in this beautiful country, the pattern is identical to that of great Britain and Australia. The old-line churches are greying and declining and the growth among evangelical, charismatic and Pentecostal churches doesn't offset the trend. In the fifties, 40% of New Zealanders were attending church once a month. In the early nineties that had declined to 29%. This survey indicated weekly attendance rates of 17%. Again the greying and declining of the Anglican, Presbyterian, Lutheran and Methodist congregations is primarily responsible for the overall demographic decline.[19]

It would be important to report, however, that both the Anglicans and Methodists began to see a bit of growth again starting in 1993. The groups in the eighties and nineties that have experienced robust growth in New Zealand are the Assembly of God, the Apostolic Churches, the Elim Churches and the Vineyard Churches.[20]

One researcher, Hugh Dickey, reported that only 12.7% of the nation's children are on Sunday and church school registers. Of this number he states that on average only 73% actually attend. There has been a precipitous drop in Sunday school attendance since the early sixties that threatens the Church's future.[21] Not surprisingly, 81% who identify themselves as of 'no religion' in New Zealand are under forty.[22]

The future of the Church in Canada

Toronto was 'Mecca' in the nineties for charismatics from all over the Western world. However, in spite of the 'Toronto blessing' Canada has experienced less growth in the Church than that which we described in the UK and Down Under. However, like New Zealand, The Evangelical Fellowship of Canada started a thrust in the late eighties called 'Vision 2000'. The aim of this umbrella organisation is to promote evangelism and church planting to expand the Church in Canada. And they have seen fruit from their initiatives.

While there has been growth among some conservative Protestants in Canada, there is also an array of emerging expressions of the Church that are very encouraging. Regent College is, in my opinion, one of the finest centres for Christian learning in North America. Intervarsity in Canada is doing a brilliant job in preparing a new generation of high school and university students to serve God. 100 Huntley Street Television productions and Brian Stiller Reports create Christian television with more substance and taste than almost anything that is offered south of the border. And Canadian Christians are involved in a much broader range of social issues than many of their American Christian neighbours.

Reginald Bibby has been writing about the demographic profile of the Church in Canada since he published his first book *Fragmented Gods*. Bibby reports that in 1957 you would find 53% of Canadians in church on Sunday morning. By 1990 it had declined to 23% and is reportedly still declining.[23] Bibby discovered that one of the reasons for declining attendance in Canada is mobility. He explained that every time Canadians move, half of them stop attending church regularly.[24] But again the major problem is the greying and declining of the United and Anglican churches. The membership patterns of these mainline denominations between 1957 and 1990 tell the story. They suffered membership declines from 80% to 30%.[25]

If we want to know where the Church is going in the future our best indicator is the involvement and commitment of the Canadian young. In the early eighties, according to Bibby, 23% of Canadian teenagers were weekly attendees and 39% described themselves as religiously committed. By the early nineties weekly attendees had fallen to 18% and the religiously committed to 24%. Even more stark are the contrasting attendance and membership patterns for eighteen to twenty-nine year olds between 1957 and 1990. In 1957 36% of this population would be found in attendance at church. By 1990 that had fallen to 14%. In 1957 68% of these young adults were church members. By 1990 that figure plummeted to 17%.[26] If the Church in Canada is to have a future it must find ways to reach and keep its youth.[27]

The future of the Church in the United States

The Church in the United States has enjoyed a period of growth in the last two decades. Mega churches like Willow Creek and Saddle Back have emerged. Alpha programmes in evangelism, imported from Britain, are resulting in thousands coming to vital faith in Jesus Christ. Prayer initiatives are involving millions of American believers. Promise Keepers is not only calling men back to a vital faith but also promoting racial reconciliation. And there are significant levels of growth among Black, Hispanic and Asian congregations in the US.

However, I am very concerned about the future of the mainline Protestant churches in America. I am seeing a small but growing number of mainline churches buying into a religious pluralism in which they are openly embracing all forms of spirituality the mind can imagine from neo-paganism to New Age. As they move away from biblical orthodoxy and

Christology at warp speed, I am wondering how they can retain any genuine sense of Christian identity. We Evangelicals have another problem. Nowhere else in the Western world do Evangelicals have to be right-wing republicans or the equivalent to be considered born-again Christians. Many have unwittingly confused their faith with American nationalism and a narrow political ideology.

I am also concerned about the future of the Evangelical movement in the US because of a growing disconnection between middle of the road Evangelical organisations like World Vision, Intervarsity, the spectrum of Evangelical colleges and seminaries, and the Evangelical rank and file. These organisations tend to understand Christian life and responsibility in broader terms than their constituents who don't read broadly and tend to rely on talk radio and Christian radio to help them understand the world. I urge these Evangelical organisations to launch new initiatives to do much more, using Christian radio, to educate their constituents to a broader vision for Christian social responsibility in order to avoid a potential break-up of American Evangelicalism.

In the United States, while the Catholic Church is still experiencing a bit of growth, virtually all mainline churches are greying and declining as in other Western countries. In 1968 eleven mainline Protestant denominations represented 13% of the US population. By 1993 it had plummeted to 7.8%—a 40% decrease. If the present trends continue uninterrupted these denominations will be totally out of business by the year 2032.[28]

Add to the problem of declining numbers that of aging congregations. For example, there are twice as many ELCA Lutherans over seventy-five as the general population.[29] The Presbyterians, the United Church of Christ, the American Baptist and the United Methodists are all dealing with the twin hits of declining numbers and greying congregations. The 2.5

million member Episcopal Church lost 1 million members from 1965 to 1989. As we will see, that has already begun to hit the pocket books of a number of major denominations.

Wade Roof and William McKinney, in their important book *American Mainline Religion*, stated that 'the churches of the Protestant establishment, long in a state of relative decline, will continue to lose ground both in numbers and in social power and influence. The proportion of the population that is Protestant will continue its gradual decline in the decades to come, and within Protestantism denominations and revitalisation movements will continue their contest for power and influence.'[30]

However, Gustav Niebuhr, religion editor for *The New York Times*, has recently reported that there is a bit of good news. Several mainline denominations including the Episcopal Church, the United Methodist, the ELCA Lutherans, The Presbyterian Church USA, saw their rate of decline begin to slow in the past three to four years. However, this doesn't alter the reality that they are slowly going out of business. It is only slowing the rate of decline.

Even the Southern Baptist Church which has enjoyed strong growth since the end of the Second World War is in trouble. Fraught with internal conflicts they have seen their growth almost come to a halt at 0.5% or less from 1994 to 1997.[31] The major growth in the US as elsewhere is among conservative Protestant groups including Black and Hispanic congregations, Assemblies of God, The Vineyard, The Evangelical Free and the Covenant Church in America.

John and Sylvia Ronsvalle state that fifteen conservative and evangelical denominations have grown between 1968 and 1993 but that isn't the whole story. They point out that between 1985 and 1993 this rate of growth slowed and the portion of the US population involved in the Church actually declined.[32] In the past ten years I have seen several conservative denominations like the Mennonite Church shift from slow growth to no growth.

Figure 1

Trend in membership as a percent of US Population, 29 Protestant denominations, linear and exponential regression based on data for 1968-1985, with actual data 1986-1995.

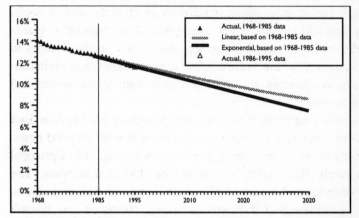

Sources: *Yearbook of American and Canadian Churches*, adjusted series; US Bureau of Economic Analysis   empty tomb, inc. 1997

It is essential to mention that the Church in the United States is the only one that appears to vary from the attendance patterns of the Church in other English-speaking Western countries. As we have seen, in spite of often significant growth in evangelism and church planting, Britain, Australia, New Zealand and Canada have over the past three to four decades all suffered a steady erosion in attendance that threatens their future.

However, in America George Gallup researchers insist that in spite of the greying and decline of the old-line churches, attendance of American Christians has remained fairly constant since the fifties at between 40% and 45%. George Barna, who has only been tracking attendance patterns since the early eighties, puts average US attendance nearer 40%.[33]

For the past decade other demographers have begun questioning the validity of American church attendance patterns remaining constant when there seems to be anecdotal evidence contradicting this profile. Kirk Hadaway, chief statistician for the United Church of Christ, has seriously questioned the validity of these surveys because he believes Americans are over-reporting their attendance. Hadaway states, 'Interest in spirituality is up. But active participation in a faith community or institution is dropping.' He points out that mainline churches have lost one fourth of their members in the last thirty years. Roughly 48% of the children in Episcopal families leave church at eighteen. Since 1965 the United Methodists have lost almost 1,000 members a week.

To check the validity of the self-reporting methods, Hadaway's research team counted cars in church car-parks in a small Ohio county over a period of several months. 'His finding: Americans over-report their actual church attendance by a marked degree. Actual attendance is closer to 24 percent, Hadaway said, and is falling slowly.'[34]

If Hadaway's observational research is more accurate than the self-reporting approach, US attendance patterns would be more similar to the kind of attendance patterns we find among churches in other Western English-speaking countries. One trend that is identical in all these countries is that the more theologically conservative, evangelical side of the Church is the lively and growing edge. This is certainly true in the US as well.

'For both the United States and Canada, evangelicals— whether defined by denominational attachment, personal beliefs and practices, or both—now constitute the largest and most active component of religious life in North America,' states Mark Noll and Lyman Kellstedt.[35]

In response to the question, 'How many Evangelicals are there in the United States?' Lyman Kellstedt responds, 'If you mean how many claim a conversion experience of being "born again"?—The answer is that nearly a third of the population is evangelical. If you mean—how many believe that the Bible is true?—the total rises to nearly half the population. If you mean—how many Americans are adherents to a church in the evangelical tradition?—we find that about one fourth of Americans are evangelicals.'[36]

Those of us from the Evangelical tradition in America, rather than celebrating our growing numbers should be asking how we can be such a large part of the population and apparently have so little influence. In the next chapter I will argue that the reason we have had so little influence on the larger secular culture is that we have allowed modern culture instead of our Christian faith to define what is important and what is of value. Most social science research that I have read reports that we Evangelicals are simply not that different from our non-church-going neighbours. We will need to place much more emphasis on quality growth instead of simply celebrating numerical growth.

Another trend in the American Church that is identical to what we have seen in all other national profiles is that the under-thirty-fives are the missing generation within the American Church too. In a recent survey of college freshers in the US, 15% indicated no religious preference. This is the highest figure ever for college freshers and two and a half times that of the nation as a whole.[37]

In his seminars George Barna says that the Buster generation (born between 1965 and 1983), aged between eighteen and thirty-two, is the first generation in America who aren't starting their lives with some kind of clear Christian heritage. Over the past ten years Barna Research reports that while older generation attendance patterns range from roughly 40% to 60%, Busters come in dead last with about 34% attendance.[38]

The incredible shrinking Western Church and the future of mission

The cold hard fact is that in spite of the welcome growth of the Evangelical church in North America and everywhere else we have examined, that isn't the entire story. As we look into the future we are witnessing the incredible shrinking Western Church. While the human needs in our McWorld future are mounting and the Western Church will need to do much more in mission at home and abroad, how will this be possible if it continues to grey and decline? Within two decades the entire Western Church is likely to see even more rapid decline because of our inability to keep and reach the young in our Western Churches.

It is my reluctant conclusion that unless something dramatic happens to change the present trends, the Church is likely to become significantly smaller in the first two decades of the twenty-first century and we will have significantly less time and resources to invest in mission to growing needs that are likely to fill tomorrow's world.

The problem with declining numbers, of course, is that it will automatically reduce the amount of time and money available to be invested in the advancement of God's kingdom. Simply put, declining numbers inevitably mean declining resources. The second section of this chapter examines specifically how the giving patterns of the Church are likely to change as we gallop into a new millennium. Because of the limited availability of research on this topic I am going to have to limit this examination to giving patterns of the Church in North America.

The incredible shrinking Western purse

It is becoming increasingly evident that in an increasingly competitive McWorld future many middle-class people will have to work not only harder but longer. So we are likely to continue to see a steady erosion of our discretionary time available for family time, relationships, prayer, Scripture study, service and being involved in our churches. As we have seen there will also be growing pressure to persuade us and particularly our young to relinquish a growing percentage of whatever is left of our discretionary time and money at the McWorld macro-mall.

Fund raisers frozen in a time warp

As I work with Christian fund raisers in North America they all seem to work from the twin unstated assumptions: 1. That the Christian giving pool in our Western countries will be at least as large in the future as it is today; 2. That this new generation will have at least as much discretionary time and money left over to support the Church as older generations.

We have already seen that the first assumption isn't valid. The donor pool is seriously shrinking. The second assumption isn't valid either. The under-thirty-fives have hit the economy at a much tougher time than the over-forty-fives. As we have shown, the relationship between what the young earn and what they can afford to buy has changed, therefore they will have both less time and money left over to invest in the work of the Church than older generations. The declining purchasing power of the under-thirty-fives is documented in *The State of Working America 1996-1997*.[39] If the young succumb to the growing pressures of McWorld to work longer and consume more, they could have even less left over to invest in the cause. Therefore given these trends I believe that the under-thirty-fives will not even be able to sustain the present giving levels to the Church and its mission let alone increase them.

At the very core of this emerging crisis is the dawning reality that my generation sold their generation the wrong dream. For all the talk about the Lordship of Jesus, my generation sold the young the Western dream or the American dream with a little Jesus overlay. For all the talk about lordship the real message to the Christian young is the message that drives McWorld. Agenda one is getting ahead in your job, getting ahead in the suburbs, getting your upscale lifestyle started and then with whatever you have left over follow Jesus. As we have seen, if this generation puts the Western dream first they will have very little time or money left over to invest in the mission of the mustard seed.

Future of fund raising in the North American Church

Dean Hoge, in his important study *Money Matters: Personal Giving in American Churches*, informs us that 20,000 – 40,000 professionals plus support staff are on the front lines of the very competitive field of fund raising in the US.[40] Even with the economy slowing right now many of them are having a very good ride. Research indicates for the last seven years that income is up to charitable organisations including the Church. However, the rate of increased giving is not beginning to keep pace with the rate of economic growth in the US in the last seven years.

But there is another very concerning trend. While corporate profits have been soaring during this boom time, corporate giving has declined. In 1980 corporate donations were 2.1% of pretax profits. In 1996 it had fallen to less than 1%.[41] In their efforts to maximise profits for shareholders, corporations aren't only scaling back their contributions but increasingly tailoring them in a way that focuses on advancing corporate objectives rather than addressing the most urgent needs in their communities.

Since governments everywhere are likely to continue to cut back services for those in need, people of faith must persuade both the Church and the business sector to increase not decrease their funding of programmes to enable our poorest neighbours participate in the lift-off of the McWorld economy.

My greatest area of concern in terms of Church giving is how much time and money Christians invest in God's mission to our poorest, most vulnerable neighbours. Hoge tells us that in 1994 Christians gave a total of $1.41 billion. But of that amount, total giving to foreign missions was only $109 million.[42] As I work with mission executives, frankly they aren't all having the same levels of success at raising money in these boom times as other organisations are enjoying. Let's look at the future of giving in the US Church and discuss the implications for the future of the Church in America and its mission into the third millennium.

Giving American style

Buoyed by recent economic growth, donations to all kinds of charities in the US after inflation increased by 7.8% during 1995. However, giving to social services like youth, family and employment services actually declined by 3%. For those counting on the private sector to pick up the slack this isn't welcome news. If giving to social services is declining in economic times as good as these what will the future hold if we enter a full blown recession? Giving to religion, including the Church, increased only by 2.5%.[43]

The Empty Tomb, which does some of the most helpful research on giving patterns in the American Church, has some very concerning information on giving over the last twenty-eight years. First they report that the real growth in US per capita income, after taxes and inflation have been factored out, increased by 68% between 1968 and 1995. However, during the same period the percentage of per capita income contributed to the Church actually declined by 21% from 3.11% to 2.46%.[44] Even more concerning is the decline in benevolent giving in the American funds that are designed to address human needs outside the church building. Between 1968 and 1995 income given to benevolence actually declined by 38%.[45]

The researchers divided the American Church between those mainline churches that affiliate with the National Council and those Evangelical churches that affiliate with the National Association of Evangelicals. Both groups reflected the decline. The NAE group declined from 6% giving in 1968 to 4% in 1995—a 33% decline. The NCC group declined less sharply from 3.3% in 1968 to 2.9% in 1995. Of particular concern was the rate of decline in benevolent giving. Between 1985 and 1995 the giving to benevolence by NAE affiliated churches declined by 18%. During the same period benevolent giving declined by 14% in NCC affiliated churches.[46]

Figure 2

Projected trends for 29 denominations, giving as a percentage of income to benevolences, using linear and exponential regression based on data for 1968-1985, with actual data for 1986-1995.

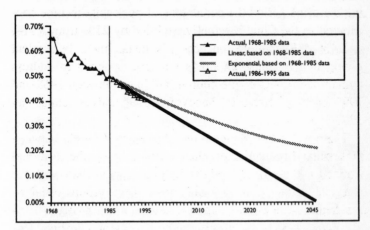

Sources: *Yearbook of American and Canadian Churches*, adjusted series; US Bureau of Economic Analysis
empty tomb, inc. 1997

The forecast for the future of benevolent giving in the United States by The Empty Tomb is truly alarming: 'If the giving patterns of the past twenty-eight years continue in an uninterrupted fashion, then per member giving as a portion of income to the category of benevolence will reach 0% of income . . . in 2045.'[47] While this linear forecast seems very improbable, the downward trend of giving should profoundly concern all those in Christian leadership.

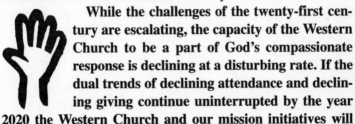

While the challenges of the twenty-first century are escalating, the capacity of the Western Church to be a part of God's compassionate response is declining at a disturbing rate. If the dual trends of declining attendance and declining giving continue uninterrupted by the year 2020 the Western Church and our mission initiatives will

be a shadow of what exists today. I sincerely pray that this assessment will sound an alarm among leaders in the Western Church. I urge Christian leaders in local churches, denominational offices and missions organisations to convene forums with missiologists and demographers and develop innovative new strategies to grow and fund the mission of the Church into a new century.

Opportunities for Christian leaders

The obvious implications of this assessment of the changing attendance patterns of the Western English-speaking Church is that to reverse the trends of decline will take a major new initiative in all our countries. This presents an opportunity for leaders to mount several new initiatives.

1. In the light of this analysis we will need to strategically target our evangelistic efforts to reach the under-thirty-fives if the Western Church is to have a future. Much of the leadership for this initiative will need to come from the under-thirty-fives.

2. However, for this initiative to be successful we must create a new spectrum of church plants, mentoring programmes and genuinely bring the young into leadership, inviting them to use their creativity to help reinvent the Church for the twenty-first century.

3. We will also need to call Christians of all ages to a much more biblically radical form of whole-life discipleship and stewardship—where we are sharing much more than the scanty left overs of our lives in the advancement of God's kingdom.

4. We will need to fundamentally reinvent not only our lives but our communities of faith so they more authentically incarnate the values of God's kingdom and prioritise a larger share

of resources to advance God's kingdom in mission to the growing needs of millennium 3.

5. We desperately need a new critique of how we got off the tracks to replace the secular humanist critique. We need a new critique that takes seriously the extent to which McWorld and the aspirations and values of modern culture have seduced Western Christians.

6. We need to enable our members to find in Scripture a compelling new alternative vision for their lives to the one offered by McWorld.

Questions for discussion and action

1. How are the attendance patterns changing in the churches in your country and in your denomination or local congregation? What are creative ways you can respond to these trends?

2. In particular, what are the attendance patterns of the under-thirty-fives and what creative ways can you use to reach this population in your community?

3. How are giving and volunteering patterns changing in your church or denomination? What are innovative ways to increase these figures?

4. What are some specific ways you and your church could alter your priorities in the use of time and money to invest more in evangelism, church planting and mission to the poor to expand the church again?

Notes

1 Philip Adams, 'Faith Heelers', *The Weekend Review*, 12-13 April, 1997.

2 Richard N. Ostling, 'Kingdoms to Come', *Time*

Magazine, Autumn 1992, p.61.

3 'Bon Fire of the Futilities: Nevada's Burning Man Festival: Ritual Without Dogma', *re:generation quarterly,* Autumn 1997, pp.14-17.

4 Robert Marquand, 'Religious Reading Digs Deeper', *The Christian Science Monitor,* 27 August, 1997, p.1.

5 Daniel B. Wood, 'New Treatment Showing Up in Hospitals: Prayer', *The Christian Science Monitor,* 18 March, 1987, p.4.

6 'Church and People Worldwide', *CRA: Quadrant,* March 1977, p.1.

7 J. Dudley Woodberry, 'Toward the Twenty-first Century: Educating People for God's Mission', Congress on the World Mission of the Church, St Paul Minnesota, 23-27 June, 1998, p.15.

8 Patrick Johnstone, *The Church is Bigger Than You Think: Structures and Strategies for the Church in the Twenty-first Century* (Christian Focus Publications/WEC: London, 1998).

9 *Ibid.,* p.231.

10 'The Power of Partnership', Interdev, Seattle, 1998, p.21.

11 Mark Hutchison, 'It's a Small Church After All', *Christianity Today,* 16 November, 1998, p.48.

12 Rick Hampson, 'Missionaries set sights on American souls', *USA Today,* 19 November, 1997, p.17A.

13 Table 2.12.1 Adult church attendance in England 1980-2000, Christian Research Association, London, England.

14 Table 14: English church attendance by age-group 1989, Christian Research Association, London, England.

15 Peter Kaldor, *Winds of Change: The Experience of Church in a Changing Australia* (National Church Life Survey: Homebush West, NSW, 1994), p.263.

16 Peter Bentley, Philip Hughes, *Religion in Australia: Facts and Figures* (Christian Research Association: Kew,

Victoria, 1997), p.52.

17 Peter Kaldor, *Ibid.*, pp.280-281.

18 Bruce Patrick, editor, *New Vision New Zealand: Calling the Whole Church to Take the Whole Gospel to the Whole Nation* (Vision New Zealand: Auckland, 1993), p.20.

19 Peter Lineham, 'The Condition of the Church', Bruce Patrick, editor, *Ibid.,* p.108.

20 Lynne Taylor, 'Denominational Growth', Bruce Patrick, editor, *New Vision New Zealand* (Vision New Zealand: Auckland, 1997), pp.48-53.

21 Peter Lineham, *op. cit.,* p.107.

22 Bruce Patrick, 'Multiplication the Key to Growth', *Ibid.* p.250.

23 Reginald W. Bibby, *Unknown Gods: The Ongoing Story of Religion In Canada* (Stoddart: Toronto, 1993), p.10.

24 Reginald W. Bibby, *There's Got To Be More! Connecting Churches and Canadians* (Wood Lake Books: Infield, BC, 1995), p.78.

25 Reginald W. Bibby, *Unknown Gods*, p.8.

26 *Ibid.,* pp.10,99.

27 Reginald W. Bibby, *There's Got To Be More! Connecting Churches and Canadians*, pp.51-151.

28 John and Sylvia Ronsvalle, 'The end of benevolence? Alarming trends in church giving', *The Christian Century*, 23 October, 1996, p.1012.

29 'Trends Affecting the Evangelical Lutheran Church in America', ELCA Department of Research and Evaluation, 27 December, 1966, p.1.

30 Wade Clark Roof and William McKinney, *American Mainline Religion: Its Changing Shape and Future* (Rutgers University Press: New Brunswick, 1987), p.233.

31 Gustav Niebuhr, 'Makeup of American Religion Is Looking More Like Mosaic, Data Say', *The New York Times*, 12 April, 1998, p.12.

32 John and Sylvia Ronsvalle, 'The end of benevolence? Alarming trends in church giving', *The Christian Century*, 23 October, 1996, p.1016.

33 'Church Attendance by Generation', Barna Research Group Limited, 1998.

34 Robert Marquand, 'Preaching to Empty Pews', *Chicago Sun Times*, 22 February, 1998, p.45.

35 Mark Noll and Lyman Kellstedt, 'The Changing Face of Evangelicalism', *Pro Ecclesia*, Vol.IV, No.2, p.147.

36 Lyman Kellstedt, 'Simple Questions, Complex Answers What do we mean by "evangelical"? What difference does it make?', *Evangelical Studies Bulletin*, Autumn 1995, Vol.12, No.2, pp.2-3.

37 'Godlessness 101', *The New York Times Magazine*, 7 December, 1997, p.61.

38 'Church Attendance by Generation', Barna Research Group Limited, 8 July, 1998

39 Lawrence Mishel, Jared Bernstein, John Schmitt, *The State of Working America 1996-1997* (M. E. Sharpe: New York, 1997), p.47.

40 Dean R. Hoge, Charles E. Zech, Patrick H. McNamara and Michael J. Donahue, *Money Matters: Personal Giving in American Churches* (Westminister John Knox Press: Louisville, Kentucky, 1996), p.5.

41 'Minuses: A Culture Where...', *Sweet's Soul Cafe*, 1997, Volume 3, Nos. 3-4, p.9.

42 Dean Hoge, *op. cit.,* p.17.

43 Karen W. Arenson, 'Donations to Charities Rose 11% Last Year, Report Says', *The New York Times*, 15 May, 1996, p.A9.

44 John L. Ronsvalle and Sylvia Ronsvalle, *The State of Church giving through 1995* (The Empty Tomb, inc: Champaign, Ill., 1997), p.11-12.

45 *Ibid.,* p.15.

46 *Ibid.*, pp.25-27.
47 *Ibid.*, pp.42-45.

SECTION TWO
A Crisis of Vision

Western progress is the centre-piece of modernity and the power house propelling McWorld into a new millennium. More than we recognise it defines for many of us our notion of home and our image of the better future. Richard Middleton and Brian Walsh state:

> The progress ideal functions as an article of faith, the unifying commitment or civil religion of the Western Civilization . . . Just as the story of Babel (recounted in Genesis 11:1-9) summarises the primordial cultural aspirations of the human race . . . of the building of a 'a city with a tower reaching to the heavens', so we could characterise the modern Western dream of progress as the building of a vast, towering civilization.[1]

Post-modernists have, in recent years, busied themselves deconstructing everything they don't like about modernity. One of the things they particularly don't like is the orchestrating vision of modernity—Western progress. They do a brilliant job of dismantling the vision of inevitable economic and social progress, but by the very nature of post-modernity they are incapable of offering an alternative vision of home or of hope. As a consequence Brian Walsh describes a post-modern generation as wandering homeless through the universe in search of something more.

Walsh pictures post-moderns as Arthur Dent, a cosmic nomad from *The Hitch Hiker's Guide to the Galaxy*, and Lily Tomlin's character Trudy the bag lady. Arthur wanders through an apparently meaningless universe homeless and alone. Somehow he realises that reality is not what it ought to be so he travels in search of counsel. He meets a prophet who encourages him to solve his problem by creating his own universe, his own reality. But Arthur realises there is an inherent problem with this post-modern solution. If anything goes awry in his self-created universe it is essentially his fault. This answer doesn't solve Arthur's deepest longings.

The narrator says

> He so much wanted to be home. He so much wanted his own home world . . . He so much wanted that when he opened his eyes again he would be standing on the doorstep of his little cottage in the western country of England, that the sun would be shining over the green hills, the post van would be going up the lane, the daffodils would be blooming in the garden, and in the distance the pub would be open for lunch.[2]

Trudy the bag lady is trying to help some aliens from outer space in search of intelligent life in the universe to consider relocating on planet earth. 'The prospects do not seem too promising!' Walsh intones, 'But not only do we have the alien's cultural perspective, Trudy herself sees things aslant.'

Speaking of her own madness, Trudy exclaims:

> 'I refuse to be intimidated by reality any more. After all, what is reality anyway? Nothin' but a collective hunch. My space chums think reality was once a primitive method of crowd control that got out of hand. In my view, it's absurdity dressed up in a three piece business suit. I made some studies, and reality is the leading cause of stress among those in touch with it. I take it in small doses, but as a lifestyle I found it too confining.' Trudy figures that being 'out of touch' with reality isn't such a bad idea. After all it's less stressful. But what is reality anyway? Nothing but a collective hunch.[3]

More and more of the Western young, like Dent and Trudy, are homeless in our world, left to define their own reality and manufacture their own hope. They have joined Trudy in rejecting the dominant reality and live in an increasingly tribal world in which everything is morally relative. But like Dent they also share a tremendous longing for home. But they have no idea of how to get there. Post-modernity is highly skilled in dismantling the dominant reality but is totally impotent to offer us a home or a hope.

Since much of the Western Church is locked into a dualistic world view that accepts unquestioningly modernity's view of reality and the better future, we aren't able to offer much hope to a post-modern generation either. Middleton and Walsh conclude, 'While modern culture was self-assured in its control of the world and taming of nature in order to make a human home, postmodern culture is plagued by a profound sense of homelessness.'[4]

Crisis I—a crisis of vision

I am convinced that the number one crisis in both society and the Church today is a crisis of vision. It isn't just a post-modern generation that is having difficulty finding their way home. We all seem to be struggling in many different ways to find purpose and meaning in our existence.

When I use the phrase 'a crisis of vision' I am not talking about anything hyper-spiritual in the clouds. I simply mean the imagery of the better future that we want for ourselves and those we care about. Kenneth Boulding, a Christian and a scholar, said, 'No people society or organisation can long exist without a compelling image of the better future that calls us forward into tomorrow.' The Bible says, 'Without a vision the people perish.' Not only are we perishing but the people we are called to serve in Christ's name are perishing because we lack a compelling image of the better future that comes from our faith instead of from modern culture.

A crisis of reflection

I believe that this crisis of vision is at the core a crisis of reflection. We simply don't spend enough time reflecting on *why we do what we do*. As a consequence, at many different levels the images and values of modern culture subvert our lives, families and Christian organisations and we scarcely seem to notice. 'What is wrong with elementary or secondary education—or for that matter higher education, journalism or television . . . has less to do with incompetence or indifference', charged Charles Silberman, than with 'mindlessness' and 'venality'. He added, 'We must find ways of stimulating educators . . . to think seriously about what they are doing and why they are doing it.'[5]

When I lectured for seven years in the doctoral programme in Educational Policy Studies at Seattle University, I was repeatedly astonished at how excruciatingly difficult it was for professionals who had worked their entire lives in education to explain *what they are doing and why they are doing it.* These professionals were brilliant at curriculum design, reading computer spread sheets and matching teaching styles and learning styles. But when I asked them what their assumptions were regarding what learning is (Is it information transfer? The systematic reinforcement of desired behaviours? Demonstrating the ability to work critically and synthetically with ideas? Or something else?) they visibly blanched and often became speechless.

A crisis of reflection in the Church

I believe this is a particular problem in the American Church.

As Mark Noll documents in *The Scandal of the Evangelical Mind,* there is a strong strain of anti-intellectualism in American Protestantism, particularly the conservative or Evangelical tradition.[6] When I ask Christian leaders to explain to me their assumptions underlying their programmes in church planting, youth ministries or missions I receive the same kind of response as I do from educators. They can describe in detail the latest approaches in planting 'user-friendly churches' but they are often at a total loss to define their ecclesiology (their theology of the Church).

A few years ago I attended an international conference that had a single task: to enable participants to define the relationship between Church and para-church. When the conference ended we were more confused than when we began, largely because as Evangelicals many of us had never biblically defined clearly for ourselves what the Church was. Therefore we were at a total loss to define the relationship of the Church to the para-church.

In a course I teach for Fuller Theological Seminary on Christian World View, we spend a good deal of time discussing how we Western Christians tend to appropriate the secular models of almost everything, baptise them and do them in Christ's name. Virtually all our Christian schooling, for example, is simply an appropriation of secular Greek models of education in which we plug in chapel and a few Bible courses and call it Christian education. We don't seem to recognise that a lot of the assumptions that come with the secular model are often in serious tension with biblical assumptions.

The problem isn't just with education. When Christians set up counselling programmes, establish health clinics or work with the poor, we tend to appropriate the secular models without ever critically evaluating the assumptions that are part of the package. In our effort to reach the unchurched, too often we plant consumer-oriented churches that are more reminiscent of an upscale shopping mall than anything like that first informal band who followed Jesus. Os Guiness observes in his incisive book, *Fit Bodies, Fat Minds* that 'failing to think Christianly evangelicals have been forced into the role of cultural imitators and adapters rather than originators. In biblical terms it is worldly and conformist, not decisively Christian.'[7]

Nowhere is this situation more critical than the extent to which we have unquestioningly embraced modernity's notion of the good life and better future for ourselves, our children and our communities of faith and made it our home. This crisis of vision is subverting our ability to provide an authentic witness to God's new order and is fostering a very culturally accommodated view of discipleship. It is also making us more vulnerable to the marketing messages of McWorld which in turn directly affects attendance and giving patterns.

In other words, I am very concerned that we are operating as though all the conversations are completed on what it means to be disciples, what it means to be the Church and do the mission of the Church. I am convinced that these conversations are not completed, and that we are working from some assumptions which simply do not square with Scripture.

I am persuaded that for many of us the reason for both our crisis of vision and our crisis of reflection is our failure to take Scripture seriously *for all of life*. We have learned to use Scripture devotionally and liturgically in worship. But we seldom use it culturally to help us define an alternative vision to the Western dream. The Black Church in America is much more in touch with the rich biblical imagery of the promised home-coming of God than the white Church. Unless we take radical action to deal with this crisis of vision in the Western Church we will become little more than a culturally compromised shadow of what God intended. And we will have little ability to offer a hope or a home to others.

In Chapter 7 we will ask, 'How did we get off the track?' And in chapter 8 we will ask, 'How can we find our way home?' How can we find in a renewal of biblical imagination a vision for our lives, families and congregations that offers a compelling alternative to the aspirations of the Western dream? How can we find a way home that looks more like Jerusalem than Babylon?

7

Mustard seed versus McWorld—how we got off the track

The largest cross I have ever seen soared twenty storeys in the air above the Valley of the Fallen outside Torrejon, Spain. The lift took me down twenty storeys into the very bowels of the mountain on which the cross stood. As the lift door opened I was ushered into a Benedictine abbey built in the depths of the earth. We were in time for morning vespers. I could hear the haunting sounds of a boys' choir singing Gregorian chants echoing through corridors. We entered the sanctuary and took our seats in the back as the service began. During this trip in Europe I had visited a Cistercian abbey in Switzerland and a Franciscan community in Italy but I was totally unprepared for what I experienced in the depths of this mountain in Spain.

As I sat down I found myself in a sanctuary chillingly different from any I had ever visited before. The severe grey vaulted chamber looked like it had been designed as a railway tunnel by fascist architects of the thirties. It came complete with heroic sculptures of biblical figures which resembled the women of war that decorate some structures I had seen in Germany.

In the very centre of the sombre chamber, suspended above

us where two grey tunnels intersected, was a breath-taking sight. As though suspended in space was the most human Christ figure I have ever seen. It was carved out of a single piece of wood firmly nailed to a rough-hewn log cross. Jesus' body shone with a warm golden glow that seemed totally out of place in that dark fascist cavern.

I found the contrasting images and the emotions they provoked so disturbing that I was totally unable to focus on the mass. As the Abbott led me out of the sanctuary I questioned him regarding the disturbing images in an effort to make sense of what I had just experienced. He explained that the Valley of the Fallen was the sight of one of the most brutal battles of the Spanish Civil War. The cross and the Benedictine abbey were dedicated to the victory of the nationalists in that war.

He paused and then said, 'You have been worshipping in the midst of 35,000 soldiers from both sides buried in this mountain. Franco not only ordered the construction of this religious shrine to celebrate his victory, he personally cut down the tree on which the figure of Christ was hanging. We Benedictines hope this place can somehow be a centre for reconciliation.' As he said that a chill went down my spine.

I found myself reeling from the conflicting images of a national monument dedicated to the victory of a brutal dictator and his Fascist government and a sanctuary dedicated to reconciliation; the thousands of young men forever entombed in the walls of that sanctuary; the sight of young Spanish lads in the choir, some of whom were undoubtedly related to those who had fallen, chanting the praises of the Almighty; this most human Christ forever nailed to Franco's cross and eternally entombed with the fallen in this monument to war, Fascism and nationalism.

I struggled because I found everything I had come to treasure as a follower of Jesus powerfully co-opted by images and agendas that not only bore no similarity to his peaceable kingdom but in so many ways profoundly violated everything the servant Jesus represented. The obsessions of nationalism have dominated the twentieth century and created this disturbing spectre. However, as we cross the threshold of a new millennium the forces of nationalism are rapidly losing ground to the forces of globalism. But I believe that the aspirations and values that power McWorld's intentions for our common future are no less alien to the aspirations of God's kingdom than what I experienced in the bowels of that Spanish mountain.

Babylon revisited

Finding our way out of town

Once when my son Clint and I were touring England we tried to drive out of York at rush hour so we could get to London and start our trek back home. For an hour and a half I tried unsuccessfully to get out of town. Every road I tried brought us right back into the centre of York. And we tried yet again to get out of town. It was like the film *Ground Hog Day—déjà vu* all over again. In many ways that is reminiscent of our common human journey. We tend to get stuck in a place that isn't home and seem to have a lot of trouble finding our way out of town.

Finding our way home

Walter Brueggemann tells us that the children of Israel, when they were in captivity in Babylon, came down with another problem regarding home. They contracted a serious case of amnesia. Somehow they forgot that Babylon was a place of bondage. They forgot that Babylon had defied the authority of the creator God by declaring itself to be absolute reality. They forgot that they were in exile in a 'strange land and they came to regard it as home. They assimilated.'[8]

They assimilated into the dominant reality of their time and apparently even forgot their God and their home. It is to these serious victims of cultural amnesia that the prophet Isaiah speaks. He not only invites them to come back home to Jerusalem, he announces that Yahweh will bring down the arrogance and pretensions of Babylon to make clear that God and God alone is the Lord of history.[9]

Finding the focus

In this chapter we will explore how we seem continually to get off the track and be seduced by other Babylons that keep us from finding our way back home. We will explore *why we do what we do* in the way we seek to follow Jesus Christ in our contemporary society. We will particularly look at how, I believe, we Western Christians have often unwittingly allowed modernity, Western dualism and the Western dream to shape our lives and trivialise our faith. I am convinced that at the core of our crisis is a misplaced allegiance.

I will attempt to show that many of us have inadvertently given our primary allegiance to the same aspirations that power McWorld instead of to those that motivate the mustard seed movement. I believe this misplaced allegiance can explain why we have so little of our lives left over for the things that really matter.

Essentially I will argue that we have discipleship dead wrong. We have settled for a dualistic discipleship and have exported this flawed model all over the planet. To get discipleship right requires discovering a new sense of biblical purpose for our lives—all our lives. Therefore at the very centre of a biblical call to whole life discipleship is a reawakened imagination of the creator's vision for coming home that is a very different vision from the one promised us by McWorld.

Naming the powers and finding our way

Our deepest human longing is to find our way back home to all we are called to be. But too often we keep winding up right back in Babylon. As we saw, many people in Spain including those of Christian faith accepted the definition of ultimate reality that was offered to them by a Fascist state. The Fascist state succeeded in fabricating a feeling of national brotherhood. And even the Church accepted and celebrated its pretensions and its brutal use of power. But I think the Abbot knew that this shrine to Spanish Fascism, constructed twenty floors below ground, wasn't home.

After the Soviet Empire imploded, Orthodox clerics acknowledged that they too had allowed faith to be co-opted by the agendas of a brutally repressive communist state. Even Emilio Castro, the former head of the World Council of Churches, belatedly admitted that the WCC had often been co-opted by the agendas of the Soviet state in their efforts to support the Orthodox Church. They all confessed that they had lost their way and the communist state wasn't home either.

The arrogant human pretension of defining for ourselves what is ultimate is still very much alive and well. It simply continues to take on new forms. Hendrik Berkhof traces this arrogance to what Paul described as the 'principalities and powers of the earth'. Berkhof states, 'The powers are no longer instruments, linkages between God's love, as revealed in Christ, and the visible creation. In fact they have become gods (Galatians 4:8), behaving as though they were the ultimate ground of being, and demanding from men appropriate worship . . . No longer do the powers bind man and God together; they separate them.'[10]

Lesslie Newbigin adds, 'The principalities and powers are real. They are invisible and we cannot locate them in time or space. They do not exist as disembodied entities floating above this world, or lurking within it. They meet us as embodied in visible tangible realities—peoples, nations and institutions. And they are powerful.'[11]

In *Engaging the Powers*, Walter Wink states that the 'powers' while essentially good, have become bent on control and degenerate into the 'domination system'. The 'domination system' is not only intent on defining what is ultimate but is also determined to insert itself into every arena of human existence. In the process the powers even redefine the destination of human life.[12]

The arrogance of both the Fascist and communist states, like the original Babylon, have fallen. But Babylon lives on. As we will see, the principalities and powers are still in the business of creating 'domination systems' that seek, like the Babylons before, to define what is absolute and the values that should direct our lives and shape our institutions.

Today modernity, as expressed in a fiercely competitive global economic order, is the 'domination system' that is, I believe, playing the leading role in subverting our lives, families and congregations. Os Guiness offers a helpful definition of modernity 'Put simply, modernity can be understood as the character and system of the world produced by the forces of development, modernisation, especially capitalism, industrial technology, and telecommunications.[13] While we are all benefiting in many different ways from globalisation in other ways, as we have seen, it is also putting our future at risk. Whatever may be the respective cost and benefits of globalisation I will argue that the aspirations and values that power McWorld are in many ways in direct conflict with those that motivate the movement of the mustard seed.

How did we get off the track?

In every age Christians battle against those forces that would subvert our faith and secularise our lives. I believe that one of the major reasons we have discipleship wrong is that we haven't accurately named the principalities and powers with which we struggle. We haven't named the forces of secularisation that are having their way with us. As a consequence we haven't been able to describe very clearly why our attendance and giving patterns seem to be declining. Exactly how have we been derailed in our desire to follow Christ in a foreign land and how has that influenced us to reduce our levels of involvement?

Derailed by worldliness?

When I attended an Evangelical Christian college in the fifties, everyone knew what would derail a vital faith— 'worldliness'. Therefore, the way you maintained a vital Christian life was simply to abstain from 'worldliness'. The only problem was that the list of worldly activities differed from group to group. Which was very confusing for serious young Christian college students. Some churches had a short-list that included abstaining from the basics: dancing, movies and drinking. Others included cosmetics, jewellery and playing with face cards. I don't believe any of the groups that are still promoting the old-fashioned legalism can make any clear connection between this view of secularism and why Christian involvement in the work of God's kingdom is in decline in the Church.

Derailed by secular humanism?

By far the most popular notion of how we in the contemporary Church have become secularised is something called 'secular humanism'. Today it is virtually the only game in town when it comes to explaining how we got off the track. Francis Schaeffer gave us the term. He said the roots of modern secularism were to be found in the renaissance when 'man became the measure of all things'. Of course there is some truth to that, but I am convinced that the secularism that bedevils us has its roots much more deeply imbedded in the Enlightenment than in the humanistic period.

Popularly understood in the US, secular humanists are those people who are for abortion, gay rights and a liberal political agenda. Evangelical Christians in America, not finding themselves anywhere on the list, mistakenly assume they are pure as the driven snow. Of course nothing could be further from the truth. We are being eaten alive by a secularism we haven't named.

It is my contention that the secular humanist critique doesn't hold water either biblically or historically. Since this critique sees the problem as something largely external to the community of faith it doesn't offer much help in explaining why levels of Christian involvement are declining. The only way we can possibly hope to overcome the secularising influences of contemporary culture is to do a much better job of defining how Western Christians are being derailed. I urge Church historians, biblical scholars, pastors and the rest of us to join together in an effort to develop a fresh critique of the forces of secularisation with which we struggle. Here's my beginning attempt to add to the conversation on a quest for a new critique.

Derailed by modernity?

As we have seen, post-modernists have, in recent decades, launched a major intellectual critique of modernity. They busy themselves deconstructing everything from modernity's assumptions about the objectification of knowledge to the belief in Western progress. A number of generally younger

Christians in Britain and the United States find they resonate with the post-modern critique of modernity. For instance, *Post Evangelical*, written by Dave Tomlinson, has caused a real stir in Britain.[14] It has caused a stir because Tomlinson states that he feels more comfortable with the intellectual insights of post-moderntiy than modernity and he no longer identifies himself as part of the Evangelical community.

David Wells is a theologian who also battles with modernity. In his book *Losing our Virtue* he writes, 'While we feast on the largesse of modernity . . . we are losing our moral bearings.'[15] His critique reflects the major problem that most Evangelicals have with modern culture—the erosion of our moral values. And that is important. But Rodney Clapp is one of a handful of Christian authors who understands our fight with modernity is not only an intellectual and a moral struggle, it is a cultural contest as well. In his book *Peculiar People*, Clapp calls the Church to seek the transformation of not only our spiritual lives and moral values but our cultural values too.[16]

Unfortunately I find virtually no post-modernists, post-modern Christians or Christian authors who, like Clapp and a few others, offer a serious critique of the way we have allowed modernity to fundamentally define both the structure of our daily lives and our sense of what is important and of value. I really believe that we have permitted modern culture to define *why we do what we do* in both our personal lives and even how we organise our churches and Christian organisations and never realised we were caving into aspirations and values counter to biblical faith.

Speaking at St Luke's Anglican Church in London, where Dave Tomlinson and his 'post-evangelical' compatriots worship, I said, 'You haven't gone far enough in deconstructing modernity. It isn't enough to join the post-modernists in an intellectual critique of modernity. We also need to criticise the extent to which we have all allowed modernity to define our idea of the good life and better future and what we are raising our children for.'

Buying into the dualistic discipleship model

What we have done, I am convinced, is to succumb inadvertently to a dualistic model of discipleship and stewardship. In spite of all the talk about 'Lordship', everyone knows that the expectations of modern culture come first. Everyone knows getting ahead in the job comes first. Getting ahead in the suburbs comes first. Getting the children off to their activities comes first. And we tend to make decisions in these areas pretty much like everyone else does—based on our income, our professions and our social status.

Essentially most Western Christians unquestioningly allow modern culture to arrange most of the furniture of our lives—forty to eighty-hour work weeks, single family detached housing, congested timetables for our lives and children. Over the last fifteen years I have seen Christians becoming busier and busier which means they have less time left over for prayer, church, ministry or even family. As we have seen we are racing into a future in which McWorld wants an even larger chunk of our time and money which means even less left over for things of faith.

On the other side of this dualism, following Christ is too often trivialised to little more than a devotional lubricant to keep us from stripping our gears as we charge up the mountain trying to get ahead in our careers, the suburbs, and our children's activities. In this dualistic discipleship model, following Christ is reduced to little more than fifteen minutes in the morning and two hours on Sunday for too many of us. In this model we wind up with a highly privatised and spiritualised piety that is often largely disconnected from the rest of our lives.

Figure 3
Dualistic discipleship

* Getting ahead in the job comes first
* Getting ahead in our living situations comes first
* Getting our economic security comes first
* Getting our children off to their activities comes first

and
Jesus
too

The problem with this dualistic model is that we not only sanction giving our first allegience to decisons about where to work, live and entertain our young, we permit modern culture, as a part of the deal, to define our notions of the good life and better future. As a consequence our lives are too often driven by the same manic aspirations that propel McWorld. No wonder we are exhausted. Modernity calls the tune and we dance.

Rodney Clapp observes that we are in serious trouble when we privatise and spiritualise our faith and allow the dominant culture to define the rest of our lives. George Marsden, looking back on the revivalist roots of this kind of culturally accommodated faith, states that there was no insistence to 'abandon most of the standards of the respectable middle-class way of life. It was to these standards, in fact, that people were to be converted.'[17]

The Western Church, in its many different expressions, seems quietly to accept the demands of modern culture on its members as a given. These members then content themselves with whatever is left over to share with the Church. Virtually all the Christian books I have seen on discipleship or for that matter on finances, time management and career planning also tend to accept the demands of modern culture as an unquestioned given. We then simply try to work out our discipleship over the top as if it all goes together—which of course it doesn't.

I am convinced that one of the main reasons why Western Christians aren't terribly effective in evangelism is that we are so much like the culture around us that we have very little to call people to. We hang around church buildings more than others do. We abstain from a few things. We aren't as hedonistic as the people around us—but we certainly keep trying.

Looking back to the origins of our dualism

This dualistic model of discipleship is a product of modern culture which has its origins in our Hellenistic and Enlightenment past. Plato can take a lot of credit for our drawing a very sharp line between the material world and the world of the spirit. He characterised the material world in very negative terms as a realm we need to escape from for an ideal existence in the non-material realm of the spirit up there somewhere. Sound familiar? This early Greek dualism has decisively shaped our modern world view, our Christian faith and even our notions of God's redemptive initiative.

Francis Bacon, writing in the sixteenth century, drew another sharp line that reinforced this platonic dualism. He metaphorically took a sword and divided the world in half. He said on one side of the line are the 'words of God' which have to do with the world of the spirit. He assigned this realm to the theologians. On the other side of the line he stated are the 'works of God'—that's the larger natural world that had his keen attention. In that simple act of dividing the 'words of God' from the 'works of God' Bacon inadvertently divided spirit from body, evicted the creator from the creation and produced a dualistic world view that has come to pervade modern culture and has directly contributed to our dualistic view of life and faith.

A crisis of vision—dualistic images of coming home

Because of the pervasive influence of Western dualism, many of us have embraced two very different images of the better future, neither of which is biblical. The first is coming home to a life of individual economic upscaling where the good life and future is defined primarily in economic terms just like the aspirations that drive McWorld. Then the second image of the better future is viewed as a heaven in the clouds totally divorced from this material world.

Coming home to a disembodied future in the clouds

Many Christians, including those of Evangelical faith, envision the future of God in considerably broader, less spiritualised terms than I describe here. But I am constantly astonished at how many Christians of all traditions envision coming home to a highly spiritualised, privatised future up there somewhere that is totally disconnected from this world.

Speaking at Wheaton College to a class of forty students I asked, 'What is your image of the future of God?' A young man spoke up. He said, 'Heaven.' I asked, 'What imagery comes to mind when you think of heaven?' He thought for a moment and then said, 'Clouds, harps and angel wings.' Plato has had his way with us. It is Plato who wrote that little ditty: 'This world is not my home I am just a-passing through.' Remember it was a Greek philosopher not a Hebrew prophet who envisioned the ideal future as going home to a non-material existence in the clouds. The image of the future of God in Hebrew literature always includes the creation and is never divorced from it.

Lesslie Newbigin declares that looking forward to having our disembodied souls take up residence in a non-material heaven in the clouds simply isn't biblical. 'For a biblical

writer, continued existence as a disembodied soul is not something to be desired but feared with loathing.'[18] Of course,
when we are absent from the body we are present with the
Lord. But as we will see in the next chapter, the future God is
preparing will not be found in a non-material existence in a
heaven up there somewhere.

There are a number of problems with this very narrow,
highly spiritualised view of redemptive theology. First of all
because it is incredibly individualistic it tends to reinforce a
very self-centred spiritualised form of faith that implies that
the creator God singularly exists to meet my needs. Secondly,
since God doesn't give a rip about this world and plans to
vaporise it, why should we care about it. Thirdly, if God is
only interested in saving our 'souls' then, as a friend once
asked, 'Why should we care about hungry people?' It makes
no sense.

Finally, for many this highly spiritualised view of redemptive theology is wedded to a degenerative view of history and
a fatalistic view of the future where everything is destined to
get worse. Because of the end time theories many have
embraced, they are absolutely convinced that nothing can get
better. As I mentioned in *Cease Fire,* I seriously doubt that
these good people ever prayed that the Berlin Wall would
come down or the Soviet Union implode because they could-
n't imagine anything on that scale getting better.[19]

As a consequence many Christians actually wind up with a
dualistic view of God. Their God is active in their spiritual
lives and shows up at prayer meetings but is impotent to act in
that larger natural world until the curtain comes down. This
God has no power to act in the Middle East peace negotia-
tions, influence the direction of urban planning among the
poor in East Los Angeles or make a difference in the destruction of the rain forest in Belize. Let's look at the other image
of the better future, in our dualistic lives, that seems to play a

much greater role in determining the focus and format of our busy lives.

Coming home to a future of economic upscaling on Earth

What gave particularly strong momentum to the Enlightenment was the creation of a new image of what the better future could look like. The story-tellers of the Enlightenment told us a new story and fashioned a new imagination. They took the vertical quest for God's kingdom which had dominated European consciousness through the middle ages and tipped it over on its side. In the age of reason it became the horizontal quest for a kingdom on earth largely divorced from the reign of God or anything transcendent.

The story-tellers of the Enlightenment assured us that if we co-operated with natural law, all of society would progress. We would gradually gain greater mastery over the natural world, create a future of ever increasing levels of economic growth and be freed to pursue our own individual material happiness.

Francis Bacon, in his book the *New Atlantis*, was the first author to imagine coming home to a future of advanced technology mastering nature, synthetic foods and a society with expanding consumer choice. This is the vision of the better future that is at the very core of modernity. Someone has written, 'Marxism says all there is is matter. Capitalism says all that matters is matter.' Both are inherently materialistic visions of the future that lack any larger sense of transcendent purpose.

Modernity from John Locke on has increasingly defined life in incredibly individualistic terms. This has given rise to a radical autonomy that Craig Gay identifies in his book *The Way of the [Modern] World,*[20] as one of the most destructive features of modernity. Many in the boomer generation not only want a life of individual economic upscaling but also of self-actualisation where they are accountable to no one—including God.

What has happened over time is that modern Western society has come to define the good life in largely economic and materialistic terms. Most of us, whether we are Evangelicals, mainliners or Catholics, seem to have accepted without question that the better future means getting ahead in our individual careers, in our living conditions and in upscaling our individual lifestyles. Like our secular counterparts we seem to have bought into the notion that the more we own the more we are.

Leo Tolstoy wrote a compelling little short story entitled 'How Much Land Does A Man Need?' A Russian farmer named Paho'm buys and sells land but is never satisfied. He always wants more. A nomad offers to sell him as much land as he can walk around in a day. Driven by an insatiable appetite he attempts to make it around a huge piece of land by sunset. As the sun is about to set Paho'm rushes exhausted back to the starting point. Just before the sun disappears he reaches his goal. Paho'm's servant runs to congratulate him and finds him dead with blood flowing from his mouth. How much land does a man need? 'Six feet from his head to his heels was all he needed.'[21]

David Myers states that research shows that the average American owns and consumes much more today than in the fifties. We are twice as affluent as we were then. We own twice as many cars and TV sets plus a spectrum of new technologies that weren't available then such as VCRs and computers. On average we are considerably larger and spend two and a half times more eating out in restaurants and bars than Americans did in the sixties. But despite more than doubling our level of consumption, The National Opinion Research Center reports that people aren't any happier than they were in the fifties.[22]

Focusing on the family

In spite of evidence to the contrary, many of us still believe, deep in our guts, that increased consumerism and having more will result in increased happiness. For many, like Paho'm, this insatiable appetite for MORE can cost us everything. While Christians, on occasion, rail against materialism the aspirations of the Western dream still seem to play a major role in shaping the direction of our lives and families. For example, Christian parents want what's best for their children like all parents. But because of the pervasiveness of the Western dream we tend to define what's best, like everyone else does, in largely economic terms. For all the talk about 'raising a child up in the way he should go', the real message to the Christian young, often flying under the banner of 'excellence', is 'get the best you can for yourselves'—a driven individualism.

Robert Cole, a leading psychologist in the US, observes of the North American young: 'Very little is asked of a lot of American children with regards to compassion and thinking of others. The emphasis is to cultivate the individuality and self-importance of each child. One sees home after home where children are encouraged to look out for themselves and get what they can. Very little emphasis is put on pointing a child's eyes and ears away from himself or herself and towards others.'[23]

The number one reason Christian college students in the US give for not considering a vocation in missions is their Christian parents. Their parents typically tell them when the subject is broached, 'Look, we didn't spend $60,000 on your college education for you to go bopping off to a refugee camp in Africa. You get your career under way, your pension scheme started, then after you are established if you want to have your holidays in Africa that is up to you!'

American Christian parents, just like their non-Christian counterparts, tend to surround their children with all the 'things': their own CD player, their own phone, their own TV and when they get to be a certain age their own car. Every Christmas looks like the department store blew up in the living room. The clear message is that what is important are 'the things'. We aren't losing the Christian young to the cults and New Age, we are losing them to the new religious shrines of devotion in McWorld—the shopping malls. Too many Western Christians of all ages are succumbing to the idolatry of modern culture, placing the acquisitiveness of McWorld before the servanthood impulses of the mustard seed.

Getting to the root—confusing occupation with vocation

Frankly I am convinced that one of the major reasons why Western Christians give the modern secular world so much authority to determine the terms of our lives are the teachings regarding work and vocation born of the Reformation. These teachings have been widely, often uncritically embraced as gospel by a broad spectrum of the Western Church.

First, leaders of the Reformation correctly decried the division of life into the sacred and the secular. Martin Luther called us to a whole life faith in which all that we do we should do 'to the glory of God'. And of course he is right. Under the creation mandate all work is seen not only as legitimate but advancing the purposes of God. Wayne Boggs explains a Reformed point of view on work: 'The reason man works today—not merely to make a living, nor to 'succeed' in the eyes of the world—but because it is God's plan for man to subjugate the earth . . . All honorable work, no matter how insignificant before men offers some opportunity to subdue this earth to God's will.'[24]

Since in this view all work under the creation mandate is advancing the purposes of God, one's work automatically becomes one's calling. 'Viewing work as calling makes it something personal. If God calls us to work, then to do work is to obey God. That is why the Reformers made so much of the attitude of the worker. Work only becomes calling if we recognize God's hand in it and view it as a part of our relationship with God.'[25] No one can argue that we need to recognise God's hand in all we do but I am not sure that our occupation automatically becomes our vocation.

Let's go back to the starting point—the creation mandate. Frankly I think it is a serious mistake to look at work and calling only in terms of the creation mandate. I believe we also need to view it from the perspective of God's kingdom purposes. For example, working at Microsoft might very well enable Bill Gates to subdue his few remaining competitors but I am not convinced that has anything to do with the creation mandate 'to subdue the earth'. There are undoubtedly Christians who are helping to construct Cruise Missiles at Boeing but I am not persuaded that that is a Christian calling, even if they do it with the right attitude.

I believe the purposes of God's kingdom are directly subversive to many of the aspirations and goals of the dominant modern commercial culture. I am convinced that the purposes of God's mustard seed movement will ultimately subvert the arrogance of every Babylon that claims the authority to define what is ultimate. Therefore I believe Scripture teaches that the primary vocation for every believer is not what we do to earn a livelihood but how we intentionally devote our lives, as Christ did, to seeking to advance the subversive purposes of God's kingdom.

Beyond Christian dualism—discovering the possibilities of a whole life faith

Making the connection to declining numbers and giving

In the light of this discussion it shouldn't be a mystery to any-one why attendance and giving patterns are declining in the Western Church. In our dualistic faith many of us have pur-sued the aspirations of the Western dream with a vengeance and tried to work a little faith in around the edges like it all works together. And of course it doesn't. Many of us have permitted modernity to define not only our notion of the good life and better future but most of the priorities and rhythms of our lives instead of our faith. And not surprisingly we find we are stressed.

Beyond dualism—rediscovering whole life discipleship

Let me be as clear as possible. I really believe we have got discipleship wrong. Dualistic discipleship has become the normative model for many in the Western Church. And while dualistic discipleship has certainly become normative it sim-ply isn't biblical. The solution that we will present more fully in the next two chapters is to call Christians back to a radical biblical approach to discipleship—a whole life discipleship.

Farmers will tell you that you can milk a cow on a one-legged or a three-legged stool. But a two-legged stool is terri-bly unstable. I believe that most of us are practising our disci-pleship on a two-legged stool. The first leg on the stool is get-ting our spiritual lives transformed. The second is the trans-formation of our moral values. Both essential. But the missing leg on the stool is cultural transformation. I believe that the Bible teaches that God not only wants to transform us spiritu-ally and morally but culturally too.

There is no way that we can try to be disciples in the biblical sense over the top of the acquisitiveness, materialism, individualism and consumerism of modern culture and wind up with anything that bears much resemblance to Jesus and his mustard seed movement. Listen again to Jesus' words, 'Do not store up for yourselves treasures on earth, where moth and rust destroy, and where thieves break in and steal. For where your treasure is your heart is also . . . No one can serve two masters. Either he will hate the one and love the other, or he will be devoted to the one and despise the other. You cannot serve both God and Money' (Matthew 6:19-21,24, NIV).

In the New Testament following Christ was clearly a whole-life proposition. It wasn't something you worked in around the edges. In the first century being a disciple of Christ meant putting a third leg on the stool. God is not just interested in changing our spiritual condition and moral values but our cultural values too.

In Christ we are crucified to the world. That simply means we are crucified to the secular values and the idolatries of the age. And we are crucified to the principalities and powers behind those values and idols. Remember that Jesus in his life and teachings was radically counter-cultural to his age and ours. And Jesus formed a new community of disciples that began to give people in that day a glimpse of God's new order that was clearly at odds with the domination system of his day.

It doesn't seem to have occurred to many of us that we are in no way obligated to accept all the arrangements that modernity hands us. We can take charge of our lives, families and communities. If we can find within Scripture an alternative vision for the better future then we can imagine and create new alternatives for how we use our time, new less expensive ways to shelter ourselves and gain greater control of our working lives. Instead of living dualistic lives in which there is little connection between our faith and where we spend our time and our money, we can fashion whole new options for our lives that are both more festive and free up more of our lives to advance God's kingdom.

Beyond the commodification of the Church

We have unwittingly allowed modernity to define for many sincere Christians our sense of what is important and of value, including how we function as a church. In *A Peculiar People,* Rodney Clapp traces our problems back to Christianity's accommodation with the Constantinian state. Before that accommodation the Christian community was clearly seen as beyond the pale of acceptable society and persecution was a fact of life for believers.

Since the 'Constantinian Compromise' Anabaptists have helped us to understand that we unwittingly blended together the agendas of state and Church and we have never recovered. In the Reformation, according to theologian John Milbank, the dualism we have been discussing, was augmented by privatising, spiritualising the sacred and making faith transcendent to the rest of human experience.[26]

Subsequently the contemporary Church in the US has learned from the apostles of McWorld how to package, commodify and market the Church using the most sophisticated marketing research. A growing number of mega churches have become essentially 'Christian' consumer malls. They include weight-loss programmes, gyms, saunas and snack bars just like in the malls—except these symbols of modern culture are all offered in Jesus' name.[27]

Many of the heralded 'new paradigm' churches have

achieved their growth by becoming very skilled at marketing their religious wares to an essentially boomer market. Since we view the Church primarily as *a place where people go,* the marketing challenge is to make your place more attractive than their place—by offering a better array of consumer offerings. In their book *Selling Out the Church: the Dangers of Church Marketing,* Phillip Kenneson and James Street state, 'The fundamental question is whether the church and its faith should be viewed as just another marketable commodity.'[28] Rodney Clapp calls this form of the Church 'you deserve a break today Christianity.'[29]

We have allowed modernity to help commodify our faith and define how we organise many of our churches. Many have embraced a very Western bureaucratic model of organisation complete with a professionalisation of ministry. Not only is this a very expensive expression of the Church, the values that are reflected in it are more reminiscent of a corporation than the values of that first community of itinerant servants, healers and teachers.

That first community of disciples was known as those 'who turned the world upside down'. They were constantly challenging the dominant values of their culture and paying the price. The contemporary Church is often one of the strongest apologists for protecting the dominant values of modern culture and it is very uncomfortable with those who challenge it.

The reason this happens, I believe, is that we have settled for a model of discipleship that ignores cultural transformation and also accepted a model of the Church that has too often chosen to silently sanction all the values of the dominant culture—unless they are blatantly immoral. And we have become domesticated. Somehow it has escaped our attention that McWorld isn't really our home. We are called to be sojourners, 'resident aliens' in this world.

In other words my ecclesiology leads me to believe that the

Church isn't just a place where we come to worship, have our needs met and consume activities and programmes, but rather a countercultural community that is committed to unmasking the values of the dominant culture rather than sanctioning them and helping both those inside and outside the Church to find a new way home.

Babylon revisited

We are entering an astonishing new world in which we will benefit from many different aspects of globalisation. What's new is that Marxism is in total eclipse and capitalism has gone global. My quarrel is not with the architects of McWorld future and their well-intended efforts to improve the human condition or even to make a profit doing it. My problem is that like Babylon of old they are making a conscious effort to redefine what is ultimate. 'It is the economy, stupid.' As we saw earlier in this book Francis Fukuyama heralded the triumph of free market capitalism as 'the end of history'.[30]

The McWorld economy has taken on a life of its own. There is not a day that goes by when one doesn't see this new globalised economy reaching into every corner of our planet and every part of our lives. It is clear that to promote this new global economy people must do much more than just create an environment for the free exchange of goods and services. They have to develop comprehensive, systematic ways to persuade us all to redefine not only what is ultimate but also what is important and what is of value to ratchet up our appetites for MORE.

We are all people who long for a destination that gives all of life a sense of significance and purpose. Even though the post-modernists have deconstructed Western progress and its sense of purpose for our future, they have done little to slow the growth of McWorld. But it has caused many of us, like

Dent, Trudy and other post-moderns, to realise that Western progress and the Western dream will never be home.

We need to remember that as followers of God we are exiles in search of a better land. As people called to a whole life faith we must, in every age, unmask the powers and expose the pretensions of Babylon. We need to join with other exiles and create new communities of celebration and subversion that have more of the aroma of God's new order than the stench of the dominant reality. In the next chapter we will search for a homeland in an ancient faith and a pre-modern imagination.

Planting a seed in San Francisco

 The Church of the Sojourners is a church with a difference. They have bought a number of homes together in the mission district where they are seeking to be a part of the living, breathing body of Christ in their community. This small congregation of thirty-five finds that by living in a residential setting together they are able to help one another resist the seductions of the secular culture more effectively than by simply commuting to a church building once a week. Families and singles share meals together in the evening and prayer before they begin their work day. They worship together on Sunday and meet in small home groups once a week to study Scripture and pray. They are one of the few communities I have found that invite God not only to change their spiritual lives and moral values but their cultural values too.

Planting a seed ministering to at-risk youth

David and Mike are a couple of twenty year olds who view the call to follow Christ as a whole life proposition, not something they work in around the edge of their 'normal' lives. They sense a strong call to make a difference in the lives of at-risk youth in Christchurch, New Zealand through Youth For Christ. They can't find anyone to pay them to do it. So they deliberately simplified their lifestyles so that they could get by on a twenty-hour a week job. As a result they could free up thirty hours a week for the ministry God calls them to. They are also buying a modest house together with some of their other mates to reduce their living costs and provide living space for others involved in the ministry.

Planting a seed in a Celtic prayer retreat centre

Christine and I are planning to build a celtic prayer retreat centre on some land we own north of Seattle. We want to design it so that it captures the spirit of a sixth-century Irish monastery. The purpose of the centre would be to provide a location where we could enable young people to develop their own spiritual disciplines while learning to live a simpler, more festive, community-based lifestyle that reflects more the values of the kingdom than those of the dominant culture.

Opportunities for Christian leaders

This critique of dualistic discipleship and the commodification of the Church offers those in leadership a number of opportunities.

1. To work with others in our seminaries, colleges and congregations to engage in a fresh analysis of how we got off the track that takes seriously the powerful influence of modernity and McWorld on our lives, our children's lives and our congregations, to become much clearer about *why we do what we do*.

2. To study the relationship between declining attendance and giving patterns of much of the Western Church in the light of the growing pressures and seductions of modern culture on the lives of our members.

3. To develop new educational resources on whole life discipleship and stewardship to enable Christians to deal with the mounting pressures of McWorld on their lives and families.

4. To examine the extent to which the contemporary Church has not only accommodated itself to modern culture but embraced its values, and to examine how we can plant churches that seek to challenge the values of the dominant cultures.

Questions for discussion and action

1. Why is it important for Christians to think about *why we do what we do*?

2. Where have you seen examples of dualistic discipleship? What ideas do you have for countering the growing influence of modern culture?

3. List where you spent your time last week. Now identify how much of the decisions about

where to spend your time came out of the expectations of modern culture and how much came out of the impulses of your faith?

4. Where have you seen examples of how the Church has apparently accommodated the values of modern culture? What are ways to help the Church create models based on biblical values?

Notes

1 J. Richard Middleton and Brian J. Walsh, *Truth Is Stranger Than It Used to Be: Biblical Faith in a Postmodern Age* (InterVarsity Press: Downers Grove, Ill., 1995), p.15.

2 Brian J. Walsh, 'Homemaking in Exile: Homelessness, Postmodernity and Theological Reflection', Doug Blomberg and Ian Lambert, editors, *Reminding: Renewing the Mind in Learning* (Centre for the Study of Australian Christianity: Sydney, 1998), pp.1-2.

3 *Ibid.*, pp.2-3.

4 J. Richard Middleton and Brian J. Walsh, *op. cit.*, p.145.

5 Charles E. Silberman, 'High Schools That Work, Murder in the Classroom, Part III', *The Atlantic Monthly*, August 1970, p.226.

6 Mark Noll, *The Scandal of the Evangelical Mind* (William B. Eerdmans: Grand Rapids, Mi., 1994).

7 Os Guiness, *Fit Bodies, Fat Minds: Why Evangelicals Don't Think and What To Do About It* (Baker Books: Grand Rapids, Mi., 1994), p.14.

8 Walter Brueggemann, *Hopeful Imagination: Prophetic Voices in Exile* (Fortress Press: Philadelphia, 1986), p.126.

9 Brueggemann, *Ibid.*, p.111.

10 Hendrik Berkhof, *Christ and the Powers* (Herald Press: Scottdale Penn., 1977), p.30.

11 Lesslie Newbigin, *The Gospel in a Pluralist Society* (William B. Eerdmans: Grand Rapids, Mi., 1989), p.204.

12 Walter Wink, *Engaging the Powers: Discernment and Resistance in a World of Domination* (Fortress Press: Minneapolis, 1992), pp.33-104.

13 Os Guiness, *Dining With the Devil: the mega Church movement flirts with modernity* (Baker Books: Grand Rapids, Mi., 1993), p.16.

14 Dave Tomlinson, *Post Evangelical* (Triangle: London, 1995).

15 David F. Wells, *Losing Our Virtue: Why the Church Must Recover Its Moral Vision* (InterVarsity Press: Leicester, England, 1988), p.12.

16 Rodney Clapp, *A Peculiar People: The Church as a Culture in a Post-Christian Society* (InterVarsity Press: Downers Grove, Ill., 1996), pp.164-171.

17 *Ibid.,* p.164.

18 Lesslie Newbigin, 'Cross Currents in Ecumenical and Evangelical Mission', *International Bulletin of Missionary Research* (October 1982), p.149.

19 Tom Sine, *Cease Fire: Searching For Sanity in America's Culture War* (William B. Eerdmans: Grand Rapids, Mi., 1995).

20 Craig M. Gay, *The Way of the [Modern World]: Or Why it's Tempting to Live As if God Doesn't Exist* (William B. Eerdmans: Grand Rapids, Mi., 1998).

21 Leo Tolstoy, 'How Much Land Does a Man Need?', translated by Loise and Aylmer Maude.

22 David Myers, 'Money and Misery', Rodney Clapp, editor, *The Consuming Passion: Christianity, the Consumer and Culture* (InterVarsity Press: Downers Grove, Ill., 1998), pp.58-59.

23 Robert Cole, 'Our Self-Centered Children—Heirs of the "Me" Decade', *US News and World Report*, 15 February,

1981, p.80.

24 Wayne L. Boggs, *All Ye Who Labor* (John Knox: Richmond, 1962), p.13.

25 Leland Ryken, *Redeeming the Time: A Christian Approach to Work and Leisure* (Baker Books: Grand Rapids, Mi., 1995), p.197.

26 Rodney Clapp, *A Peculiar People: The Church as Culture in a Post-Christian Society* (InverVarsity Press: Downers Grove, Ill., 1996), pp.25-32.

27 Abraham McLaughlin, 'Churches' Many New Services', *The Christian Science Monitor*, 30 September, 1998, pp.1, 5.

28 Phillip D. Kenneson and James I. Street, *Selling Out the Church: the Dangers of Church Marketing* (Abingdon Press: Nashville, Tn., 1997).

29 Rodney Clapp, *op. cit.,* p.21.

30 Francis Fukuyama, *The End of History and the Last Man* (Hamish Hammond: London, 1992).

8

How can we find our way home?

You could smell the fragrant aroma of lamb roasting over an open fire as you walked up the dusty road in Biram, a small village in Palestine. The group of beleaguered soldiers cleared the final hill and saw a table in the yard by a small rustic cottage laden with fruit, vegetables and freshly baked home-made bread and the lamb on the spit. As they approached the feast the father of this Palestinian Christian family explained to his children why he had prepared this lavish banquet for these Jewish soldiers.

> In Europe there was a man called Hitler. A Satan. For a long time he was killing Jewish people. Men and women, grandparents— even boys and girls like you. He killed them because they were Jews. For no other reason . . . Now this Hitler is dead . . . but our Jewish brothers have been badly hurt and frightened. They can't go back to their homes in Europe, and they have not been wel-comed by the rest of the world. So they are coming here to look for a home.[1]

The children from the Chacour family helped load the plates of their guests at this home-coming feast.

Longing for home

I have never met a person of Jewish faith who doesn't look forward some day to returning home—to Jerusalem—many of them for the first time. David Swarr, a friend of mine raised in Israel, reports what it is like to come back home to Jerusalem. As soon as planes with Jewish people from other parts of the world land at Ben Gurion Airport the passengers 'all burst into spontaneous applause. First time returnees descend the steps of the plane to kiss the tarmac. There are often tearful reunions between family members who have not seen one another for many decades. There are stories of families being reunited with loved ones they thought had been lost in the holocaust.'

I have been fortunate enough to travel to the Holy Land several times. The more I study Scripture the more I find myself looking forward to returning home to Jerusalem too. As we will see, the prophetic imaginations of Isaiah, Jeremiah and a number of other Old Testament authors all looked forward to a grand home-coming in a new Jerusalem.

Certainly one of our deepest human longings is for home. There are some 28 million refugees in the world who have no home and their numbers are growing. Homelessness is growing in a number of Western countries including the United States. Millions more have adequate shelter but no real home. Hundreds of millions have absolutely no sense of the future that God has prepared for God's people and God's world. The creator built into us all a profound longing to come home.

When I think of returning home my mind races back to warmer summer days at my grandparents' farm in Blackfoot, Idaho. Suddenly I am five again sitting splay-legged on the grass intently watching a parcel of new-born kittens frolicking on the lawn in front of me. Above me is a white arbour covered with red climbing roses permanently attached to the old white clap-board house my grandfather built. I can smell the aroma of home-made bread wafting out of the kitchen window. Inside my grandmother is just slicing the fresh bread and I can hear my name being called.

The creator God has built deep within us all a longing for home—a place where we belong, where we hear our name being called and a place that gives all of life a much more compelling sense of meaning. The author of the letter to the Hebrews gives us a list of the great heroes of the faith. The Scripture reads, 'These all died in faith, not having received what was promised, but having seen it and greeted it from afar, and having acknowledged they were strangers and exiles on the earth. For people speaking thus make it clear that they are seeking a homeland' (Hebrews 11:13-14).

In a very real sense we are all exiles seeking a homeland. As we have seen, a lot of folks all over the world, including many Christians, have bought into modernity's notion of what the homeland looks like. We meet so many people who are literally stripping their gears trying to climb McWorld's mountain accepting the mythology that the ultimate can be defined in economic terms—if they can only earn a little more or buy a little more they will be home free.

Like the children of Israel who were taken captive in Babylon, many of the community of God's people today seem to have contracted a serious case of amnesia. We seem to have forgotten not only whose we are but also the homeland towards which we are headed. When we succumb to a dualistic faith in which the future of God is pictured as a disembodied existence in the clouds then baubles that Babylon offers can start looking pretty good. That is why I argued earlier that crisis number one for the Western Church is a crisis of vision. We have unwittingly embraced two very different notions of what the better future looks like and neither of them happens to be biblical.

Finding the focus

 Therefore, in this chapter we are calling for the Spirit of the living God to blow through our imaginations until we are totally captivated by the astonishing vision of the great homecoming of God. We are all caught up in a historic contest between the aspirations and values that power McWorld and those which motivate the mustard seed.

We will argue that if we can both understand and embrace something of the creator's loving purposes for a people and a world it can help us to find what Walter Brueggemann calls 'a new reason for being'. It can help us to find a much clearer and compelling sense of purpose for our lives, families and communities of faith. It can help us to move from a dualistic to a whole life faith. And it can help us to create a way of life that is more festive than anything McWorld can offer.

I am confident that we will be absolutely flabbergasted at how much of our time and resources we could free up if we decided to put God's purposes first. I think we will be even more astonished at how the creator God will use our mustard seeds to make a difference in our world today and tomorrow.

In search of a new way home

Reports from the front indicate that people are exhausted by long hours of work and they are not finding the consumers' delights of McWorld nearly as satisfying as they thought they would. Growing numbers of people both inside and outside the Church are looking for a way to get off the jet-skis and find a way of life with a clearer sense of direction and a deeper spirituality. We particularly find that a number of young people are looking for a faith that impacts every aspect of life.

If you are among those who are in search of a greater sense of significance and a faith—for all of life—read on.

In search of a whole life faith

When my wife, Christine, was a missionary working in Ghana she found her faith seriously challenged by animism. The spirituality of the people she worked with touched every facet of their lives; from drawing water to harvesting crops, all of life was connected to the spiritual realm. She realised that this wasn't true for her or the other missionaries she worked with. It was through the influence of these animists that her journey began in search of a whole life Christian faith.

We don't have to look to animism to find a whole life faith—all we have to do is look to our own Judeo-Christian roots. The Israelites understood that their faith was intended to transform every part of their lives from their spiritual lives and dietary codes to their politics and economics. Clearly God intended them to be a counter-cultural alternative to the people around them—not just in their spiritual lives but in every aspect of their lives.

In the first century being a Christ-follower was not something you worked in around the edges of an already over-committed life. Following Jesus was clearly a whole life proposition which caused people in that first community to fundamentally reorder their lives to put God's purposes first.

John Alexander writes, 'Christians spend a lot of time and energy explaining why Jesus couldn't have meant what he said. This is understandable; Jesus was an extremist and we are all moderates. What's worse he was an extremist in his whole life—not just in the narrowly spiritual areas—but in everything, so we have to find ways to dilute his teachings.'[2] I think Alexander is spot on. For all the talk about lordship, few of us have much experience of applying the teachings of

Christ to all of life, including how we use our time and resources.

Look at the monastic movement in Europe. The Desert Fathers, the Cistercians, Benedictines and Franciscans were all creative experiments in whole life Christian faith. They deliberately sought to create a new rhythm which for many of these groups meant a focus of four hours a day in prayer, four hours a day in study and four hours a day in work. At their best they were compelling witnesses to a whole faith. The Desert Fathers had seekers come out to visit them in the Egyptian desert. They characterised those who came with a sincere hunger as 'visitors from Jerusalem' and those who were merely curious as 'visitors from Babylon'.

There is a spiritual renewal going on in many parts of the Church in Britain as people reconnect with their Celtic Christian roots. One of the reasons they seem to find Celtic spirituality so inviting is that for Celtic Christians following Christ was very much a whole life proposition too. In fact the Celtic saints talked about the door into that other realm being constantly ajar. The Spirit of the living God permeated all of their life from making the fire to milking the cows. There was no division between the sacred and the secular. For the Celtic monks their faith led them to adopt a way of life in which all of life was devoted to the mission purposes of God. By putting the mission purposes at the centre of life, God used these Celtic Christians to evangelise Scotland, England and much of continental Europe.

The Wesleyan lay movement called followers of Jesus Christ to share much more than the left-overs of their lives. They participated in communities in which they helped one another reorder their priorities to put first things first. One cannot read Howard Snyder's *The Radical Wesley* without being struck by the impact this rag-tag band of whole life disciples had on their world for Jesus Christ in the eighteenth century.[3] Deep down I think we know that we only come home to all we are intended to be when we join this great company of those who have gone before us and choose to become whole life disciples.

In search of a mustard seed faith

In 1981 I published a book entitled *The Mustard Seed Conspiracy* that stirred a surprising but welcome response by many who read it. In the introduction I wrote:

> Jesus let us in on an astonishing secret. God has chosen to change the world through the lowly, unassuming, and the imperceptible. Jesus said, 'With what can we compare the kingdom of God, or what parable shall we use for it? It is like a grain of mustard seed, which when sown upon the ground is the smallest of all seeds on earth; yet when it grows up it becomes the greatest of all shrubs, and puts forth large branches, so that the birds of the air can make their nests in its shade' (Mark 4:30-32).

That has always been God's strategy—changing the world through the conspiracy of the insignificant. He chose a ragged bunch of Semite slaves to become the insurgents of his new order. He sent a vast army to flight with three hundred men carrying lamps and blowing horns. He chose an undersized shepherd boy with a slingshot to lead his chosen people. And who would ever dream that God would work through a baby in a stable to turn the world right side up! 'God chose the foolish things of the world to shame the wise; God chose the weak things of the earth to shame the strong. He chose the lowly things of this world and despised things—and the things that are not—to nullify the things that are, so that no one may boast before him' (1 Corinthians 1:27-29).

 **It is still God's policy to work through the embarrassingly insignificant to change the world and create his future. He has chosen to work through the foolishness of human instrumentality. And he wants to use your life and mine to make a difference in the world. Just as Jesus invited that first bunch of fishermen, he invites us to drop our nets, abandon our boats and join him in the adventure of changing the world.[4]**

As we race into a future of economic globalisation, ruthless domination and commercial conquest on a scale never seen before, it is very difficult to believe that there is a force in heaven or on earth that can challenge the principalities and powers behind the globalisation of our planet. But I am convinced that the creator God is indeed quietly conspiring through the insignificant and unassuming to transform our world with a very different form of globalisation. The Bible reminds us that God's global agenda is not to create a global super mall but to redeem a people and transform a world. It is a kingdom that is both present and coming both now and not yet.

Jesus invites us to a subversive hope

'Hope is the refusal to accept the reading of reality which is the majority opinion' declares Walter Brueggemann. 'Hope is subversive, for it limits the grandiose pretensions of the present daring to announce to the present to which we have all made commitments is now called into question.'[5] Brueggemann sees this subversive hope being kept alive in the 'ministry of imagination'. Jesus was a part of this prophetic 'ministry of imagination'. He came proclaiming a very different vision for the future than the dominant vision in his time or ours.[6]

Jesus Christ walked the streets of Palestine proclaiming a single message: good news, good news, the future of God has broken in upon you! He not only proclaimed it, he demonstrated it. Every time he fed the hungry, opened the eyes of the blind and hugged the children we are given a preview of coming attractions—we are shown a small glimpse of the home-coming that God has in mind for us and many of our family we have never met. 'Jesus rejects "the world of grasping" and affirms "the world of the gift." He comes as an agent of the kingdom of God, dispensing the gifts of the kingdom to those who are dispossessed. His ministry of healing exorcism, table fellowship and teaching restored the broken, freed the oppressed, welcomed the outcast and taught a new pathway home.'[7]

Jesus formed a new community that was intended not only to be counter-point to the dominant culture but a foretaste of the future of God that he preached. It was a collection of those who were dispossessed by their culture becoming a new family making their way home together. It is through the death and the resurrection of Jesus that we are all invited to become a part of this new community. And it is through the bread and the wine that we receive a foretaste of that great home-coming banquet.

Through parables Jesus shows us tantalising samples of the great home-coming that connect directly back to the imagination of the prophets. British New Testament scholar N. T. Wright states that the parables were 'subversive stories' to 'bring to birth a new way of being the people of God'.[8]

For example, in the parable of the mustard seed we are not only shown how God is working subversively through the small and insignificant but we are also given a glimpse of the promised home-coming as well. Jesus said that the mustard seed 'when planted becomes the largest of all the garden plants, with big branches in which the birds of the air can perch in its shade' (Mark 4:32). Luke said that 'It grew and became a tree and the birds of the air perched in its branches' (Luke 13:19). The imagery of the sheltering tree directly connects to the imagery of the great home-coming of God in Ezekiel 17:22-24.

In Ezekiel 17 God promised to bring down the imposing imperial powers of that day. But God also promised to make the 'low tree grow tall'. 'This is what the sovereign Lord says: I myself will take a shoot from the very top of a cedar and plant it; I will break a tender shoot from the top most shoots and plant it high on a lofty mountain. On the mountain heights of Israel I will plant it; it will produce branches and bear fruit and become a splendid cedar. Birds of every kind will nest in it; they will find shelter in the shade of its branches. All the trees of the field will know that I the Lord bring down the tall tree and make the low trees grow tall. I dry up the green tree and make the dry tree flourish. I the Lord have spoken and will do it' (Ezekiel 17:22-24).

Bernard Brandon Scott stated that the imagery of this passage in Ezekiel parallels the imagery in Christ's parable of the mustard seed. It also pictures the mountain of God as a great 'world tree' under which the creatures of earth will dwell in the great home-coming.[9] Darrell Bock in his commentary on Luke suggests that the birds of the air represent not only an ingathering of Jews who have been scattered but all of God's children including the Gentiles.[10] God intends to bring his people home to a future made new.

Welcome to the great home-coming of God!

Let's take a trip back to the past through the rich imaginations of the prophets to discover a fuller picture of what the great home-coming of God looked like to those early poets. The prophet Isaiah develops the most breath-taking tapestry of imagery of the creator's loving purposes for a people and a world. It is not our aim here to discuss theology in a sophisticated way but rather to rediscover some of the powerful imagery of God's intentions for the human future that can give us purpose today.

First of all it is important to emphasise that the setting for the future of God is not in the clouds. The Hebrews always saw God's purposes as embracing creation, not divorced from it. As you will see, Isaiah's vision fully embraces the created world while bringing it into complete union with that realm in which God dwells. Isaiah's vision is for all of life and can provide a springboard for us to rediscover a whole life faith.

In the early chapters of Isaiah in the seventh century BCE the Assyrians are at the gates threatening the very existence of Jerusalem. But God has mercy and spares Jerusalem. However, in later chapters God allows Babylon to capture Jerusalem to punish the children of Israel for their chronic disobedience. As a consequence they wind up in exile in Babylon and, of course, that's where they begin to treat Babylon as though it were home. We will borrow images from all three parts of Isaiah.

I will briefly share some of the images that Isaiah used to remind the forgetful followers about the hope and the home that God had in mind for them. But as you will see, these images were not just intended for those in Babylonian captivity. These are images that are intended for all the people of God who are looking forward to coming home to all that God has promised. After we revisit the panoramic vision of the great home-coming, be ready to answer two questions:
1. What appear to be God's purposes for the human future and the created order in these passages?
2. Are the aspirations and values that motivate the great home-coming of God the same as those that power McWorld?

Listen to the vision of the prophet Isaiah: 'Behold, I will

create a new heaven and a new earth. The former things will not be remembered or come to mind. But be glad and rejoice forever in what I create, for I will create Jerusalem to be a delight and its people a joy. I will rejoice over Jerusalem and take delight in my people; the sound of weeping and of crying will be heard in it no more' (Isaiah 65:17-19). C. S. Lewis writes about how the realm in which God dwells will one day be fused together with the created order and we will come home to a new heaven and a new earth.

Commentator J. Alec Motyer states, 'Heaven and earth represent the totality of things . . . Former things picks up the reference to "former troubles" that includes "everything about the old order" . . . The awareness will be of a total newness without anything even prompting a recollection of what used to be.'[11]

Remember that the author of Revelation also looked forward to a new heaven and a new earth in which the new Jerusalem comes down to earth. Listen to the home-coming welcome: 'Now the dwelling of God is with men and he will live with them. They will be his people and God himself will be with them and be their God. He will wipe away every tear from their eyes. There will be no more death or mourning or crying or pain, for the old order of things has passed away. He who is seated on the throne said, "I am making all things new!" Then he said "write this down, for these words are trustworthy and true"' (Revelation 21:1-5).

The setting for the future of God is a new heaven and a new earth. But the focal point of home-coming is a new mountain and a new city—Zion and Jerusalem. When Isaiah states that God will 'create Jerusalem to be a delight and its people a joy, I will rejoice over Jerusalem and take delight in my people' (Isaiah 65:18-19), the prophet is describing a renewed Jerusalem.[12] Earlier in Isaiah is one of the most compelling images of the great home-coming of God—one in which

Mount Zion is transformed from a tiny hill to a transcendent peak that welcomes home family from every tongue and tribe and nation.

In the last days the mountain of the Lord's temple will be established as chief among the mountains; it will be raised above the hills, and all nations will stream to it. Many people will come and say, 'Come let us go up to the mountain of the Lord, to the house of the God of Jacob. He will teach us his ways, so that we may walk in his paths.' The law will go out from Zion, the word of the Lord from Jerusalem. He will judge between the nations and settle disputes for many peoples. They will beat their swords into ploughshares and their spears into pruning hooks. Nation will not take up sword against nation neither will they train for war anymore (Isaiah 2:1-4).

The people of God will be magnetically drawn home to Jerusalem, many for the first time. The pretentious spokespersons of the dominant reality will be given an early retirement and Jerusalem will become a centre for wisdom and learning. Another passage in Isaiah states that 'the knowledge of God will cover the earth as the waters cover the seas.' Paul said, 'now we know in part but then we will know even as we are known.' We will finally get it. No more squinting through a glass darkly. And the nations and the ruling economic powers will finally get it too. Mary was absolutely right about the advent of God's new order—the high and mighty will be brought down and the poor and humble will be lifted up.

The centre-piece of the great home-coming of God, at the top of the mountain of God, is going to be a huge international home-coming feast. Tony Campolo has it right—the kingdom of God is going to be a party! Watch the spectacle, enter into the celebration, savour the fare. The best that has ever been will be alive again.

'On this mountain the Lord Almighty will prepare a feast of

rich food for all peoples, a banquet of aged wines—the best of meats and the finest of wines. On this mountain he will destroy the shroud that enfolds all peoples, the sheet that covers all nations; he will swallow up death for ever. The sovereign Lord will wipe away the tears from all faces; he will remove the disgrace of his people from all the earth. The Lord has spoken. In that day they will say, "Surely this is our God, we trusted in him and he saved us. This is the Lord, we trusted in him; let us rejoice and be glad in his salvation"' (Isaiah 25:6-9).

⁻What we are witnessing is not only the great home-coming banquet of God but the consummation of God's great redemptive initiative in Jesus Christ. Through the cross, God's grace is extended to all of us in Christ. The New Testament makes clear that even as the one whom we follow rose from the dead, at the return of Christ we too will be resurrected—mind, body, soul and spirit—to be welcomed home to a new heaven and a new earth. The prophets not only picture the redemption of a new humanity, including all those who are disabled, but also the restoration of God's good creation. Even the creation gets in on this incredible home-coming celebration.

The desert and the parched land will be glad; the wilderness will rejoice and blossom. Like the crocus it will burst into bloom; it will rejoice and greatly shout for joy. The glory of Lebanon will be given to it, the splendour of Carmel and Sharon; they will see the glory of the Lord, the splendour of our God. Strengthen the feeble hands, steady the knees that give way; say to those with fearful hearts, be strong, do not fear; your God will come, he will come with vengeance; with divine retribution he will come to save you. Then will the eyes of the blind be opened and the ears of the deaf unstopped. The lame will leap like a deer, and the mute tongue will shout for joy. Water will gush forth in the wilderness and streams in the desert. The burning sands will become a pool, the thirsty ground bubbling springs. In the haunts where jackals once lay, grass reeds and papyrus will grow. And a highway will be there; it will be called the Way of Holiness. The unclean will not journey on it; it will be for those who walk in the Way; wicked fools will not go about on it. No lion will be there, nor will any ferocious beasts get up on it; they will not be found there, and the ransomed of the Lord will return. They will enter Zion with singing; everlasting joy will crown their heads. Gladness and joy will overtake them, and sorrow and sighing will flee away. (Isaiah 35:1-10)

'The day of the Lord is coming when the final pilgrimage will be made through a transformed desert. The motif of a transformed world speaks . . . of the end of sin's reign and the reversal of the Lord's curse. (Genesis 3:17ff). The burgeoning wilderness, at long last released from bondage (Romans 8:22ff), is actually shouting its welcome.'[13] The Pentecostals and charismatics are right—God's will is healing. You can be sure that the pilgrimage through that transformed desert is going to be littered with abandoned wheelchairs and white canes. The ransomed will return home to Zion with ecstatic celebration.

The final passage we will use to weave something of Isaiah's vision of the purposes of God is a passage that liturgical churches use during advent. It pictures the coming of the chosen one of God who ushers in this new order. Influenced by the dualism that is widespread, I have frequently heard commentators on Christian radio in the US state that the coming of the Messiah only focused on spiritual matters and was nothing to do with economics or politics. Watch in this passage what happens to the rod of their oppressors across their shoulders and the military uniforms rolled in blood from the warfare at the coming of the chosen one of God.

The people walking in darkness have seen a great light; on those living in the land of the shadow of death a light has dawned. You have enlarged the nation and increased their joy; they rejoice before you as people rejoice at the harvest, as men rejoice when dividing the plunder. For as in the day of Midian's defeat, you have shattered the yoke that burdens them, the bar across their shoulders, the rod of their oppressor. Every warrior's boot used in battle and every garment rolled in blood will be destined for burning, will be fuel for the fire. For unto us a child is born, to us a son is given, and the government will be on his shoulders. And he will be called Wonderful Counsellor, Mighty God, Everlasting Father, Prince of [Shalom]. Of the increase of his government and [shalom] there will be no end. He will reign on David's throne and over his kingdom, establishing and upholding it with justice and righteousness from that time on and forever. The zeal of the Lord Almighty will accomplish this (Isaiah 9:2-7).

The zeal of the Lord will accomplish all this! God will indeed multiply the nation beyond the people of Israel. And the prince of shalom will bring this expanded family home to a future of justice, righteousness and shalom in which the Messiah reigns, exuberance is the order of the day and the shouts of elation are deafening. Let's attempt to answer the questions posed when we began this quest to find an alternative to modernity's view of home-coming and post-modernity's chronic homelessness. It is through the imagination of an ancient faith and a pre-modern vision that we discover the imagery of the great home-coming of God for the human future.

Question 1: What are God's purposes for the human future and the created order in these passages from Isaiah?

We are invited into a vast waste land, a wilderness in which there is not a single blade of living grass. As we look to the horizon we see small dots coming towards us across the desert. As they get closer we see they are people from every tongue, tribe and nation. There is a family from Bosnia, an older couple from India and some children from an inner-city community in the United States—all pressing forward together. Rising up out of the desert is a huge mountain. As the throngs start to go up the mountain something remarkable happens. Suddenly the waste land is transformed into an abundant garden. They go up the mountain arm in arm and crutches are discarded, wheelchairs abandoned and the singing in hundreds of different tongues is deafening. When we reach the summit an incredible banquet is spread before us. The tables visibly sag under the weight of bountiful fare. And God is in the midst of this huge international feast, welcoming us home.

What are God's purposes for the human future and the created order? The short answer is that God intends to redeem a people and transform a world. God certainly intends to redeem us spiritually. But that's where the redemptive process begins not where it ends. The imagery makes clear that at the time of the resurrection of God's new community God intends to redeem us as whole persons, physically, intellectually and emotionally. The Scripture couldn't be clearer. The blind will see, the deaf will hear, the 'lame will leap like a deer'.

And we won't be redeemed individually. This is a corporate celebration. The creator God will redeem us, at the great home-coming, as a huge multi-cultural family from different times and places. And it is going to be more festive and celebratory than World Cup soccer, Disneyland and a holiday in the Caribbean all rolled into one.

Clearly in the stirring imagery of the home-coming initiative, God purposes to bring justice to the poor so that those at the margins are no longer excluded or oppressed. In fact, in both Mary's Magnificat and in the imagery of the home-coming banquet in the Gospels, the poor and vulnerable ones are the guests of honour and the wealthy and powerful apparently find themselves on the outside looking in.

We see weapons of war being transformed into implements of peace. And we see the military equipment that can't be transformed being incinerated. In another portion in Isaiah we are told that the lion will bed down with a lamb and a child shall play in a serpent's den. All violence, exploitation and predation will be at an end: 'They will neither harm nor destroy on all my Holy Mountain.'

God not only intends to bring an end to all violence, but Isaiah reminds us that all suffering, sin and death will also be vanquished as we come home to a world made new. 'The former things have passed away. Behold I am making all things new.' 'All things' certainly includes the renewal and restoration of God's good creation. As we have seen, the creation is going to be fully involved in this historic home-coming celebration.

When people of Jewish faith greet one another with 'shalom', they aren't simply saying peace. This Hebrew word means much more than that. Shalom means 'may you live in anticipation of that day when God makes all things whole again.' What the prophets are describing in the imagery of the great home-coming is really the shalom future of God.

Walter Brueggemann states:

Shalom is an enduring vision . . . Among the eloquent spokesmen for the vision . . . is this letter [Jeremiah] wrote to the exiles urging the validity of the vision even among displaced persons: 'I will fulfil to you my promise and bring you back to this place. For I know the plans I have for you, says the Lord, plans for shalom and not for evil, to give you a future and a hope . . . You will seek me and find me; when you seek me with all your heart, I will be found by you, says the Lord, and I will restore your fortunes' (Jeremiah 29:10-14).[14]

Question 2: Are the aspirations and values that motivate the great home-coming the same as those that power McWorld?

Think about it. How are modernity's aspirations, expressed in the Western dream, different from the purposes of God? First of all the Western dream defines the better future in largely individual terms. The vision of the future of God is clearly corporate. While the Western dream or the American dream defines the good life and better future largely in terms of economic upscaling and self actualisation, the imagery of God's great home-coming has a very different definition of what the better future looks like. While the biblical vision embraces the material world it isn't materialistic. It doesn't define the good life primarily in economic terms.

Rather the shalom vision defines the good life and better future in terms of renewed relationships with our creator, one another and the created order. The focus is on giving life away instead of sanctioning the self-interest that propels the market and preoccupies our lives. While modernity's aspirations focus exclusively on the here and now, the biblical vision is rooted in the reign of the creator God and a forever-after hope. And while modern culture is obsessed with power, the future of God comes on a donkey's back.

 **The themes of the Western dream are accumulating, upscaling, status, power, consumerism, individualism and self-actualisation. The themes of the home-coming future of God are justice for the poor, peace for the nations, the redemption of the people of God, a restoration of community, a renewal of creation and a celebration of the shalom purposes of God for a people and a world. These are not two versions of the same dream. These are totally different dreams. One is born out of an**

ancient faith. The other is the product of an Enlighten-ment vision of Western progress.

The brutal cross and the empty tomb are our way back home

In the dualistic model God is only active in the spiritual realm. The God we find in Scripture is the Lord of history and is involved in the totality of human experience. The creator God has invaded creation in Jesus Christ. Through the brutal crucifixion of Jesus, this God has redeemed all things. 'In him we have redemption through his blood, the forgiveness of sins, in accordance with the riches of God's grace' (Ephesians 1:7). Paul goes on to tell us that we are no longer outsiders but through the death and the resurrection of Jesus Christ we have been included in the family of God (Ephesians 2:19-22). Through the humiliation of the cross God has defeated the principalities and powers and all the pretensions of our global society. God has forever brought an end to sin, suffering and death. And it is through the cross and the empty tomb that God invites us home to a future made new.

Jürgen Moltmann writes:

> The manner in which God mediates his future through this partic-ular one is the form of substitutionary suffering, sacrificial death, and accepting love. If one looks from the future of God into the godless and forsaken present, the cross of Christ becomes the present form of the resurrection . . . The kingdom of God can only be understood as the real future of the world if it becomes present in history and as the goal of human striving . . . which we discover in the resurrection of the crucified one.[15]

Jesus putting first things first

Jesus stood up in the synagogue in his home town, at the

beginning of his ministry, and announced his vocation to an attentive audience. 'The Spirit of the Lord is on me, because he has anointed me to preach good news to the poor. He has sent me to proclaim freedom to the prisoners and recovery of sight to the blind, to release the oppressed, to proclaim the year of the Lord's favour' (Luke 4:18-19). He rolled up the scroll, handed it back to the attendant, sat down and then said something quite startling, 'Today this scripture is fulfilled in your hearing.'

This scripture, of course, comes out of the same compelling tapestry of imagery we have just read out of Isaiah and that is no accident. What it meant for him to be Messiah of God was not only to commit himself to God but to God's purposes for a people and a world. In this inaugural address he was announcing that the future of God had quite literally broken into the present and he was the one who would usher us home to a future made new.

> When understood literally, the passage says the Christ is God's servant who will bring to reality the longing and the hope of the poor, the oppressed, and the imprisoned. The Christ will also usher in the amnesty, the liberation, and the restorations associated with the proclamation of the year of jubilee (v.19; Leviticus 25:8-12) . . . The age of God's reign; the eschatological time when God's promises are fulfilled and God's purpose comes to fruition has arrived.[16]

Somehow John didn't get it. He wasn't convinced that Jesus was the one. So in Luke 7 he sends two of his disciples to find out if Jesus was really the chosen one of God. What proof does he offer John's disciples that he is indeed the Messiah? 'Go back and report to John what you have seen and heard: The blind receive sight, the lame walk, those who have leprosy are cured, the deaf hear, the dead are raised, and the good news is preached to the poor. Blessed is the man who does not fall away on account of me' (Luke 7:22-23).

The evidence he offers that he is indeed the Messiah of God is that he has committed his life to working for God's purposes that directly parallel his vocational statement drawn from Isaiah 61. By the power of God's Spirit, something of God's new order is indeed bursting into the present. What greater proof could Jesus offer? People must have been astonished as the blind threw away their canes, the lame danced, cleansed lepers sang and those that had died even joined in this amazing foretaste of the great home-coming.

Disciples called to put first things first

What did it mean to be a disciple in the first century? Something very different than it does today. Today as a direct result of many of us buying into Western dualism we often move things of faith and Spirit to the margins of our life. In this dualism everyone knows your job comes first, your des. res. comes first, getting ahead comes first. Then we work our faith in around the edges.

As we will see in the next chapter, to be a follower of this Jesus you were expected to do exactly what Jesus did. You not only committed your life to God but to the purposes of God: 'sight to the blind, release to the captives, good news to the poor.' You were expected to reorder your entire life around this new sense of purpose—to be whole life disciples. And those first disciples reordered their *entire* lives not only around their commitment to God but the purposes of God.

It all starts with a party

 Recently Christine and I had the opportunity to work with some students at Messiah College. They read these passages out of Isaiah aloud. Then we divided them into three groups each with a different assignment regarding the great home-coming of God. The first group planned a weekend party called a 'taste of the Kingdom' in which African American, Hispanic, Asian and Anglo churches would be invited to bring their food, dance and music and invite the entire community. The second group sketched a mural portraying people going up the mountain to the great home-coming feast arm in arm with singing and celebration. The third group actually composed a song about the great home-coming of God that was so compelling we had them perform it in chapel the next day.

Every time we share the bread and the wine we are not simply remembering the death and resurrection of Jesus Christ. In the mystery of the Eucharist we are actually joining in that great home-coming banquet with our God and all those who have gone before us in anticipation of the return of Christ and when we are all welcomed home. Frederick Buechner Rominesus 'No matter how much the world shatters us to pieces, we carry within us a *vision* of wholeness that we sense is our true home that belongs to us.' (Frederick Buechner, *The Longing for Home* [Harper: San Francisco, 1996], p.110.)

Babylon revisited

What God offers us as a group of exiles in the world is not just a new destination—the great home-coming—but also 'a new reason for being'. While McWorld comes as Babylon with power and pretension to establish absolute dominance, the creator God comes through the small, the powerless and the unpretentious to turn the world right side up. Incredibly God can even use your mustard seed and mine to make a difference in some small ways now in anticipation of that day when the creator will make all things new.

I am convinced that not all the upscaling and accumulating of McWorld can ever satisfy our deepest longing to find significance in life. But what could give life greater significance than to be a part of God's subversive mustard-seed movement that is quietly changing our world and offering people a hope and a home-coming?

Opportunities for Christian leaders

There is no greater opportunity for those in Christian leadership than enabling believers to discover in Scripture a new vision for the future of God that not only inspires hope but also offers a sense of direction for life. Leaders have specific opportunities:

1. To enable those with whom you work to discover in Scripture an alternative vision to the aspirations of the Western dream and the addictions of McWorld—for all of life; people need particular help in bringing the imagery of God's great home-coming into their lives through celebrations, music and liturgy;

2. To enable your members to use the biblical vision as a basis to define a new sense of focus for their lives and families as the first step in putting first things first;

3. To enable your members to use their sense of biblical vocation as a basis to help them redefine their notion of the good life as the first step in reordering their priorities;

4. To examine the assumptions and values implicit in how we

live our lives, order our churches and operate our Christian organisations in light of the aspirations and values of God's new order.

Questions for discussion and action

1. What is your most welcome image of coming home? What is your deepest longing for home?

2. As you read the imagery of the great home-coming, how is it different from the aspirations of the Western dream?

3. How could you put the vision of Isaiah and the vocation of Jesus at the centre of your life, family and congregation?

4. Draw a picture, write a song or plan a party that brings to life the spirit of the great home-coming and invite over some friends to enjoy the celebration.

Notes

1 Elias Chacour with David Hazard, *Blood Brothers* (Chosen: Grand Rapids, Mi., 1984), pp.11-12.

2 John Alexander, 'Why We Must Ignore Jesus', *The Other Side Magazine*, October 1977, p.8.

3 Howard Snyder, *The Radical Wesley: and Patterns for Church Renewal* (InterVarsity Press: Downers Grove, Ill., 1980).

4 Tom Sine, *The Mustard Seed Conspiracy* (Word Books: Waco, Texas, 1981), pp.11-12.

5 Walter Brueggemann, *The Prophetic Imagination* (Fortress Press: Philadelphia, 1978), p.67.

6 *Ibid.*, pp.45, 97.

7 J. Richard Middleton and Brian J. Walsh, *Truth Is*

Stranger Than It Used to Be: Biblical Faith in a Postmodern Age (InterVarsity Press: Downers Grove, Ill., 1995), p.161.

8 N. T. Wright, *Jesus And The Victory of God* (Fortress Press: Minneapolis, 1996), p.181.

9 Bernard Brandon Scott, *Hear Then the Parable: A Commentary on the Parables of Jesus* (Fortress Press: Minneapolis, 1989), pp.384-385.

10 Darrell Bock, *Luke,* Volume 2: 9: 51- 24: 53 (Baker Books: Grand Rapids, Mi., 1996), p.1226.

11˙ J. Alec Motyer, *The Prophecy of Isaiah: An Introduction and Commentary* (InterVarsity Press: Downers Grove, Ill., 1993), p.529.

12 *Ibid.,* p.530.

13 *Ibid.,* p.273.

14 Walter Brueggemann, *Living Towards a Vision: Biblical Reflections on Shalom* (United Church Press: New York, 1984), p.22.

15 Jürgen Moltmann, 'Toward the Waiting God', Frederick Herzog, ed., *The Future of Hope: Theology as Eschatology* (Herder and Herder: New York, 1970), pp.31- 50.

16 Fred B. Craddock, *Luke: Interpretation, A Bible Commentary for Teaching and Preaching* (John Knox Press: Louisville, 1990), p.63.

SECTION THREE
A Crisis of Creativity

A grand old-fashioned funeral hearse drove up in front of Cascade College auditorium just as we were getting out of chapel one bright spring morning. To my delight I spotted Paul Byers, a good friend, behind the wheel. As we gathered around he explained that he had spotted the old hearse the day before not far from the college with a 'for sale' sign in its window. Purely on a whim he came up with $250 and was now the proud owner of this stately vehicle with Victorian curtains at each of the windows.

It didn't take long for Paul and the rest of us to realise that this was more than a classic funeral hearse. It represented a serious challenge to our collective creativity. Just what are the possible uses for an ancient funeral hearse? After about twenty minutes of brainstorming we discovered that with very careful packing we could get thirteen students lying down in the back of the hearse at the same time. We cut classes and Paul proceeded to drive all over Portland, Oregon. Every time he approached a red light or a stop sign he would accelerate. Then at the last moment he would slam on the brakes and all thirteen of us would abruptly sit bolt upright at the same time. Cars drove up on lawns, one guy almost swallowed his cigarette. We would lie back down and wait for the next stop sign. We caused chaos all over Portland. It was very gratifying.

One of God's greatest gifts to us is the gift of creativity. 'The story of God begins with creation—with the spectacular, extravagant creativity of God. Before anything existed, the creator God, out of nothing created everything. Our creator has graciously gifted us, as divine image-bearers, with creativity. Though we are not able, like God, to create something from nothing, we are able to imagine and bring into being a lavish array of new possibilities for ourselves and God's world.'[1]

Corporate executives tell me that the most satisfying part of their work is not simply increasing corporate profits but the challenge of using their creativity to achieve corporate objectives. I know of no other segment of society that makes greater use of imagination and creativity than the world of commerce. One can see their creativity in some of the very imaginative ads.

However, Emil Brunner states that any time we use our creativity autonomously apart from God, we risk the 'gravest consequences'.[2] Clearly much of humankind's creativity has added to the beauty and bounty of God's good creation. But human imagination has also been used in ways that undermine our humanity and threaten the viability of creation itself. Harvey Cox charges that the human creature, 'While gaining the whole world . . . has been losing his own soul. He has purchased prosperity at the staggering impoverishment of the vital elements of his life. These elements are festivity— the capacity for genuine revelry and joyous celebration, and fantasy—the faculty for envisioning radically alternative life situations.'[3]

As we saw in the last chapter, God is clearly at work creating a new heaven and a new earth where we will come home to a future made new. The creator God invites us, through the mustard seed, to be a part of the adventure of creating new ways to manifest something of God's new order.

A crisis of creativity

In the American Church there is a widespread view that the Church is essentially on track as we race into a new millennium. But in Britain, Australia and New Zealand there is a much greater sense that it is in serious trouble and needs to be fundamentally reinvented to address more effectively the new challenges of a very uncertain future. I am convinced that one of the major under-utilised resources to help us with the task of reinvention is our creativity.

Everywhere that Christine and I minister, people tell us that they feel trapped by the pressures of the modern world and are convinced there is no way out. These sincere believers don't seem to realise that they aren't as boxed in as they think they are. They can, through their imagination, create alternatives that offer a way of life with a much greater sense of significance, that is more festive and less stressed than anything that modern culture has to offer.

This crisis of creativity not only impacts our lives and families but it also impacts how we function as Church. There are many churches in which there is no shortage of innovation. But much of the innovation we see is faddish. Churches simply attempt to copy other models of what's going on whether it is buying inflatable playthings for their youth group or jumping on board the newest church-growth bandwagon.

Candidly I find that even mission executives and missiologists tend to get caught up in bandwagon approaches to missions instead of being more intentional in their creativity. But we have found that there are very few resources available to enable mission organisations, churches or individuals to create the new possibilities for life and mission in a changing world.

Through Mustard Seed Associates, Christine and I try to respond to this need by conducting futures/creativity workshops. [Email 103213.2024@compuserve.com] In the final two chapters we are going to challenge those in leadership to replace random innovation by showing you how to get creative on purpose. We will show how to use our creativity for two purposes: 1) to create new ways to advance biblical purposes; 2) to create new ways to respond to tomorrow's challenges.

1. To create new ways to advance biblical purposes

As we saw in chapter 6, there are astonishingly few models of Christian approaches to education, health care or even church structures that aren't simply dull reflections of modern secular models—sanctified by doing them in Jesus' name. Those in leadership don't seem to notice that many of the implicit values in these models are diametrically opposed to biblical values. We really give very little thought to *why we do what we do*. As we saw in the last chapter, while we hold Scripture in great esteem we tend to use it devotionally or liturgically but seldom use it as a launching pad to create new alternatives.

A group of Mennonites in the US wanted to have a modest witness for the gospel of Christ in the criminal justice field. Instead of simply borrowing the standard model of criminal techniques and doing them in Jesus' name they created a new model to implement biblical purpose. They started with the biblical call to reconciliation ('All this is from God, who reconciled us to him through Christ and gave us the ministry of reconciliation: that God was reconciling the world to himself in Christ, not counting men's sins against them. And he has committed to us the message of reconciliation' [2 Corinthians 5:18, NIV]). And the message of reconciliation is not only that we are to be reconciled to God but also to one another. Therefore these Mennonites created a modest new ministry called VORP.

VORP stands for the Victim Offender Reconciliation Programme. Essentially in this programme they bring together the guy that got his house burgled and the kid that did it. They work for reconciliation and restitution.

Out of this innovative ministry VORP staff tell me that friendships often emerge. Sometimes the guy that got his house broken into actually spends his money to send the young offender to college and helps him find a new sense of direction for his life. I can guarantee that any Christian leader who moves from bandwagon innovation to creating models flowing directly from biblical principles will be astonished at how God enables them to create brand-new models that reflect more the values of the kingdom than those of modern culture.

2. To create new ways to intentionally respond to tomorrow's challenges

Christine and I are testing a process with Intervarsity Christian Fellowship in the US to help prepare a new generation to create new options for their lives in order to enable them to respond to the new opportunities of tomorrow's world. For example, I talked to a student recently who is studying electrical engineering but feels God is calling him into missions. In exploring with him I found that his view of mission vocations was quite limited as it is for many students. He visualised missionaries as essentially preachers or perhaps educators but he had no idea his training in electrical engineering had any application. I explained that one of the exciting new missions vocations for the twenty-first century is photovoltaic engineering. In other words he could use his engineering training to help construct solar collecters to turn the sun's energy into electricity to start clinics or small businesses in communities of need in the Two Thirds World. We hope through this process to enable college students to do a much better job of anticipating new options in the future and creating new lifestyle and vocational possibilities to take advantage of those opportunities.

In these final two chapters we will argue that business as usual in our lives, churches and missions organisations will not be adequate to address the escalating challenges of a new century. Therefore, in the next chapter we will explore creative new ways we can put God's purposes first in addressing the new challenges of a new millennium in our lives and communities of faith. In the final chapter we will explore how to reinvent our approach to mission in a changing world.

9

Reinventing Christian life and community

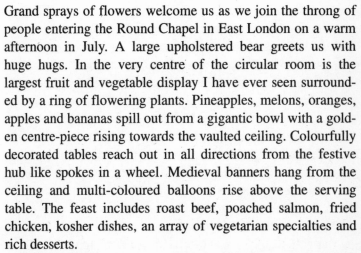

Grand sprays of flowers welcome us as we join the throng of people entering the Round Chapel in East London on a warm afternoon in July. A large upholstered bear greets us with huge hugs. In the very centre of the circular room is the largest fruit and vegetable display I have ever seen surrounded by a ring of flowering plants. Pineapples, melons, oranges, apples and bananas spill out from a gigantic bowl with a golden centre-piece rising towards the vaulted ceiling. Colourfully decorated tables reach out in all directions from the festive hub like spokes in a wheel. Medieval banners hang from the ceiling and multi-coloured balloons rise above the serving table. The feast includes roast beef, poached salmon, fried chicken, kosher dishes, an array of vegetarian specialties and rich desserts.

Those pouring in for this lavish feast pay only a pound a head (less than $2 each). The hosts deliberately priced it so that every person in this richly multi-cultural community could afford to come. As far as they know this is the first time anyone has successfully brought together the entire community. We stand in line for our food behind a mum and three children who are originally from Jamaica. Those behind us in line are from a local drama group which often performs in this large circular room now primarily used as a centre for the performing arts.

As we sit down to join the feast a local string ensemble begins entertaining the 350 guests. Different local groups take turns in performing during the entire feast. Looking around I can see that members of this London neighbourhood are thoroughly enjoying not only the lavish banquet and the music but one another. Listen to the comments that people wrote as they left: 'Simply amazing. Could we have it again please?' 'I thought today was a great innovative idea. To get people from everywhere together is very refreshing.' 'Felt a bit like a wedding without the bride and groom!' And it reminded me of that final grand wedding banquet that we will share at the great home-coming of God.

Who was responsible for the feast? A lot of people from all over the community and a small group of young Christians were the moving force. They are part of a Reformed congregation determined to creatively reinvent what it looks like to follow Christ in a fragmented, alienated community. At least a half a dozen young couples have deliberately moved house to a transitional neighbourhood and become united in common cause as an expression of the reconciling gospel of Christ. And they are finding the satisfaction of creating a way of life with a difference.

They have started a food co-operative that enables those at the margins to buy a much broader array of food in bulk at cost. They have also started a community equipment loan scheme to share gardening tools. Their most recent ministry creation is the provision of a place in the community where parents with pre-schoolers have a drop-in place to come.

Finding the focus

 The Round Chapel Neighbourhood Project is a sample of the inbreaking of God's kingdom and an example of the kind of innovative approach to life, community and mission that Christians are initiating all over the world. This is an invitation to discover how God can use your mustard seed, in community with others, to make a difference in the world. The purpose of this chapter is to explore specific imaginative ways that Christians can both reinvent how we do discipleship and create communities of faith that both advance God's purposes and prepare us to live creatively in tomorrow's world. And it all begins by our critically re-examining *why we do what we do* in nurturing disciples and in growing churches.

Back to the future one more time

The challenges of our McWorld future will require that we radically recreate how we live our lives as disciples of Jesus Christ, raise our young and form our communities. Remember we are heading into a future in which we are likely to come under mounting pressure to work harder and longer. If we return to the future of the 'long boom' we and our children are also going to be under growing pressure to consume more to keep the economy booming.

If we experience the future of the 'slow meltdown' many people in Western societies are likely to experience the same dislocations that have caused such enormous pain to millions of people in Asia and Russia. The Church needs to prepare people for both boom or bust.

Beyond Christian dualism—back to the Bible one more time

The good news is that we don't have to settle for modern culture arranging the furniture of our lives or defining where we spend our time and money. We don't have to settle for high stressed lifestyles that are disconnected from vital faith—where we have precious little time for prayer, service or celebration. Like the young people in East London, God can help us to create life with a difference.

Call to biblical discipleship—putting first things first

Think about it! Those first disciples of Christ weren't immersed in Roman culture nine to five with a house church on the weekend. No dualistic, compartmentalised faith for them. They understood that following Christ was a whole life proposition. Unlike the kind of dualistic discipleship offered today they didn't simply invite God to transform their hearts and forgive their sins and go about life as usual. For all those committed to equipping Christians to do the work of the Church we must reinvent our programmes calling believers to whole life discipleship and stewardship in which they place God's purposes at the centre of life.

In the first century you were expected not only to commit your life to God but also to the purposes of God. As followers of Jesus you no longer settled for the dominant culture defining the focus of your lives. You expected to make Jesus' vocation your vocation 'sight to the blind, release to the captives and good news to the poor.'

That's why those first disciples did wild, outrageous things like quitting jobs and leaving homes because they had a new reason for being. Listen again to Jesus' call to whole life discipleship: 'If anyone comes to me and does not hate his father and mother, his wife and children, his brothers and sisters—yes, even his own life—he cannot be my disciple . . . any of you who does not give up everything cannot be my disciple' (Luke 14:25,33).

Dietrich Bonhoeffer reflecting on this radical call to follow Christ, presents one way we often get off the hook.

> If Jesus said to someone, 'Leave all else behind and follow me; resign your profession, quit your family, your people, and the home of your fathers,' then he knew that to this call there was only one answer—the answer of single-minded obedience but we would tend to rationalise away the clear intent of Christ's call by arguing, 'Of course we are meant to take the call of Jesus with "absolute seriousness" but after all the true way of obedience would be to continue all the more in our present occupations, to stay with our families, and serve there in a spirit of true inward detachment.'[4]

Bonhoeffer is right. In the dualistic discipleship model it is fascinating to see how we have been carefully nurtured to side-step the radical demands of whole life discipleship. We are typically taught to tip our hat to this radical call and give passive assent to Christ's claim on all our life. In this dualistic model we are routinely taught to say 'that everything we have is God's and if he hits us with a blinding vision we will give it all back . . . but in the meantime we will continue enjoying for God.'

Those first disciples didn't passively wait for a bolt out of the blue to call them to devote their entire lives to Christ and his kingdom. And neither should we. In contrast we find that many Christian college students are being nurtured in a dualistic discipleship model in which they are encouraged to put the agendas of modern culture first.

Message to the young—agenda one is putting first things first

Too often the real message to the Christian young, for all the talk about Lordship, is 'agenda one is getting your job underway, getting your house in the suburbs, getting your upscale lifestyle started and then with whatever you have left over (like older generations), serve Jesus.' But because many of the young are hitting the economy at a much tougher time than those of us who are older, they don't have much left over.

When Christine and I speak at Christian colleges we offer a different message. We state that 'agenda number one is not where to work, where to live or even who to marry. Life decision number one is to determine how God wants to use my life to advance his purposes!' Then, like the first followers of Jesus, we have the opportunity to actively reorder all of life to put God's mustard seed purposes first.

What I am suggesting is pretty radical. I am suggesting that Christians of all ages need to discover how God is calling us to put God's mission purposes first. Then we can begin the creative adventure of reordering every area of our lives to put first things first just like Jesus did.[5]

At the beginning of his ministry Jesus Christ stood up in his home town and read, 'The Spirit of the Lord is on me because he has anointed me to preach good news to the poor. He has sent me to proclaim freedom for the prisoners, and recovery of sight for the blind, to release the oppressed, to proclaim the year of the Lord's favour' (Luke 4:17-18, NIV). Then in the rest of the gospel narrative we witness Jesus consciously devoting the remainder of his life with a single focus—to advance the purposes of God.

Remember, Jesus' vocation is directly related to the promise of the great home-coming of God. If we try to follow Christ on automatic pilot I can guarantee that the values of modern culture will wind up defining the direction and the character of our lives. I am arguing that the call to follow Christ is a call to intentionally live out the purposes of God in every aspect of our lives.

Drafting a mission statement for a difference

What does it look like today when disciples seek to put God's purposes first like Jesus and that first band of disciples did? Recently Jerry Sitzer, who teaches theology at Whitworth College in Spokane, experienced a devastating tragedy. He lost his wife and one of his children in a violent car accident. Left as a single parent to raise three children by himself he told me that he was overwhelmed by grief. After weeks of prayer and struggle it dawned on him that one of the ways to honour those who died was to sit down with his three children and write a family mission statement—to raise his children with a definite purpose in mind.

He sat down with his three children, and with his biblical training, drafted a family mission statement. Jerry told me that they check it every week to ensure they are finding creative ways to bring faith to every dimension of their life as a family.

Christine and I followed Jerry's example. We have both had the opportunity to live with the poor in the Two Thirds World and we will never be the same. As a consequence we have chosen Proverbs 31:8-9 as a basis for our mission statement: 'Speak up for those who cannot speak for themselves, for the rights of all who are destitute. Speak up and judge fairly; defend the rights of the poor and needy.'

Reinventing our timestyles to put first things first

At other times both Christine and I were out of control in how much we were taking on and we paid a very dear price. We have discovered the hard way that Jesus needs our service not our exhaustion.

Christine and I aren't alone in struggling with stressful timetables. Speaking at the Greenbelt Festival in England I asked, 'How many are under serious pressure in your time schedules?' Virtually all of the 250 people in the tent raised their hands. We had the same overwhelming response to the question in a Baptist church in Vancouver BC and a Presbyterian church in Seattle.

Planting a seed in a prayer retreat

One way we have found of getting in control of our timetables and focusing our lives is to go on a prayer retreat four times a year. Typically we take two days for prayer, biblical reflection, writing journals and refocusing. All we take with us are our Bibles, our journals and our mission statement.

We usually begin our retreat with an extended time of prayer and biblical meditation waiting for God to show us where we have come off the track and become distracted from our sense of calling. Then we prayerfully set new goals for every part of our lives that we believe clearly reflect our sense of calling, including our ministry, our spiritual disciplines, our marriage, our relationships, our hospitality, celebrations and finances.

Then we draft a new time schedule that reflects the goals flowing out of our mission statement. Finally we take a couple of hours every Sunday morning before church, drive to a viewpoint and have a time of discussion and sharing with each other.

We have discovered that a strong part of our sense of vocation is hospitality. Therefore we have deliberately set aside more of our time and money to entertain and honour those dear friends God has given us. Another part of our sense of calling is celebrating the great home-coming of God with our friends. Every Christmas season we put on a party called Advent 2—home-coming in which we celebrate not only the advent of the king but also the new kingdom of banqueting and celebration. This approach may not work for everyone, but I am convinced we all need to find a way to discover God's mission call on our lives.

Ten-week course on reinventing our lives to put God's purposes first

Week one—life beyond the stress race

 Everywhere we work we find people searching for a way of life that is less exhausting where they can find the satisfaction of putting God's purposes first. Christians simply don't know how to connect whatever they hear in the Sunday morning sermon with their lives from Monday to Saturday. I am persuaded that one thing that could help is a ten-week course to help Christians put first things first. Christine is actually writing a book on this subject. But I will give you a quick outline that you can use with this book, in any Sunday school class or small group, to discover how God can help you reorder your life to put God's purposes first.

I find that it is essential to begin by giving people time to share their sense of exhaustion and frustration with one another as the first step in a journey towards freedom. It is also essential for the leaders to help people to identify the specific reasons that their timetables are out of control and begin exploring how they could reduce some of their involvements. As God's Spirit speaks, people will need time for repentance too.

Weeks two to four—living life on purpose

Three weeks is probably a bare minimum for people to draft a personal or family mission statement on the basis of what they have studied in Scripture. You might start by helping people to focus on God's passionate purposes for a people and a world. The imagery of the great home-coming of God in chapter 9 might be of help. Like the young people I mentioned at Messiah College, have your folks plan a party, draw a picture and write a song that captures something of God's intentions for the human future. Next enable them to understand how Jesus and his first disciples very deliberately made God's purposes their purposes—and how that sense of biblical vocation shaped every single aspect of our master's life.

Weeks five to seven—creating a life with a difference

The aim of drafting a mission statement is to enable every believer to discover how God wants to use their mustard seed to make a small difference in the world for God's kingdom. For example, a lawyer could use her training to create a practice to work for reconciliation in broken families. An engineer could use engineering design and computer systems to help disabled persons become more self-reliant. A mother who stays at home could become involved in the vitally important ministry of foster care for unwanted children.

Others might even feel called into the huge range of 'full-time' Christian ministries, from working in Scripture translation with Wycliffe in Indonesia to working in urban evangelism with Youth For Christ in Glasgow among the at-risk young. Intervarsity Christian Fellowship has persuaded hundreds of graduates to give God the first year or two out of college to work with the urban poor.

A book entitled *Your Money or Your Life* explains innovative ways in which individuals can simplify their lifestyles for five to seven years and then place a significant amount of what they save in investments and live off the interest.[6] I find very few Christians who have ever considered schemes like this so that they can invest the rest of their life in their mission vocation.

With the greying of our Western societies, many older Christians have the opportunity to use the second half of their lives to invest in the work of God's kingdom. In his challenging book *Half Time,* Bob Buford writes to those in the middle of their lives

> If you do not take responsibility for going into half-time and ordering your life so that your second half is better than your first, you will join the ranks of those who are coasting their way to retirement . . . But if you take responsibility for the way you play out the rest of the game, you will begin to experience the abundant life that our Lord intended for you.[7]

But if we are not called to advance God's kingdom purposes through our occupation, full-time Christian mission or substantial lifestyle change, then we need to enable everyone to change their timetables to free up two to four hours a week to be actively involved in witness or service beyond the doors of the church.

Planting a seed—families for others

One idea from one of our creativity workshops was for families to visit neglected senior citizens in nursing homes together. The creative twist was for the children to read stories to the elderly people while their parents listened too. What kind of children would we raise up if, instead of eighteen years of highly indulgent living, our young were involved during those years with their parents in ministry to others?

Weeks eight to ten—creating a life you can love

The Christian lifestyle literature of the late seventies gave the impression that the call to lifestyle change was simply a scaled-down version of the Western dream. I am arguing that the kind of change Scripture calls us to isn't primarily economic downscaling but cultural transformation.

You see, the rat race is a fraud! It never was the good life. It is disturbing how many of us, like the children of Israel have contracted a serious case of amnesia. We are people in exile who will never be at home in McWorld. We need to find a sense of God's call on our lives and to invite him to transform our values from those that pervade the dominant culture to those that motivate the mustard seed movement. Study the Gospel of Luke and compare the cultural values Jesus taught and reflected in his life with those promoted by McWorld and help people to begin to redefine their notions of the good life.

Planting a seed—learning to party the kingdom

Speaking in a charismatic church in London recently, I said, 'You folks are fun to be with during praise worship on Sunday but the rest of the week you are a bit of a drag.' Of course I was being a bit facetious. But the point I was trying to make was that in our dualistic faith we tend to keep our Christian celebrations of faith to one small compartment of our lives. And then like everyone else we passively become dependent on modern culture to entertain us.

Where I encourage people to begin to change their timetables and lifestyles to more authentically reflect God's new order is not to cut back or give up anything. I urge people to throw a party that begins to express the kingdom of God in Scripture: the wedding feast, the international banquet, the jubilee. Encourage your people to take one of these biblical images and plan a party.

One of the most intriguing aspects of the monastic movement is the way in which it enabled adherents to live out their faith by altering the rhythm of their lives. Try to help one another to create an easier rhythm for your lives. As Anglicans we love celebrating the rhythm of the Church calendar.

At the very centre of whole life discipleship is the need to set aside generous daily time for Scripture study and prayer. We are called to be people of deep spirituality who are growing in intimacy with our God. In one of Richard Foster's most recent books, *Streams of Living Water*, he introduces us to a rich spectrum of Christian prayer traditions that provide resources to help us deepen our spiritual life. Foster's organisation, Renovare, provides excellent resources to help people in your congregation deepen their life of prayer.[8] (Email: 103165.327@compuserve.com)

I recommend you create a brainstorming time in which people are invited to create new rituals for their lives and families. One particularly helpful resource here is the Treasury of Celebrations that is put out each year by Alternatives for Simple Living, PO Box 2857, Sioux City, Ia 51106. [800-821-6153]

We need to enable people to be more innovative in creating a new rhythm in their timetables and also a new pattern of stewardship in how to use our other resources including money. Once we have biblically redefined the good life it is time we all asked the question, 'How much is enough?' How much do we need to spend on ourselves in a way that is consistent with our sense of vocation.

Part of our serious problem here is that our view of Christian stewardship is wrong. The standard teaching in most Protestant churches is tithe stewardship. I believe it fragments our sense of responsibility. Understanding the Old Testament

origins of the tithe, a growing number of New Testament
scholars tell us there is no basis for 10% stewardship in the
New Testament. The call to follow Christ in the New
Testament is a whole life proposition.

Dualistic Christianity typically teaches that after you bring
your tithe (or some part of your tithe) into the store house you
can pretty much do what you want with the rest. You can buy
whatever toys you want and live as lavishly as you want—as
long as you don't get a materialistic hang-up about all your
things. It is amazing how many American Christians seem to
be able to live palatially without ever getting hung up about
materialism. Too often our Christian leaders in the US are the
pace setters for this kind of economic upscaling.

What isn't taught very often is that the issue isn't just one
of 'materialistic hang-ups'. We are part of the international
body of Jesus Christ. There is something profoundly wrong
when some of us live lavishly and other Christians in our
world can't feed their children. The only way the Church has
any hope of reversing our declining giving patterns is to
enable people to find creative ways to become whole life
stewards.

Planting a seed in communities of support and accountability

A ten-week course will not be enough to
keep us on track in this tough area. We will
need community and accountability. In a
Mennonite church in Goshen, Indiana, every
member is a part of a small group in which
they pray and study Scripture together. But
twice a year they do something that terrifies
American Evangelicals when I tell them
about it. Twice a year they bring their timetables and their
budgets to the group. They ask everyone in their group to hold

them mutually accountable for how they plan to use their time and money in the next six months in their struggle to put God's purposes first.

I would encourage you to have a celebration at the end of the course as people begin their journey into a more purposeful way of life. We need to remind one another that the decision to follow Christ may also cost us our very lives as it has done for many of our sisters and brothers in other parts of the world. The only way we can possibly be whole life disciples and stand against the principalities and powers of our age is to be part of communities of faith where we are known, loved and held accountable like the Mennonites.

Beyond culturally accommodated churches— reinventing communities of faith for a new millennium

In *Reinventing American Protestantism,* Donald Miller identifies the most creative expression of the Church in America today as the 'new paradigm churches' because they are doing a better job meeting the needs of their clientele than mainline churches.[9] While the seeker-friendly churches, like Calvary Chapel, Vineyard Christian Fellowship, Saddleback and Willow Creek are often displaying more growth and vitality than their mainline counterparts, I am not sure they are any longer the innovative edge of the Church as we enter a new millennium. But they have been the growing edge in the nineties.

There is a tremendous amount of creativity going on in church planting globally that is causing many to rethink and reinvent what it means to be the Church. The Web Chapel has a chaplain, a Bible study opportunity and offers counselling and prayer. But is an on-line community really a church?

A new generation of young leaders all over the world are

creating some very innovative models of the Church for a new millennium. For instance, a string of innovative twenty-something churches are being planted all over the US and are connected and resourced by the Leadership Network that is providing support without control. This network of twenty-something churches rejects the user-friendly, highly programmatic mega-church models. They are busy fashioning a more relational post-modern model of what the Church could look like.[10]

Planting a seed in the Brown Bear pub

Some twenty year olds in Britain planted yet another model of tomorrow's church to reach out to Caribbean young people—the Brown Bear pub in London. They created a reggae band to lead worship and opened their doors for witness. One night during a foot-washing service a Jamaican drug dealer slipped into the back of the worship space. He didn't realise he was in a 'church' and when he saw this white guy down on the floor washing his Nikes it got his attention. He is now the sergeant of arms at the Brown Bear pub, seriously considering the claims of Christ.

Planting a seed in the parallel universe

Mark Pierson and Mike Riddell created an alternative worship experience for twenty to forty year olds in Auckland, New Zealand called Parallel Universe. They rented a night club, set up floor-to-ceiling screens on three sides of the space with tables and chairs in the middle. They have created a highly visual, innovative worship space with everything happening on all three screens at the same time. One night the focus for this largely non-believing audience was on the grace of God. They started out with limbo dancing, 'how low can you go?'

Rethinking what it means to be the Church

What I am arguing is not that we simply need to be more innovative but rather we need to be more innovative on purpose. We need to fundamentally reinvent the Church in a way that more authentically reflects a biblical theology of the Church and equips believers to serve God in the very demanding world of the twenty-first century.

It is past time for Protestants, particularly conservative Protestants, to do some fresh biblical work on the theology of the Church. We need to be much clearer as to *why we do what we do*. Avery Dulles, in his classic book on ecclesiology, *Models of the Church*, offers ten models of the Church from Church as institution and sacrament to the Church as community and servant.

In *Resident Aliens,* Stanley Hauerwas and William H. Willimon compellingly remind us that as the exiled people of God our home is not in this modern world. They describe the community of faith as 'a colony . . . a beachhead, an outpost, an island of one culture in the middle of another, a place where the values of home are reiterated and passed on to the young, a place where the distinctive language and lifestyle of resident aliens are lovingly nurtured and reinforced.'[11] Part of the problem with our view of the Church is that we tend to see it more as a place we go to than as an alien community we are part of.

Missiologist David Bosch explained that the view of church as *a place to go* was an unintentional product of the Reformation. George Hunsberger adds, 'This perception of church gives little attention to the church as communal entity or presence, and it stressed less the community's role as the bearer of missional responsibility throughout the world, both near and far away. "Church" is conceived in this view as *the place where* a Christianized civilization gathers for worship, and *the place where* the Christian character of society is cultivated.'[12]

As one reads the book of Acts, the Church, that first alien community, really wasn't defined as a building you go to once a week. It was much more of a living breathing community that was 'breaking bread from house to house', sharing life, sharing resources all centred in the worship of the living God.

I am firmly convinced that the first call of the gospel isn't to proclamation and I am committed to evangelism. And I don't believe that the first call of the gospel is to social action and I am very concerned for the poor. I believe the first call of the gospel is to incarnation. Only as we flesh out in community something of the right-side-up values of God's new order do we have any basis to speak or act.

Marcus Borg describes this new community of the Spirit as a counter-cultural community in the dominant Roman-Jewish culture of their day. 'Jesus sought to transform his social world by creating an alternative community structured around compassion . . . Thus Jesus saw the life of the Spirit as incarnational, informing and transforming the life of the culture.'[13]

British theologian Michael Green understood that the first church wasn't a place you go. It was an incarnational community where people found a home and were being transformed in every part of their lives.

They made the grace of God credible by a society of love and mutual care which astonished pagans and was recognised as something entirely new. It lent persuasiveness to the claim that the new age had dawned in Christ. The word was not only announced but seen in the community of those who were giving it flesh. The message of the kingdom became more than an idea. A new human community had sprung up and looked very much like the new order to which the evangelist had pointed. Here love was given daily expression; reconciliation was actually occurring; people were no longer divided into Jews and Gentiles, slave and free, male and female. In this community the weak were protected, the stranger welcomed. People were healed, the poor and dispossessed were cared for and found justice. Everything was shared. Joy abounded and ordinary lives were filled with praise.[14]

Rodney Clapp argues that the Church wasn't primarily intended to be an institution but a family. To follow the Christ of the New Testament requires that we give our first allegiance to a new family—'the first family' of God. Listen to Rodney Clapp: 'Jesus creates a new family. It is the new first family, a family of his followers that now demands primary allegiance. In fact, it demands allegiance over the old first family, the biological family. Those who do the will of the Father (ie, live under the reign of God) are now brothers and sisters to one another.'[15]

In other words, I believe that the Church at its best is called to be a new community centred in the worship of the living God, offering a glimpse of the character of the great home-coming of God and sharing life and resources like a large extended family. Robert Banks tells us that becoming a part of this family altered how members stewarded their resources. 'The principle of mutual financial support . . . lay at the heart' of this new community.[16] One of the major reasons they formed communities and shared resources was to focus their lives outwardly in witness and service to others.

If we began creating churches that weren't institutions quietly sanctioning the values of the dominant culture but rather communities for resident aliens, how would we redesign our churches? If we started planting churches that weren't places where people worshipped once a week but extended families where believers shared life and resources, how would we reinvent our churches? What kind of churches will we need to equip people to live in either the future of the long boom or the slow melt down?

A radical proposal for planting churches for the third millennium

I have a radical proposal. I recommend that we experiment in planting some new 'church plants' that are less buildings we worship in once a week and more new human settlements we live in seven days a week where we also happen to worship. Much is being written by architects on new village design, new urban community design and co-operative housing projects.

One of the new design groups in the US calls themselves the Congress for the New Urbanism. In Britain the counterpart organisation is called the Urban Village Group. What they share in common is a commitment to creating living urban environments that are more than roads, houses and gardens. They are trying to create people-friendly communities that foster neighbourliness and community co-operation rarely found in suburban communities.[17]

Planting a seed in a new Christian settlement

 If we invented new models of the Church that were first of all new human settlements centred in worship and committed to mutual care and mission, what might they look like? To be honest I am not exactly sure but let me sketch a bit. Imagine a 'church plant' that is actually a newly designed intergenerational community for sixty people. Architects, the-ologians and Christians committed to more radical biblical discipleship would design this community from the ground up in a way that reflected more the values and rhythms of the great home-coming than the values and rigours of the Western dream. They would be designed in a way that facilitated community and mutual care, becoming a large extended family in Christ committed to mission in the world.

In a Southern Baptist home in Tennessee, a nine-year-old comes home from school and spends an hour every day helping an older woman with her chores before he plays or does his homework. Imagine a community in which every member covenants to barter three hours a week to provide mutual care so we become the body of Christ in real terms and reduce the amount of resources every nuclear family has to set aside for pensions and disability care.

One of the major benefits of such a model is that monthly living costs could be significantly reduced through building less expensive dwellings, providing low interest loans and mutual care. Residents could have more of their lives back to invest in worship, prayer, weekly ministry in their neighbourhood and celebration of their faith. This community could become highly self-reliant, growing much of their own food and caring for creation as a part of their witness.

I am not suggesting that every believer should be part of

this kind of unusual residential church plant. But with the mounting pressures of a McWorld future we are all going to need to be in communities where we are known, loved and held accountable. Building strong mutually supportive Christian community committed to mission will be one of the most important tasks for the Church in the twenty-first century.

Planting a cooperative seed in Denmark

 Part of the imagination for designing new residential settlements for mutual support comes out of studying the co-housing movement. Over twenty years ago people in Denmark, who weren't particularly religious, concluded, based on their own experience, that single detached family housing wasn't necessarily the good life that modern culture contended it was. They invented something new. It is called co-housing. Essentially it is like a condominium with a purpose. It bears no resemblance to the hippie communes of the sixties.

Envision a two-storey dwelling that houses seventy-five people. Instead of every family having their own back garden and front garden this co-housing complex has one co-operative area where all the children play together and another where everyone gardens together. Instead of every dwelling in the co-op. having their own large recreation room they constructed one recreation room for the entire community. They have meals in this common room every evening at a cost of roughly a dollar a person. Each couple cooks once every two months. However, you don't have to eat there. Everyone has their own kitchen too.

People who live in these co-operative housing complexes report they much prefer a way of life that is more co-operative where they share child care, gardening and meals. Widows and singles state they much prefer it to living alone. In fact, they report it is as though they have been engrafted into a larger family where people care for one another.

This co-housing movement is growing at a very rapid rate in the US and Britain. But virtually all of those involved in this kind of experimentation are social progressives. They want to create new living arrangements for themselves and their children that more genuinely reflect their values instead of those handed to them by the culture. (You can contact the *Co-housing Magazine* for more info at: cohomag@aol.com)

In our dualistic Christianity it doesn't seem to have occurred to us very often that we aren't obligated to accept all the models that modern culture hands to us. The single family detached house didn't come with the ark of the covenant—and it is among the most expensive ways to live.

Considering co-operative stewardship in a needy world

Looking at the costs of the single family detached model

Let's look at the cost of the single family detached model in the North American context. Many Christians will wind up spending over two and a half times what their homes are worth on interest. Many of the couples we work with in the US and Canada will spend from $500,000 to $1 or 2 million US dollars over thirty years for shelter.

It costs roughly $250,000 to raise a child in this model. A report on CNN estimated that the average couple who are fifty-five will need to put away $1.5 million to retire comfortably in the US. Calculate the enormous amount that must be taken out of the life income of your congregation over twenty years to meet these kinds of legitimate needs. As we have seen, in a McWorld future the state is likely to shift more of the costs of education, health care and retirement back to the individual raising the costs still higher. And these costs are rising for many of our young in particular.

Considering the possibilities of a co-operative stewardship model

Let's look at the cost savings of one group of Christians who have been sharing the costs of a co-operative model in North America for almost a hundred years. Some 30,000 Hutterites live in co-operative communities in Canada and the US. I visited one of these communities and was impressed by how they attempt to authentically live out the kingdom in every aspect of their life together.

They explained that as a result of living a co-operative lifestyle they are able to significantly reduce their living costs compared to the single family detached model. The cost of constructing a three-bedroomed home connected to other units is only $32,000. The monthly per person cost is only $190, for everything including shelter, food, health care and retirement. That is less than $800 a month for a family of four. Which frees up a lot of time and money for other uses.

This particular community is very generous with the resources they free up. They give generously to those in need in Bosnia and to urban ministries in the US. And families from this community routinely spend a few hours every week outside their community visiting prisons, working with the poor and helping senior citizens and the disabled in their neighbourhood.

I am not for a minute suggesting that we all become Hutterites. But I think we can learn from their co-operative stewardship model of ways we can in community, be better stewards of the time and money God has entrusted to us. I am certain we could all find ways to be more a part of God's loving response to the growing needs of tomorrow's world. Couldn't people of Christian faith also create new living arrangements that more authentically reflect the values of the kingdom instead of the values of modern culture? Couldn't we create not a single model but a range of models that more authentically reflect the biblical values that we claim?

Planting a seed in a six plex to set the young free

I am very concerned about the rising costs of shelter for a new generation. For the last six years I have been presenting a modest diagram of a six-unit co-operative community that is intentionally designed to help the under-thirty-fives get out from under the burden of huge mortgages so they have more of their life to invest in the advance of God's mustard-seed movement. Assume this six-plex co-op. will be planted in a community where a two-bedroomed house sells for $150,000. (But remember that a young couple who purchases that house will end up spending close to half a million for it over thirty years.) LeeRoy Troyer, a Mennonite architect, helped me design this co-op model.

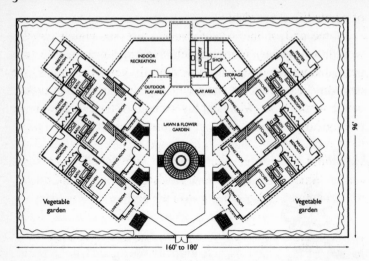

In the co-op I am presenting, a three-bedroomed, bath and a half unit could probably be constructed for $60-70,000 a unit (with some invested labour) on a third of an acre site. This six-plex would also include a shared recreation room, shared laundry and a common garden area for the children to play in. There are two more bedrooms upstairs in each of the six units.

I am proposing an alternative mortgage scheme in which six older Christian couples in the same church who are well financed each provide a $60,000 no-interest loan for each of these six younger couples. They would get their $60,000 back in five years. All they would 'lose' is the interest. For that small sacrifice they would be responsible for a double whammy. These six young couples, instead of spending half a million dollars over thirty years, would spend $60,000 over five years to provide a home for themselves and their families.

If these six young couples were willing to pay two more years after payout for the kingdom, that would free up $144,000 to provide housing for a hundred families in Uganda or three to four Habitat for Humanity houses in the same neighbourhood where they live. Do you see the possibilities of whole life stewardship?

At the end of the seventh year, these six young couples wouldn't have any mortgage left. Nothing in the Bible suggests that we are obligated to work thirty years for a mortgage company. We could set some young people free. Then if they could work it out with employers both spouses could work twenty hours a week instead of forty to eighty—not just to have more time for their children and leisure activities. Then we would have some young people who would have some serious time available to work for 'sight to the blind, release to the captives and good news to the poor'.

Reinventing the Church to put first things first

Let me share one fresh model of those who are reinventing the Church in a way that both compellingly reflects biblical principles and is preparing the believers to become more engaged in compassionate response to the challenges of tomorrow's world. Rockridge United Methodist Church is located in a multi-cultural urban neighbourhood in Oakland, California. They began the process of reinventing themselves from a typical mainline church that was fairly corporate in its structure to a much more organic relational model of church as family modelled after the Church of the Savior in Washington DC.

While the church growth movement has largely focused on numerical growth, Rockridge church is much more focused on qualitative growth. They are intent on making disciples who attempt to observe all of Christ's teachings. You will remember their primary vehicle for this. They not only call their members to whole life discipleship and stewardship, they institute disciplines, like good Methodists, to ensure they grow in every area of their life. All members are encouraged to become covenant members which calls for a yearly commitment to the disciplines of a covenant group which includes:

1. A daily commitment to at least thirty minutes in prayer and Scripture study;

2. A commitment to allow the rhythms of our lives to be dictated by our faith instead of the culture—including keeping the Sabbath holy;

3. They covenant to consistent participation in the worship and educational life of the community 'unless prevented';

4. They covenant to develop and use their spiritual gifts not only in the church but out in the community. They devote one evening a week to be part of a small mission covenant group. Then they invest an additional two to four hours a week to do ministry with their group;

5. They covenant to manifest, with God's help, something of the fruit of the Spirit and strive against sin. It is in these covenant groups that believers are both nurtured and held accountable as they are formed into God's new family;

6. They covenant to a form of whole life stewardship that begins with the tithe and then goes up from there. They report, 'From this foundation we find God making us more generous. We are becoming aware of the dangers of our society's consumerism, and we can see how to be better stewards of God's creation.'[18]

A seed planted in a co-op community in Oakland

One of the most intriguing Mission Covenant Groups are the Community Builders. This MCG is committed to planting a new 'expression of God's love in . . . North Oakland'. These folks are the first Christians I have found anywhere who actually began constructing a co-housing project, called the Temescal Co-housing project, to provide another model of how to be the community of God's people in a rapidly changing world. Six church families are designing a nine-unit co-housing project built around a lovely old Victorian house. The common space includes: a dining hall, a children's play room, a workshop, guest rooms, laundry facilities and garden.[19]

The Temescal Co-housing project first of all aims to create an intergenerational multicultural community that will operate like a large extended family sharing evening meals, child care, prayer and Bible study, vehicles and engagement with their immediate neighbourhood. These folks are already providing a homework centre for neighbourhood children, a computer centre for adults and youth and providing affordable housing. They want to show hospitality to their local neighbours and host community celebrations like the young people in East London. They are designing the whole co-housing project in a way that models sustainable gardening and responsible stewardship of God's good creation.

I am convinced that this small planting of God's kingdom is going to grow a much larger tree than they realise. I believe it will have an impact not only in their own lives, congregation and community but will become a model for many other high-risk disciples who want to put first things first. It is a small foretaste of the great home-coming of God.

Anglican Franciscan, Brother Samuel SSF, is one of a growing number who are calling for a remonking of the Church. Brother Samuel reflects, 'Monastic life may seem utterly out of tune with the spirit of our times, yet if we are entering another Dark Age, it may be to the wisdom of such a way the Church of today needs to turn . . . I sense that the renewal of both the Church and society will come through the re-emerging forms of Christian community that are homes of generous hospitality, places of challenging reconciliation, and centres of attentiveness to the living God.'[20]

We are galloping into a future that is changing at breakneck speed. As we race into a globalised future, a little faith worked in around the edges won't begin to equip us for the challenges of a new millennium. We will need to call the people of God to a more biblically radical whole life faith and whole life communities that more authentically reflect the mission of the mustard seed than the addictions of modern culture. This provides a unique opportunity for Christian leaders who are willing to take some risks.

Opportunities for Christian leaders

How should leaders prepare Christians to reinvent their lives to put God's purposes first in order to creatively engage the challenges of a new millennium? Leaders have the opportunities:

1. To both call and enable their members to become whole life disciples and whole life stewards;

2. To begin this process through assisting individuals and families to use Scripture to draft personal and family mission statements;

3. To design a ten-week course (using the outline in this chapter) to enable the people to use their mission statement to reorder their private worlds and reinvent their lives;

4. To help members create small support communities where they are known, loved and held accountable. Some leaders then may want to explore creating new co-operative or co-housing communities where believers can more authentically flesh out the values of the mustard seed in a McWorld future.

Questions for discussion and action

1. What is the difference between whole life discipleship and dualistic discipleship?
2. What was the result of Jesus Christ and that first community of disciples putting the purposes of God at the centre of their lives?
3. Working from Scripture and prayer, try to discern how God is calling you to use your life to be a part of what God is doing to make a difference in the world. Write down your personal mission statement and share it with your family and your small group.
4. Begin the creative adventure of reinventing your timetable and lifestyle to put your sense of mission purpose first. Ask your small group to hold you accountable and be sure to add some celebration to your life.
5. If you are not part of a small group where you are known, loved and held accountable, prayerfully create one. If you are part of a small group, consider creating a residential model where, together with others, you can more authentically live out the values of faith in an alien culture and reduce your lifestyle costs so you have more of your life to invest in the advance in kingdom mission.
6. Create a celebration for people in your church that helps them enter into the celebration of the great home-coming of God.

Notes

1 Tom Sine, *Live It Up! How to Create a Life You Can Love* (Herald Press: Scottdale, Az., 1993), p.185.
2 Emil Brunner, *Christianity and Civilisation* (Charles Scribner's Sons: New York), 1948, p.157.
3 Harvey Cox, *Feast of Fools: A Theological Essay on*

Festivity and Fantasy (Harvard University Press: Cambridge, 1969), pp.9-10.

4 Dietrich Bonhoeffer, *The Cost of Discipleship* (Macmillan Publishing Co. Inc: New York, 1959), p.89.

5 Athol Gill, *The Fringes of Freedom: Following Jesus, Living Together, Working for Justice* (Lancer: Homebush, Australia, 1990), p.30.

6 Joe Dominguez and Vicki Robin, *Your Money or Your Life: Transforming Your Relationship with Money and Achieving Financial Independence* (Penguin Books: New York, 1992).

7 Bob Buford, *Half Time: Changing Your Game Plan from Success to Significance* (Zondervan: Grand Rapids, Mi., 1994), p.164.

8 Richard Foster, *Streams of Living Water: Celebrating the Great Traditions of Christian Faith* (Harper: San Francisco, Ca., 1998).

9 Donald E. Miller, *Reinventing American Protestantism: Christianity in the New Millennium* (University of California Press: Berkeley, 1997), p.3.

10 Sally Morgenthaler, 'Out of the Box: Authentic Worship in a Postmodern Culture', *Worship Leader*, May/June 1998, p.25.

11 Stanley Hauerwas and William H.Willimon, *Resident Aliens: Life in the Christian Colony* (Abingdon Press: Nashville, Tn., 1990), p.12.

12 George Hunsberger, 'Missional Vocation: Called and Sent to Represent the Reign of God', Darrell L. Guder, editor, *Missional Church: A Vision for the Sending of the Church in North America* (William B. Eerdmans: Grand Rapids, Mi., 1988), p.78.

13 Marcus J. Borg, *Jesus A New Vision: Spirit, Culture, and the Life of Discipleship* (Harper and Row: San Francisco, 1987), p.142.

14 Quoted in Jim Wallis, *The Call to Conversion: Recovering the Gospel for These Times* (Harper & Row: San Francisco, 1981), p.15.

15 Rodney Clapp, *Family at the Crossroads: Beyond Traditional and Modern Options* (InterVarsity Press: Downers Grove, Ill., 1993), pp.76, 77.

16 Robert Banks, *Paul's Idea of Community: The Early House Churches in Their Historical Setting* (William B. Eerdmans: Grand Rapids, Mi., 1980), p.90.

17 Sarah Boxer, 'A remedy for the Rootlessness of Modern Suburban Life?' *The New York Times*, 1 August, 1998, p.13.

18 Rockridge United Methodist, 'Our Covenant', Annotated and Updated, pp.7.7 and 7.8.

19 Rockridge United Methodist Church Mission Covenant Groups: Hearing and Following The Spirit's Call, On the Inward Journey and Sanctification and the Outward Journey of Mission.

20 Brother Samuel SSF, 'Mission and Community' (British Bible Society, 18 July – 9 August 1998), p.14.

10
Reinventing Christian mission for the third millennium

Torrential rains and floods swept down a steep ravine in Jalapa, Mexico where the poorest families live in little flimsy shacks which hug the hillside. It was 1.30 in the morning and Saul Cruz's wife Pilar had not come home. He was praying fervently because he feared his wife had been lost in the floods. She had left home early in the evening to try to help one of her friends who lived in one of those little shanties. Finally she returned home exhausted at 2.00am. Saul and their children welcomed her with tremendous relief and joy.

In this devastating flood back in 1989, hundreds of homes were destroyed and thirty-one people lost their lives. Pilar sat down with her husband, Saul, and declared that the solution to this problem must be helping people like her friend in Jalapa build safe houses so they and their families wouldn't be at risk every time the torrential rain and floods came. But Saul knew nothing about construction. He had brought his family to this community to plant a church. But in response to Pilar's passionate concern he found a man who was a builder and organised a handful of volunteers from the community. Together they built two sturdy basic homes. It was a very small beginning—a mustard seed.

If you had seen Jalapa in 1989 you wouldn't recognise it today. 'Two million people living on the sides of a precipitous ravine, often muddy, always dangerous. Raw sewage poured down the hillsides into the streams where children played and the poorest built their shacks out of milk cartons. Now the area has been transformed. Electricity, paved streets, piped drinking water, concrete channels for sewers. Hardly a shack to be seen.'[1]

Originally Saul and Pilar came to this community to bring good news to the poor and plant an Evangelical church. But they had absolutely no idea of what that good news would be or how God would use their lives to make a difference for God's kingdom. Someone gave them a rubbish tip and Saul prayed over the tip. For three months Saul prayed over the rubbish tip every day for wisdom. God answered those prayers.

One of the leaders of the community volunteered to help Saul and Pilar make a start on their garbage dump and the community pitched in. Slowly a community centre emerged from the rubbish heap that became the centre for the transformation of the entire community. Pilar, working with mothers and children in the community started homework clubs and a range of other children's activities. Saul solicited help from the mayor to secure resources to rebuild this shanty community. Tear Fund England was invited to partner in the project. They not only provided some of the resources for housing construction, they created micro-enterprise projects like producing red-roof tiles to provide income for the unemployed in the community.

During this entire time Paul and Pilar held a Bible study in their home. But they resisted sponsoring large evangelistic meetings. They wanted to see their demonstration of God's love touch the people. One day a man who was a chronic drunk had a dramatic conversion experience which God used to break things wide open. The people crowded out their home and they now have a thriving church in the community centre on the former rubbish tip. The centre is called Armonia which is the closest Spanish word to the Hebrew word shalom. Their dream is to see the continuing transformation of the community through the word and deed ministry of Armonia.

Saul said there are three reasons why they work in Jalapa: 'compassion, obedience and indignation. Compassion for the suffering people, for their needs; obedience to Jesus Christ who has sent us to work among the poor; and indignation, because we get indignant when people created in God's image suffer in this way.'[2]

Defining the focus

 Saul and Pilar are among a growing number of our sisters and brothers all over the world who are discovering first hand that God is working through the mustard seed to change our world. God invites all of our communities of faith to become instruments of the shalom purposes of God in a world of growing need.

In this chapter we will argue that we need to radically reinvent how we carry out missions to both more effectively address the challenges of tomorrow's world and to more authentically advance the mustard seed purposes of God. There has been a dramatic growth in short-term missions, more missionaries are being sent by the Church in the Two Thirds World and more churches have been planted among unreached people groups.

But I find that those active in missions tend to focus on the up side and not deal seriously with either the new challenges ahead or the extent to which we haven't really worked hard enough to define *why we do what we do* in missions. As a consequence I am afraid that sometimes we get the story wrong and use methods that contradict the faith we claim.

We will begin by going back to the future one last time to highlight some of the new challenges facing Christian missions in a new millennium. Then we will go back to the Bible and work to get our story straight. Finally we will share with you imaginative new ways that Christians all over the world are finding to manifest something of God's mustard seed in response to the mounting challenges of our globalised future.

Back to the future—one last time

This book opened with a ride on the wild side that reminded all of us that we are living in a world changing at blinding speed. Too many of us are also experiencing rides on the wet side because we are not spending enough time paying attention to how both the arenas in which we carry out mission and function as a church are changing.

Ray Bakke, a Christian urban specialist, stresses how important it is to understand the urban context—to 'exegete the city' before we develop missions strategies. What I am advocating is that mission executives, missiologists and leaders in local churches make our best effort to anticipate how the context in which we carry out mission is likely to change in the future—before we strategise.

The physical needs of people in many poorer countries (particularly on the African continent) are likely to increase significantly if the global meltdown spreads. The good news is that the Church in the Two Thirds World will take more leadership in missions and in the worldwide Church in the coming century.

Even if we resume the long boom worldwide, it is clear that

many of the world's poorest residents will not benefit if they don't receive help in becoming competitive players in this tough 'new economy'. The forces of globalisation are bringing unprecedented pressures on families and local communities all over the planet.

The pressures of global competition are influencing many of our Western countries to cut back programmes to the poor at home and abroad. As we have seen, we are actually losing ground in the task of world evangelisation to both population growth and McWorld's rapidly expanding borderless youth market which is proving to be much more successful at reaching the hearts and minds of that next generation. So mission organisations need to gear up to do more—much more.

Of critical concern is the growing pressures of McWorld for those of us who are part of the Western Church to work longer and consume more. Which means that if we don't find a way to resist this growing pressure we will have less time and money left over to invest in mission. As we have also seen, the Western Church is declining in numbers and giving at a very alarming rate. Particularly concerning is the rapid disappearance of the under-thirty-fives from our churches and the declining discretionary time and money of many of those who stay with the Church.

Therefore my reluctant forecast, if we don't find ways to alter these trends, is that the Church in the West and many mission organisations are likely to have difficulty even sustaining their present levels of mission investment—over the next two decades. The mounting challenges facing us in a global future and the declining capacity of the Western Church to respond deserves much thoughtful discussion and creative action by missiologists, mission executives and practitioners.

Back to the Bible one last time—putting first things first in the Church

Many Western churches are much more highly invested in maintaining a place for worship and nurture for folks inside the building than making a difference in their community or their world.

In fact it is not unusual to find American churches, with big buildings and big budgets, that don't sponsor a single ministry outside their buildings. Pastors in the US often tell me 'that they don't believe doing ministry in the community is the church's responsibility. But it's fine if their members want to volunteer at the local rescue mission or help out at Big Brothers.' In informal sampling I have found that less than 20% of our time or money ever leaves the building in the average American church. I am convinced that our problem of priorities, at its core, is theological. Too many churches have become the protectors of the dominant values of modern culture not their critics.

British theologian, Alister McGrath, brings a very direct word on the dangers of this kind of cultural accommodation. Looking back on Christians who quietly supported the values that were part of Hitler's Germany he states:

> We are doing the same thing today, by allowing ourselves and our churches to follow societal norms and values, irrespective of their origins and goals. To allow our ideas and values to become controlled by anything or anyone other than the self-revelations of God in scripture is to adopt an ideology, rather than a theology; it is to become controlled by ideas and values whose origins lie outside the Christian tradition—and potentially to become enslaved to them.[3]

The Church exists not only to meet our spiritual needs and bring us into faith communities, it is also called to help transform our values from those of the culture to those of the king-dom. The Bible reminds us that the Church doesn't exist pri-marily for itself but for others. We are called on to place mis-sion at the centre of our congregational life as 'resident aliens' who are intended, by God's grace, to be a very rough sample of God's great home-coming celebration. And we are called to share the good news of God's new order in word and deed and by unmasking the values of the dominant culture.

Recovering the theology of first things

Everywhere I work with the Church I find many Christian leaders who act as though all the questions about what it means to be the Church and carry out the mission of the Church have been answered. Now it's just up to us to go out there and do it. I for one am not convinced that all the ques-tions have been answered. I believe that too often we operate from a set of 'immaculate assumptions'. If we ever thought-fully checked out *why we do what we do* we would discover many of us are in serious trouble. And I think we will also discover why mission has been marginalised in many of our churches.

There is a great deal of talk these days among Christian leaders in Britain and North America about revival and the renewal of the Church that sometimes tends to focus us inwardly on ourselves. Wilbert Schenk, a missiologist, wrote a very compelling article in the International Bulletin of Missionary Research arguing that the renewal of the Church and mission are inseparably related.

Authentic renewal of the church cannot be separated from mis-sion; the two are integrally linked. Both arise from the same the-ological foundation: God's covenant with Abraham was for the blessing of the nations, and this covenant was renewed and reaf-firmed in Jesus Christ. The people of God exist because of God's salvific intentions for the nations and the role they are to play in God's mission.[4]

Lesslie Newbigin reminds us that 'The church is not an end in itself. The growth and the prosperity of the church is not the goal of history.' Jesus instead prepared a community to be a 'chosen bearer of the secret of the kingdom . . . to embody and announce the reign of God.'[5] The establishment of God's new order is a fulfilment of the blessing to the nations that God covenanted with Abraham and Sarah. Newbigin stresses that this is God's initiative and the creator will indeed bring into being the promised new order through the death and the resurrection of God's chosen one.

Reflecting on the current transition of the Church in North America from a modern to a post-modern culture, George Hunsberger states that we must do much more than 'mere tinkering with long assumed notions about the identity and mission of the church . . . there is a need for reinventing or rediscovering the church.' Building on Newbigin's call for the people of God to 'embody and announce the reign of God', Hunsberger proposes that we reinvent the Church to become missional communities where mission is no longer a programmatic activity but is at the centre of our shared life as a sent community.[6]

The early Celtic Christian community, in the sixth to seventh centuries, understood that to follow Christ they were called into mission and existed as a sent community that stood against the dominant culture of their time. While the Roman Church coming into England from the south was often preoccupied with power and status, the Celtic Church coming down from the north was a community of servants identifying with the poor. They were much more focused on making a difference than making a comfortable existence.

Seeds of hope

Planting a seed in Christchurch

In Britain, Australia and New Zealand the churches I have worked with seem to be more outwardly focused. They typically sponsor several ministries in the community and seem to give a larger share of their total budget to missions. For instance, Spreydon Baptist, in Christchurch, New Zealand is a church that places the biblical call to mission at the centre of congregational life, not at the margins. 60% of their total budget is invested in mission in their own community and overseas. They sponsor twenty-five thriving ministries to single-parent mothers, unemployed young people and those on welfare in Christchurch. A very high percentage of their 800 members are involved every week in these ministries.

One of their most creative ministries is called the Kingdom Trust. Essentially the Trust operates very much like a credit union in which those on the margins are given small loans so that they can start small businesses and become self-reliant. However, Spreydon Baptist not only lends the money but also makes available free business consultation. Over the years they have successfully enabled hundreds of people to become self-supporting again.

Planting a seed in London

Ichthus Fellowship in London is a mega church without a building. They rely heavily on home groups and rent a school auditorium once a month so the entire congregation can worship together. This enables them to invest a much greater share of their resources in mission to others. They sponsor a broad spectrum of ministries in London as well as overseas.

Planting a seed in La Puente

Casa de Señor is an unusual church plant that exists as a witness to God's love in La Puente, California. It is a Pentecostal Mennonite church. The church is pastored by two men and two women, all non-salaried. Consuelo Moreno is the minister of prayer. She works at a job from 3pm to 11pm to support her ministry. She arrives at the church early every morning and there is a steady stream of people from the community waiting for her to pray with them. Some are seeking prayer for healing, others for work and still others for discernment. They witness supernatural healings and deliverances which attracts others to this growing congregation. The church runs a sexual abstinence programme for young people in the community that has been so successful that the local school board is exploring adopting it. The church consists of three houses: one for worship, one for a community education centre and one for transitional housing for those in crisis.

Getting the story straight

Sometimes it is very hard work to get the story straight. Wycliffe translators working with the Illuit tribe in Alaska were stumped because they could find no word in the Illuit language for 'joy' as they were translating the New Testament. Finally, after weeks of struggle, one of the Illuit elders helped them solve their problem. Now the verse in question reads, 'There will be more tail wagging in heaven over one sinner who repents than over ninety-nine who need no repentance.'

We all need to work a little harder to make sure we get the story straight. I am concerned because some of those I have met who are the keenest for mission are, I believe, inadvertently working from the dualistic Christian model I discussed earlier. They are passionately committed to seeing people come to vital spiritual faith and begin to change their moral values. But they are oblivious of the need for disciples of Christ to invite God to change their cultural values.

While Western missionaries have learned to 'contextualise the gospel' when they go into other cultures they often seem oblivious to the extent to which we bring our own cultural values with us. As a consequence we often wind up unwittingly becoming evangelists for the aspirations and values that power McWorld instead of those that inspire the mustard seed.

Exporting the wrong message

The greater problem is that a number of Christians in the West have exported this very narrow spiritual view of the gospel all over the world. Several years ago an American missions organisation was working in a supportive relationship to the indigenous Haitian denomination of 300 churches. The head of this mission organisation, wanting to bless the president of this Baptist denomination, invited him to move into the missionary compound with the missionaries where they would construct a new home for him.

This compound, called the City of Light, was built on a hill above Les Cayes where it was cooled by the trade winds. The some forty missionaries who lived there had homes very much like they would have had back in the States, complete with electricity, stereo head phones and Haitian servants too.

Within three months of the time the president of the Haitian Baptist Church moved into his new American style home in The City of Light, a remarkable change started to take place in numbers of Baptist churches all over Haiti. Leadership cut back funding to literacy and community health projects. They then began using these funds to build a house for their pastor like the missionaries and now their president had.

The missionaries had come preaching Jesus with their lips while their lifestyles 'preached' the good news of the American dream. Jonathan Bonk documents how insidiously the affluent lifestyles of missionaries from the West have undermined Christian witness throughout the world in his important book *Missions and Money*.[7]

Latin American missiologist, Orlando Costas, indicted the Western Church for exporting a culturally accommodating gospel that calls people to 'a conscience-soothing Jesus, with an unscandalous cross; an other worldly kingdom; a private inwardly, individualistically limited Holy Spirit; a pocket God; a spiritualized Bible' and a Church that escapes the gut issues of society. It has conceived the goal of the gospel as a 'happy' comfortable, successful life. It has made possible 'the "conversion" of men and women without having to make any drastic changes in their lifestyles or world views', guaranteeing thereby 'the preservation of the status quo and the immobility of the people of God.'[8]

Mission on two tracks

One of the major afflictions of Protestantism, particularly conservative Protestantism, is that we have got the story wrong. At the core of our dualistic faith is the dualistic view of the future we discussed earlier. Too many of us have embraced a view of God's redemptive purposes as the saving of disembodied souls for a non-materialistic future in the clouds. This has inadvertently given rise to a two-track approach to mission all over the world.

One of the most concerning aspects of the Christian dualism model is that it tends to convey the impression that the good news of the gospel only has to do with the narrowly individual, spiritual aspects of personal faith. For instance, in 1996 I was invited to participate in a panel discussion of the Church's response to the poor at the Call to Renewal Conference. The other panelists included Brian Hehir, a Catholic scholar from Harvard, E. J. Dionne, a well-known Catholic author and conservative commentator Cal Thomas.

Cal Thomas made a forceful statement that illustrates the point I am trying to make. Cal stated, 'I recently interviewed Ralph Reed [then president of the Christian Coalition] and I particularly liked his response to one question I asked him. I asked, "What would happen if every member of the Christian Coalition began to live as their leader commanded them . . . and I am not talking about Pat Robertson?" Reed responded, "Loving their enemies, praying for those that persecuted them, feeding the hungry, clothing the naked, visiting those in prison." Cal stressed, "not as an end . . . not as an end . . . but as a means . . . because it gives you an entry to their hearts!'

I responded that I was raised in an Evangelical faith that saw salvation in the singularly personal and spiritual terms that Cal had emphasised. But I said that the very call to feed the hungry and visit the prisoner was a part of the vision of the prophet Isaiah that clearly reflected the purposes of God. Scripture teaches that God's redemptive purposes aren't just personal and spiritual. They are corporate and touch every aspect of human life. God's redemptive initiative 'includes the personal transformation we Evangelicals have always emphasised, but the Bible teaches that God also plans to renew a world and create a new community . . . and that is an end and not just a means.' The problem is that this viewpoint is not unique to Cal Thomas.

Beyond two-track mission—recovering the whole gospel for the whole world

This narrowly spiritual approach to the Christian message has inadvertently led to a two-track approach to mission. During the past sixty years there are those who have defined mission as simply proclamation evangelism, personal discipling and church planting. They have planted churches solely concerned with the spiritual needs of the members.[9]

Thirty years ago other Christians who held a broader view of Christian mission went to many of the same communities where church planters had been working and began doing Christian community development projects to help the poor help themselves. World Vision, Tear Fund England, World Concern (who are committed to holistic mission) are a few of dozens of Christian agencies that are all still actively involved in village level development projects.

As one travels in Africa, Asia and Latin America one can still find the legacy of this two-track approach to mission. You will still find churches focusing exclusively on the spiritual needs of their members and an agency like World Vision working in the same community to help primarily meet their economic and physical needs.

When I worked at World Concern, a CEO from a church-planting organisation asked me, 'Do you think my organisation should do community development?' I responded, 'Absolutely not. Your organisational mission is church planting. But I think you need to plant churches that find ways not only to address the spiritual but also the health care, educational and economic needs of their congregations so that Christian development agencies never have to come to their villages.' I am convinced if we, like Saul and Pilar, could do our mission on a single track the witness for the gospel would be much stronger.

Defining why we do what we do—*in search of an integrated approach to mission*

To do this we will need to do some really fresh biblical work. A very important conversation has been going on in the Church for the past thirty years regarding the nature of its mission among mainline Protestants, Roman Catholics and Evangelicals. Let me mention a few highlights. For those of us of the Evangelical tradition the Lausanne Covenant 1974 is our touchstone for a new movement into a more integrated single-track approach to mission. '[Evangelism and socio-political] involvement are both part of our Christian duty. For both are necessary expressions of our doctrines of God and man, our love for our neighbor and our obedience to Jesus Christ.'[10]

At CRESR 1982 the relationship between evangelism and social responsibility was defined as the relationship between two wings on a bird or two oars in a boat. They were seen as being inseparable. I had the responsibility of organising another conference called Wheaton 1983: The Church in Response to Human Need, where we invited Christian leaders to define our biblical responsibility to the poor.

David Bosch states:

> For the first time in an official statement emanating from an international evangelical conference the perennial dichotomy was overcome. Without ascribing priority to either evangelism or social involvement, the Wheaton '83 Statement . . . declared, 'Evil is not only in human hearts but also in social structures . . . The mission of the church includes both the proclamation of the Gospel and its demonstration. We must therefore evangelize, respond to immediate human needs and press for social transformation.[11]

Evangelical leaders in Britain, like Steve Gaukroger, are much clearer about the unity of our biblical mission than many I have worked with in other parts of the Western Church. Gaukroger writes, 'The Bible consistently describes mission in terms of compassion as well as communication, that is by works as well as words.'[12]

Since the early eighties we seem to have moved into a defacto recognition that mission is broader than simply addressing people's spiritual needs. I say defacto because this growing consensus doesn't seem to have come out of biblical reflection but simply embracing normative views of mission of the ever-changing Evangelical world view. However, I still run into numbers of people, including those in leadership, who are still pre-Lausanne '74 in their view of mission.

Let me explain. We need to do some fresh thinking about a theology of mission. When World Vision was exploring getting involved in urban mission in the United States, back in the early eighties, Paul Landry asked me to criticise one of their earliest proposals for an urban ministry project in Houston, Texas. The proposal presented strategies for meeting housing needs, economic needs and nutritional needs of an inner-city neighbourhood but there was no discussion of the theological assumptions undergirding the project. In my response I wrote, 'What if you successfully met all these unmet needs for shelter, financial income and an improved diet in Houston, would the kingdom of God come on earth? Or are we after something more than simply "need meeting"?'

Many Christians, even those who have a more wholistic theology, tend to chronically view mission on two tracks: as individual 'need meeting' and 'soul saving'. Part of the reason we haven't done a very good job of developing an integrated approach to mission is that we haven't spent enough time attempting to define a biblical picture of what God's ultimate purposes are for God's people and God's world.

Consulting with the leadership team of a Christian missions organisation in Britain, I asked the question: 'What are you trying to accomplish in the communities of the poor you work with in terms of a sense of biblical purpose?' The CEO immediately spoke up and said, 'Our organisation works with the poorest of the poor in helping them meet their basic needs and we work in partnership with a number of different agencies in this mission.'

I responded, 'I understand your programmatic goals but what would one village in India look like if you accomplished your sense of what God's purposes are for that community?' He suddenly blurted out, 'My God, we have never biblically defined what our end game is! We have never biblically defined what we are trying to accomplish in the transformation of a given community!'

Defending *why we do what we do*—listening to God through Scripture and community

Most churches and mission organisations seldom attempt to do the hard work of biblically defining *why they do what they do* in mission. Most churches I work with are afflicted by what I call 'chronic randomness', with the men's group going one direction, the women's group another and all holding a potluck supper once a year to celebrate their activities. But no one knows how it all comes together. Churches typically have a mission statement to accompany all their random activity. But it is rare to find a congregation that has developed a mission statement out of Scripture study and then refocused all their activity to reflect that mission statement.

It is even rarer to find Christian organisations that have done the hard biblical work of defining *why we do what we do* in mission . . . where they have actually drafted an operational theology of mission. I can guarantee that when we work from largely unstated assumptions in our personal lives or organisations, the values of the dominant culture are going to slip in and shape not only what we do but how we do it. And we won't even notice.

Planting a seed by listening to Scripture at Luther Place

Luther Place is a largely white congregation in Washington DC that found itself in an increasingly non-white and needy community. Like many white congregations in that situation it took a vote as to whether to move their church to the all-white suburbs or stay put. To their surpise the vote was to stay put. Before they were perfectly content simply to be a Lutheran Church doing random activities for their members. But if they were going to stay in this community they felt they needed a clear sense of biblical purpose. Members became involved in a very serious study of the Gospels and received what they believed was God's call to their congregation: 'As God is hospitality to us in the bread and the wine of the Eucharist, we feel called to be the hospitality of Christ in this needy community.' They followed up by scrapping a number of their random activities for people inside the building and created a range of new ministries in urban housing and tutoring programmes that were clearly related to their sense of biblical call. You see, not only individual believers and families need biblical mission statements—so do churches.

Planting a seed—listening to Scripture at World Concern

 In the mid-eighties I helped World Concern draft their first operational theology of mission. We secured the services of New Testament theologian Eugene Lemcio and Old Testament scholar Steven Hayner (presently the CEO of Intervarsity Christian Fellowship in the US). The mission statement focused on what they understood to be God's ultimate purpose: To reconcile us in Christ, not only to God, but to one another and to God's good creation through nurturing strong churches. One of the most startling results of making our implicit assumptions explicit was that it changed the mission focus of the organisation.

Before World Concern was content simply to do water projects and health-care projects in Jesus' name. But once we concluded that a major part of God's end game was to develop strong churches that he could use to transform the communities in which they were planted, it changed one facet of World Concern's mission strategy. They funded the development of a curriculum for a Bible school in El Salvador on how to plant churches that seek to address not only the spiritual needs but also the economic, health care and nutritional needs of the community so World Concern would never need to come to those communities to do projects. (For more info: E-mail wconcern@crista.org)

Planting a seed—Listening to community in Haiti

 Several years before I helped to draft a theology of mission at World Concern, I had the responsibility to initiate a community development project in Haiti. In preparation I invited the team we were sending to Haiti to join me in writing down our biblical assumptions about mission (*why we do what we do*). One of the assumptions we wrote down was that we affirmed 'that God was alive, well and at work in Haiti before any of the team arrived'. I realised that this principle would be self evident to many people. But the act of writing it down made it explicit and meant we felt compelled to act on it. The first thing our team did on their arrival was to tour the village asking people about their felt needs. They heard people expressing need for tractors, clinics and new buildings—very expensive stuff.

Determined to act on our assumptions that 'God was alive, well and at work' before the team arrived, we created a strategy to find out how God was at work and what kinds of dreams he was stirring up in the hearts of the people. So the team toured the valley a second time asking a very different question: 'What kinds of dreams is God giving you for the future of your family and the future of your community?'

This time the team got a very different response. People told of a strong rivalry and animosity between several families in the community. They believed that God wanted to see their community reconciled. Over 80% of the children were too poor to go to school and God stirred up a dream in many to see all the children able to go school. A number said that the Lord was leading them to pray for the spiritual renewal of their community. The answer to the second question was much more beneficial in helping to focus the direction of the project than the answers to the first. But you see we would never have asked the second question if we hadn't first written down our assumptions about mission.

Bryant Myers, in a comprehensive unpublished manuscript on transformational development, states that transformational development is a 'convergence of stories'. 'The story of the community is joined by the story of the development facilitator and . . . they share a story. God has been and is at work in both stories and God is making an invitation for a better future story. This means the biblical story must become a part of the transformational development process.'[13]

Reinventing mission as though community matters

God's purposes for a new redeemed community is much more than 'soul saving' and 'need meeting' which reflects the individualism of modernity. It is the transformation not only of individual lives but also the quality of relationships of those in this new community.

Mennonite theologian Marlin Miller describes God's end game for the transformation of community as well as individual lives: 'It includes social justice: the protection of widows and orphans, and society's dependents; the struggle against exploitation and oppression; the protection of life and property.'[14] 'From the disruption of *shalom* in the Garden of Eden to its total renewal in the new Jerusalem, the object of all of God's work is the recovery of *shalom* in his creation.'[15]

I have found no more compelling imagery of the shalom future of God than that offered us by Richard Foster in his classic *Freedom of Simplicity*:

This great vision of *shalom* begins and ends our Bible. In the creation narrative, God brought order out of chaos; in the Apocalypse of John, we have the glorious wholeness of a new heaven and a new earth. The messianic child that is born is the

Prince of Peace (Isaiah 9:6). Justice and righteousness and peace are to characterise his unending kingdom (Isaiah 9:7). Central to the dream of *shalom* is the wonderful vision of all nations streaming to the mountain of the temple of God to be taught his ways and to walk in his paths.[16]

Globalisation and the future of community

While globalisation of the economy is providing growing opportunities for numbers of those on the bottom rungs, it is also homogenising us into one huge McWorld macro culture where everywhere looks like everywhere else. Local cultures, that often reflect more of the values of God's kingdom than the invading global commercial culture are disappearing at an alarming rate. The massive efforts to centralise and globalise the economy are also, as we have seen, increasingly devastating local communities, local economies and the supporting natural environment.

Wendell Berry is very concerned that the globalisation of the economy is increasingly becoming a threat to many local economies and communities all over our planet. He writes: 'The dangers of the ideal of competition are that it neither proposes nor implies any limits. It proposes to simply lower costs at any cost, and to raise profits at any cost. It does not hesitate at the destruction of the life of a family or of the life of a community.'[17]

What will the long-term costs be to our families and communities of allowing Godzilla-size corporations to swallow farms, shops and the economies of whole communities? Do we really need to trust the future of our families and communities to the magic of the marketplace, the force of globalisation and the centralising appetites of colossus corporations? My Bible tells me that the people of God are not to sit by passively and allow centralised political or economic powers to run rough shod over our families and local communities.

Aren't we called to work actively to see the reign of God established not only in our lives and families but also in our neighbourhoods and local communities?

Mercy Corps is one of a new breed of Christian organisations working to promote the growth of civil society in communities from Lebanon to Honduras. They are committed to developing strong communities in which people have a voice in their own lives and neighbourhoods and are reconciled with their neighbours. (For more info: E-mail mercycorps@msn.co)

Berry insists that the only response we can make to the forces intent on creating a highly centralised global economy is for us to create 'a strong local economy with a strong local culture . . . A human community if it is to last long, must exert a sort of centripetal force, holding local soil and local memory in place.'[18] I believe that the creator God is already powerfully at work in all our communities seeking to provide a place to help nurture families and manifest something of the shalom purposes of God's new order.

Titou Paredes is a Christian anthropologist in Peru who said, 'God is in all cultures both affirming and judging.' I have never seen a mission's project in which there has been any effort to identify the good, the strong and the beautiful of God's new shalom order in that culture and then ask residents in the face of rapid McWorld cultural colonisation and homogenisation which aspects of their culture they want to attempt to augment and preserve. Imagine being involved in mission on a single track working and praying not only for the transformation of lives but of a community as well . . . co-operating with what God has already been doing in our local communities.

Planting a seed for community agriculture in Chicago

 As we look into the future and see the growing vulnerability that we all face in a McWorld future, it will be essential that we increase our capability for regional and community self-reliance. Wendell Berry states: 'In a healthy community, people will be richer in their neighbors . . . in the health and pleasure of neighborhood, than in their bank accounts . . . If you have money to invest, try to invest it locally, both to help the local community and to keep from helping the larger economy that is destroying local communities.'[19] A growing number of agriculture programmes are being started to enable the poor to become more self-reliant in providing their supply of nutritious food. Vegetable gardens are being planted in vacant plots, roof-top tomato patches and backyard beehives are springing up. Some 750 cities have community gardening programmes.

Perhaps one of the most imaginative urban agricultural projects was initiated by Job Ebenezar for the Evangelical Lutheran Church in America with the poor in Chicago. The food banks in Chicago received half a ton of tomatoes, aubergines, cucumbers and other vegetables from this project all grown in four shallow pools located on top of a parking garage near the O'Hare International Airport. They are even seriously considering working with the International Heifer Project to raise small livestock including goats and rabbits in the inner city.[20]

Planting a seed in Nicaragua

 One of the most interesting models I came across in my research was not a model for community transformation but really for community creation. The AGROS Foundation in Seattle has been raising funds to help the landless poor in Central America to buy land and create new communities on the land. In Nicaragua AGROS has purchased just under 200 acres of high quality land that will provide the opportunity to create a settlement for fifty landless families. Mario, who is a member of the leadership council for this project, was a contra soldier during the war. As the war ended one of his dying compatriots led him to commit his life to Christ. He in turn led Alejandro, who used to be a Sandinista soldier, to faith. Alejandro is also on this leadership council which is comprised of both Protestants and Catholics. They not only select fifty families but they help them build homes on the land, create the basis for a civil society, schools and literacy programmes and a worship facility that can be used by both Catholic and Evangelical Christians. AGROS has just received an international award from the World Bank, UN and the Inter American Foundation for the creation of one of the most successful anti-poverty programmes in Central America. (Their Email is: miracles@agros.org)

Planting a seed in Atlanta

'I think what they have done is absolutely phenomenal,' said Tiger Woods at the Tour Championship at East Lake Golf Course in Atlanta. Woods was talking about a creative project in which people of compassion in Atlanta raised $93 million to restore this aging golf course and the adjacent East Lake Community in which people lived in entrenched poverty. With leadership from Christian urban activist, Bob Lupton, they have built one of the first urban co-housing projects complete with a large organic garden to help these urban residents create a community in which residents work together to improve the quality of their life.[21]

Planting a seed for reconciliation in Mississippi

One of the most important elements of working for the transformation of our communities is working for the cause of reconciliation. The miracle in South Africa is a witness to the power of faith to begin the healing process that has so long torn a nation apart. *The Clarion-Ledger*, Mississippi's leading newspaper, reports:

The Rev. John Perkins drew applause from both the Legislative Black Caucus and the Conservative Caucus for suggesting how to help Mississippi move beyond its past . . . He suggested lawmakers set up something similar to South Africa's Truth and Reconciliation Commission to bring reconciliation between the black and white community in Mississippi. Perkins said a new commission can help the state say, 'We're bringing this to an end, that the war is over and the past is behind us. Now let's see where we go in the future . . . Whites have to overcome their guilt and ask God to forgive them and move forward. We blacks have to overcome our blame and stop being victims.'[22]

Planting a seed for reconciliation Down Under

Aboriginal Christians are seeking not only healing at the massacre sites but justice from the Australian government regarding land claims. An Aboriginal Christian writes to other Aboriginal believers:

Oppressors through violence distort reality . . . they put forward the 'narrative of the lie' . . . This lie can only be overcome by a stronger redeeming narrative. If we, together with many other Aboriginal people are going to be 'the Exodus people of God down under' then we have to learn to walk according to another covenant and learn to march to a different drum . . . We are a part of an alternative cosmic story of what God has done and is doing. And it is never dull to be on the road with Jesus . . . I am content to be on the journey and confident that the creator of this 'precious land under the southern cross' is concerned about all our people and wants all of God's diverse family at the table in God's future.[23]

Planting a seed for reconciliation in the path of the crusaders

Perhaps one of the most intriguing efforts at reconciliation is the Reconciliation Walk. 27 November, 1995 is the day that marked the nine hundredth anniversary of the call of Christendom to retrieve the holy places from the 'infidels'. This date was selected by Lynn Green and a group comprised largely of European Christians as the date to launch a Reconciliation Walk along the same path the crusaders walked to ask forgiveness of both Jews and Muslims who had been brutalised by the European crusaders.

The reconciliation message they shared with everyone they met in their journey reads:

> Nine hundred years ago, our forefathers carried the name of Jesus Christ in battle across the Middle East. Fuelled by fear, greed and hatred they betrayed the name of Christ by conducting themselves in a manner contrary to his wishes and character.
>
> The Crusaders lifted the banner of the cross above your people. By this act they corrupted its true meaning of reconciliation, forgiveness and selfless love. On the anniversary of the first crusade we also carry the name of Christ. We wish to retrace the footsteps of the crusaders in apology for their deeds and in demonstration of the true meaning of the cross. Muslims, Jews and Orthodox Christians have warmly accepted the apologies and embraced those who are coming in the name of the reconciling Christ.

Reinventing Christian stewardship to put first things first

If the Western Church has any hopes of making a serious difference in the lives, families and communities in tomorrow's world we need radically to reinvent how we carry out stewardship in our lives and also our congregations and Christian organisations as well.

Local churches need to teach their members to be whole life stewards. They also need to set new goals to focus more congregational time and money into mission. I urge every congregation to set a goal, like Spreydon Baptist did, of the percentage of time and money they want to invest in mission and conduct an annual audit to see how you are doing.

As a part of giving much more emphasis to mission I urge much more creativity in stewarding staff and church buildings costs. A more relational less bureaucratic approach to congregational life could mean real savings in staff cost. (I am certain that more pastors will need to become bi-vocational in the future.) A number of churches could go for a more decentralised approach, like Ichthus Fellowship, that doesn't require any new construction. Instead of building new facilities some churches are sharing facilities with Seven Day Adventist churches or auction studios.

Church planters need a wake-up call. Most under-thirty-five congregations will not have the resources to build the expensive church buildings my generation erected. Howard Snyder has long urged the American Church to overcome its 'edifice complex'.

Christian organisations will need to create much less cost-intensive virtual organisations that rely much less on buildings and paid staff to carry out their mission. We won't be able to afford the top heavy bureaucratic models very far into the twenty-first century with the high executive salaries paid by a number of US-based organisations. We will need to experiment with webbed and networked organisations that are building free and where growing numbers of us work bi-vocationally in ministry.

Essential to the advancement of the purposes of God will be the creation of new partnerships to maximise the use of limited resources. Increasingly the leadership for these partnerships will come from the Church in the Two Thirds World. Christian organisations will also need to learn to create a broad spectrum of partnering relationships with governments, corporations and international organisations like the United Nations.

A wave of the future will be more people-to-people partnerships. Most churches and many Christian organisations could benefit from using the services like those of Interdev to help broker relationships with churches in another part of the world. They also help Christian mission organisations to design collaborative ventures within countries to maximise impact and reduce costs. (For more information contact E-mail interdev-uk@xc.org)

Planting a seed at Pecan

When Simon Pellew started Pecan, a Christian ministry to work with the urban poor in London, he took a very different approach to staff compensation. He paid everyone the same modest salary he paid himself. He told me, 'I thought it was a good idea when we started but I think it has turned out to be an even better idea than I anticipated. Because we don't have high administrative salaries we are able to hire more staff and we work together more collegially.'

Planting a seed in old tyres

In the future we will all need to become creative Christian scroungers doing much more with much less. During a creativity workshop in Chicago on urban ministry, I gave participants some creativity assignments. I asked one group to find something that had been thrown away in the city and then to do something with it for the kingdom. They came back with their idea thirty minutes later. I asked, 'What do you have?' They responded, 'Vertical gardening. We plan to collect old tyre casings that you find all over the place in an inner-city community. We will stack the tyres nine tyres high. We will fill the stack of tyres with dirt and plant potato seed in the stack. The potato sprouts will grow out between the tyres. When it is harvest time you simply push over the tyres, pick up the potatoes and sweep up the dirt.' We need this level of creativity as we seek to expand mission to meet the growing needs of the third millennium.

Planting a seed by giving away money

Phil Wall, working with The Salvation Army in Britain, created a new model of fund raising from the parable of the talents. He took all his family's personal savings and asked others in his church to contribute money as they could afford to help raise money to support AIDS orphans in Africa. They put on a banquet in which they presented the plight of the orphans. Instead of asking people to give money to the cause, Phil gave every person there £10 ($15). He said you can take this money and spend it on yourself if you want. Or you can take a list of ideas of ways to invest this money and multiply it to assist these children in Africa. He handed out the list of ideas and gave a deadline for response. He has done this three times and each time he has received more than ten fold the original amount they gave out.

Planting a seed in Brazil

Some conscientious Christian educators have created a new low-cost approach to theological education in Brazil that only costs students $38 a month in tuition. The Seminario Teologico Sul Americano makes every effort to keep costs at an absolute minimum by using church buildings throughout the country for classes and finding teachers who are willing to donate their time to help raise a new generation of leaders who are free to serve God without the burden of debt incurred by college fees. The college even offers doctoral level studies.

This isn't your mum and dad's church any more—a new generation leading the Church into a new millennium

A new generation of leaders are coming on! You will find them planting alternative churches in Glasgow and London, creating new forms of urban ministries in Seattle and Auckland. For example, Simon Chaplin is a twenty-seven-year-old Baptist pastor to the prostitutes and gay community in the red light district of Auckland. He and his family live right in the community where he ministers. You can spot him late at night chatting with his 'parishioners' in his camouflage trousers and red dreadlocks.

God's Spirit is raising up a new generation of deeply committed young men and women who will lead the Church into a new millennium. I am particularly impressed by their keen desire to see God use their lives to make a difference in the world. And much of the cutting edge innovation I celebrate in this book is the work of twenty- and thirty-year-olds. Those of us who are older need to pay attention to what God is stirring up through their lives and ministries.

Many churches in Britain are encouraging and mentoring a new generation of leaders. Too often in North America you have to be 40 before you are invited to use your leadership gifts. I urge every church to begin mentoring the young into leadership and take seriously the visions, creative ideas and gifts God has given them.

This postmodern generation is creating a whole new expression of the Church that is more relational, local, tribal and looks very different from the mega church model of the 90s. They emphasise the creative character of a God of beauty. Growing numbers of these churches are writing their own music and bringing original art and drama into their services. We need to be open not only to encourage a new generation but to learn from their commitment and their creativity.

Planting a seed in Rolling Stone Magazine

 One of the most creative ventures in sharing the story to a new generation is the production of a new series by the International Bible Society. Initiated by CEO Paul Chandler who is in his 30s, it is entitled 'Discovering Ancient Wisdom: Practical Words of Insight and Understanding'. The Bible Society has created edited versions of selected Old Testament books like Ecclesiastes and Proverbs plus the teachings of Jesus from the New Testament in beautifully designed little booklets. They are finding a very responsive market for this 'middle eastern wisdom literature' as IBS has advertised these booklets in Rolling Stone Magazine and various New Age publications.

Planting a seed of hope in Red Square

 Intervarsity staff seeking to find new ways to share their faith with a very secular student population at the University of Washington created an imaginative new approach. There is a huge brick quad that students cross on their way to classes called Red Square. These Intervarsity folks wrote the word HOPE in huge thirty-foot chalk letters on the brick. Then they put pieces of chalk down all around the word. Both students and faculty immediately began stopping and used the chalk to write on the brick. Some wrote of their very real struggle with cynicism and despair. One young woman wrote of the hope that a new relationship gave her. A few wrote statements regarding their faith. Others

composed verse. Over the course of four hours these young Christians found many opportunities to share both life and faith with their peers.

Planting a seed in Saint Mary's, Ealing

Many of the post-modern young from outside the Church find that our churches aren't just middle classed but middle aged—and they find they don't connect with their generation. Johnny and Jenny Baker were given the opportunity to plant a new post-modern church in an existing church at Saint Mary's Anglican Church in London. They have created an alternative Celtic Christian Sunday evening service in which they are incorporating their own art, music and liturgy. This alternative church has drawn large numbers of young people who never would have shown up for a traditional Anglican service. But they are also finding ways to bring both generations together in common cause.

Planting a seed on the road to Canterbury

Matthew 28:20 reminds us that the great commission is really a call to make disciples, 'teaching them to observe everything I have commanded you'. Teaching them 'to observe everything' didn't just have to do with the spiritual compartment of life but all of life. It is a call to whole life discipleship. But I am persuaded that we not only need to rethink *why we do what we do* but how we do it. So many of the ways I have seen Western churches practising discipleship seems to reflect more of the modernity lecture model than the rabbinical one.

David Pott invited thirteen students to come to London

from different countries for a discipleship training seminar. Previously, these sessions had always taken place in a class-room. But this time David decided to try something different. The thirteen students journeyed together from London to Canterbury—a seventy-mile walk over the course of a week. They journeyed as though they were journeying with Jesus. They read and discussed the teachings of Jesus as they walked together. They gave one another foot rubs and back rubs as they went. In the evenings they would read *Pilgrim's Progress* about the slough of despondency and all the other barriers that face the pilgrims on their way.

When they began their journey they didn't get on very well together. But as they learned to journey with Jesus they found it improved how they related to each other. When they arrived in Canterbury they imagined they had arrived home to the kingdom of God and concluded the week with a rousing cele-bration of coming home. I find that a post-modern generation is drawn much more to this kind of a relational, rabbinical model than getting lectured in a box. God is raising up a new generation to lead the Church into a new millennium and we need to be open to their creative leadership.

Welcome to the wedding feast of God!

Let's return to where we began this final chapter—Jalapa, Mexico. You have just entered the community centre that God enabled Saul and Pilar and their church to build on that rub-bish tip. Picture the community centre transformed—flooded with white balloons, colourful streamers and ribbons hanging from the ceiling. At the front of the room is an enormous six-tier wedding cake. The buffet table is filled with a festive dis-play of dishes provided by the families who are being mar-ried. The centre is packed with hundreds of friends, some of whom are standing on tiptoes to see the twenty-eight couples who are being married. There are parents, grandparents and grandchildren all getting married at the same time. Not a few with tears in their eyes.

The Armonia community is conducting this mass wedding for poor couples who have never been able to afford the high costs of legal paperwork and medical certificates plus the costs of a Mexican wedding. As the final prayer is pronounced and the husbands kiss their brides, an enormous cheer goes up from the assembled, a Mexican band starts playing with tremendous energy and the celebrating begins in earnest.

The centrepiece of the great home-coming of God is going to be a huge wedding feast. Listen to Jesus making some last-minute changes in the list of invited guests: 'The wedding is ready, but those who were invited were not worthy. Go therefore to the main highways and as many as you find there, invite to the wedding feast' (Matthew 22:2-10). We dare not be among those who miss out. Like those first followers we need not only to commit our lives to God, but like Jesus, also to commit our lives to the purposes of God, giving 'sight to the blind, release to the captives and good news to the poor.'

We are entering a new millennium that is changing at blinding speed. For the Church to faithfully carry out its mission in this world we need leaders who lead with foresight, vision and imagination. We will need leaders who learn to lead with foresight, paying attention to how both the world and the Church are changing. We will need leaders who lead with vision who enable us to find in Scripture an alternative dream to the aspirations that power McWorld. And we will need leaders who enable us to use our imagination to create new ways to advance God's purposes in response to the challenges of tomorrow's world.

As we have seen, globalisation will present us with an array of new opportunities and challenges. I am convinced that if we don't seriously and prayerfully reorder our use of resources in our lives and churches we won't begin to be able to respond to the new opportunities that God is giving us. We will need to radically reinvent our lives, churches and mission programmes if we have any intention of engaging the new challenges of a new millennium.

We also need to pay much more attention to the pressures from modern culture to cave into the seductions, idolatries and addictions of McWorld. I am convinced that those pressures are largely responsible for the steady erosion of our investment of time and money in the work of God's kingdom.

At the very centre of our lives God calls us to a very different dream than the Western dream. It is the dream of a God who invites us home to a world made new. It is an opportunity to flesh out in community with others, by God's grace, something of the hope and celebration of God's great home-coming. And it is an invitation to join sisters and brothers all over the world in allowing God to use our mustard seeds to see his kingdom come in some partial ways now in anticipation of Christ's return when the wedding feast will break out in its fullness. I don't think we have any idea of how God can use our mustard seed to make a difference in a new millennium if we are willing to take the risk of reinventing our lives and congregations to put God's purposes first. Welcome home to the wedding-feast future of God!

Opportunities for those in leadership

 The opportunities for Christian leaders are:

1. To make a major effort to reach, church and mentor a new generation in our Western countries, and to challenge them to a radical biblical discipleship in which they place the purposes of the mustard seed before the aspirations of McWorld;

2. To challenge all churches to move mission to the centre of congregational life, setting goals for how much total time, prayer and money they plan to invest in mission each year (at home and abroad) and do an annual audit;

3. To enable all churches and Christian organisations to do the hard work of writing down their implicit assumptions about *why they do what they do.* Then to study Scripture and write down a set of biblically based assumptions to provide a springboard to focus mission and create new possibilities;

4. To create new ministries that work for the shalom transformation of individuals and also whole communities in order to reflect something of God's purposes;

5. To reinvent how we steward resources in our Christian organisations to do more with less;

6. To pay attention to the leadership that is being provided by a new generation and find ways to collaborate;

7. To create new forms of partnership to maximise impact while reducing costs.

8. To create new celebrations of the in-breaking of God's kingdom as we work with those at the margins for the Shalom purposes of God.

Questions for discussion and action

1. How much of the time and resources of your congregation are presently being invested in ministry in your community or abroad?

2. What emerging areas of need in your community could your church respond to? Eg, child care for mothers coming off benefits, activities for at-risk children, neglected senior citizens.

3. What are some ways you could mentor young people in your church into serious leadership roles?

4. In what ways could your church partner with churches in communities of need to not only meet individual needs but also see whole neighbourhoods experience the shalom of God?

Notes

1 'A View of The City', *Tear Times*, Spring 1995, pp.6-7.

2 *Ibid.*

3 Alister E. McGrath, *A Passion For Truth: the intellectual coherence of evangelicalism* (Apollos: Leicester, UK, 1996), p.63.

4 Wilbert R. Schenk, 'Mission Renewal, and the Future of the Church', *International Bulletin of Missionary Research*, October 1997, p.158.

5 Lesslie Newbigin, *The Gospel in a Pluralist Society* (William B. Eerdmans: Grand Rapids, Mi., 1989), pp.133-134.

6 George Hunsberger, 'Missional Vocations: Called and Sent to represent the Reign of God', Darrell L. Guder, *Missional Church: A Vision For Sending the Church in North America* (William B. Eerdmans: Grand Rapids, Mi., 1998), pp.77-81.

7 Jonathan J. Bonk, *Affluence as a Western Missionary Problem* (Orbis: Maryknoll, 1992).

8 Orlando E. Costas, *The Integrity of Mission: The inner life and the Outreach of the Church* (Harper and Row: San Francisco, 1979), p.17.

9 Of course there were also a number of conservative groups that also planted hospitals and schools as they went. But for many of these groups this initiative was seen as outside of their theology of mission—it was often seen as a door-opener for the 'real' mission which was addressing people's spiritual needs. So you still wind up with a two-track approach to mission.

10 David Bosch, *Transforming Mission: Paradigm Shifts in Theology of Mission* (Maryknoll, NY, 1993), p.405.

11 *Ibid.,* p.407.

12 Steve Gaukroger, *Why Bother With Mission?* (InterVarsity Press: Leicester, UK, 1996), p.59.

13 Bryant Myers, *Walking With the Poor: Principles and Practice of Transformational Development* [an unpublished manuscript] 6 July, 1998, chapter 7, p.21. (This manuscript will be published under the title *Walking With the Poor* by Orbis Press in 1999.)

14 Marlin E. Miller, 'The Gospel of Peace', *Mission and Peace Witness*, Robert L. Ramseyer, ed. (Herald Press: Scottdale, Az., 1978), p.30.

15 James E. Metzler, 'Shalom is the Mission', *op. cit.,* p.40.

16 Richard J. Foster, *Freedom of Simplicity* (Harper: San Francisco, 1981), pp.30-31.

17 Wendell Berry, *What are People For?* (North Point Press: San Francisco, 1990), p.131.

18 *Ibid.,* pp.155, 167.

19 Wendell Berry, *Sex, Economy, Freedom and Community* (Pantheon Books: New York, 1992), p.40.

20 Ann Scott Tyson, 'Urban Farms: How Green Is My

Barrio', *The Christian Science Monitor*, 4 December, 1996, p.4.

21 Clifton Brown, 'Golf Course At the Center of a Community', *The New York Times*, 29 October, 1998, pp.C25-C29.

22 Jerry Mitchell, *The Clarion-Ledger*.

23 Don Carrington, 'Christians and the Struggle for Reconciliation', *Indigenous Leadership: A Journal for Aboriginal and Islander People*, Issue 12, August 1997, pp.18-19.

INVITING PEOPLE TO SHARE SEEDS

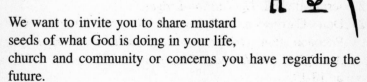

We want to invite you to share mustard
seeds of what God is doing in your life,
church and community or concerns you have regarding the
future.

In other words we want to make this an interactive book.
We plan to set up a chat room in which Christians all over the
world can share creative ways they are finding to put God's
purposes first. To join this conversation all you have to do is
go to: www.bakerbooks.com and then go to <u>Mustard Seed vs
McWorld</u> and click on. I will be looking forward to learning
what God is doing in your life, church and ministry to respond
to the new challenges of a new millennium.

Again the web page address is: www.bakerbooks.com